EIGHTH EDITION

LOCATING AND CORRECTING READING DIFFICULTIES

James L. Shanker

California State University, Hayward

Eldon E. Ekwall

Late of University of Texas at El Paso

Merrill
Prentice Hall

Upper Saddle River, New Jersey
Columbus, Ohio

Library of Congress Cataloging-in-Publication Data

Shanker, James L.
  Locating and correcting reading difficulties/James L. Shanker, Eldon E. Ekwall.—8th ed.
    p. cm.
  Includes bibliographical references and index.
  ISBN 0-13-031395-5 (pbk.)
    1. Reading—Remedial teaching. I. Ekwall, Eldon E. II. Title.

LB1050.5 .E38 2003
372.43—dc21
2002032599

Vice President and Publisher: Jeffery W. Johnston
Editor: Linda Ashe Montgomery
Editorial Assistant: Evelyn Olson
Production Editor: Linda Hillis Bayma
Production Coordination and Text Design: Emily Hatteberg, Carlisle Publishers Services
Design Coordinator: Diane C. Lorenzo
Cover Designer: Megan Sykes
Cover image: Getty Images
Production Manager: Pamela D. Bennett
Director of Marketing: Ann Castel Davis
Marketing Manager: Darcy Betts Prybella
Marketing Coordinator: Tyra Poole

This book was set in Century Book by Carlisle Communications, Ltd. It was printed and bound by R.R. Donnelley & Sons Company. The cover was printed by Phoenix Color Corp.

Pearson Education Ltd.
Pearson Education Australia Pty. Limited
Pearson Education Singapore Ptd. Ltd.
Pearson Education North Asia Ltd.
Pearson Education Canada, Ltd.
Pearson Educación de Mexico, S.A. de C.V.
Pearson Education—Japan
Pearson Education Malaysia Pte. Ltd.
Pearson Education, *Upper Saddle River, New Jersey*

10 9 8 7 6 5 4 3 2
ISBN 0-13-031395-5

For Tracy Lindman Shanker—
May you and Michael have a joyous life together

Preface

The eighth edition of this book, like previous editions, is organized to provide reading specialists, teachers, tutors, and reading education students with specific, concrete methods for locating and correcting reading difficulties. It can be used in classroom or remedial situations and is designed so that busy practitioners can find in one place the essential information they need to help struggling readers overcome their literacy difficulties. Direct instruction, motivational learning activities, and abundant practice in the act of reading are stressed. As in the previous editions, instruction in individual reading skills is recommended where appropriate; however, emphasis is also placed on the use of strategic approaches to the teaching of reading.

ORGANIZING TO ASSIST STRUGGLING READERS

This book is composed of 29 chapters, divided into six major parts, which cover the full range of reading and reading-related skills. While the major features of the previous edition have been retained, this new edition has been updated and reorganized to make the information within more accessible to the reader.

Methods and Approaches.   The first section of this book is an introductory chapter that provides information on important principles of effective instruction for students who have reading difficulties. It is hoped that these principles will guide your reading throughout the remainder of the book. This chapter also presents useful techniques or approaches for teaching students with reading difficulties. These techniques/approaches are included in this chapter because they apply to many of the specific reading problems that are the focus of subsequent chapters. The first approach describes a number of oral reading techniques that have been shown to be unusually effective in helping students as they struggle to master decoding skills. Equally important, these techniques are among the most powerful teachers can use to develop students' reading fluency and build a foundation for better reading comprehension. A second method is the language-experience approach, which benefits both beginning and remedial readers. In this section, you will find a thorough description of these approaches and many practical activities for application in the classroom or tutorial setting.

As with previous editions, the Reading Diagnosis Chart (see page xiii) matches the logical development of various reading skills and corresponds to the order of the chapters. The basic format of each chapter is the same. A section titled "Recognized By" defines and/or describes the reading difficulty. The "Discussion" section provides additional background information and explains how to test or otherwise determine if a student is experiencing difficulty in this area. The "Recommendations" section offers an alphabetical listing of specific strategies or activities you may use to help the student overcome the problem. In most chapters, these suggestions are followed by a variety of "Games and Exercises" that may be used to provide students with independent practice.

Emergent Literacy.   Part 2 addresses emergent literacy skills. In this edition, Chapter 1 is now devoted entirely to phonemic awareness, reflecting recent research affirming the importance of this area in early reading development. Alphabet knowledge is now addressed separately in Chapter 2. Tests for phonemic awareness (in Appendix B-4) assess rhyming ability, initial sound recognition, phoneme blending, and phoneme segmentation. Specific instructional procedures added to Chapter 1 are matched to each of the skills tested.

Decoding Skills.   In previous editions, Part 3 consisted of chapters focusing on a variety of different oral reading problems. In nearly every case, these problems are caused by some weakness in the reader's decoding skills. For this reason, decoding skills are now presented *before* oral reading difficulties. In these chapters you will learn how to assess and teach various decoding skills such as sight vocabulary, phonics, structural analysis, and the use of context clues.

Oral Reading, Comprehension, and Study Skills.   Part 4 consists of 10 chapters on specific oral reading difficulties such as poor pronunciation, omissions, repetitions, and so on. Part 5 addresses comprehension skills. Part 6 addresses instruction in study skills and other skills essential to success in school.

THE APPENDICES: TOOLS FOR LOCATING AND CORRECTING READING DIFFICULTIES

We encourage readers to use the materials provided in the appendices for *locating* reading difficulties to construct their own diagnostic kits. These appendices include a code for marking in oral diagnosis and, as previously noted, a new set of tests for phonemic awareness. The appendices also include materials and directions for assessing students' knowledge of the alphabet, basic sight words and phrases, phonics, structural analysis, contractions, the use of context clues, and two reading interest surveys. A new test for assessing the reading interests of older students and adults has been added to this edition. Altogether, more than 30 different diagnostic tests are provided in these appendices. Specific directions and important points to remember are provided for administering each test or survey instrument.

Thirteen appendices have been provided for *correcting* reading difficulties. The first, a new appendix titled "Books for Emergent Readers," consists of lists of rhyming books, books with alliteration, and alphabet books. You will also find appendices for basic sight word sentences, a phonics primer, and newly revised phonogram lists, including sentences and other new features in this popular phonics instructional program. Next is an appendix titled "Words for Teaching Short and Long Vowels," followed by "Words, Sentences, and Stories for Teaching Structural Analysis." The remaining appendices address prepositional phrases, prefixes and suffixes, the cloze procedure, a chart for graphing students' progress in using the technique of repeated readings, a description of and charts for graphing students' progress in using the precision reading technique, charts for graphing words per minute and comprehension, and suggestions for interviewing parents of disabled readers.

Finally, definitions of terms appear in a glossary at the end of the book.

ACKNOWLEDGMENTS

Special thanks are extended to Carol Huntington, Katrina Kistler, Alison Kuehner, and Kathy Terrell for their assistance in researching instructional methods and for their help in creating the new appendices for this addition. I also thank the many individuals who made contributions to previous editions of this book, notably Cheryl Milner, who created the structural analysis program that appears in Appendix B-6. I greatly appreciate the conscientious work of the following individuals who reviewed this text: Lois C. Catrambone, Concordia University; Elizabeth Darvas, Nova Southeastern University; Susan Blair Larsen, The College of New Jersey; David C. Little, Samford University; Donna Ortiz, Fort Hays State University; James Sabin, Louisiana State University, Shreveport; and Maria Slack, University of Phoenix. Their insights, thoughtful comments, and constructive suggestions have made this a more useful book.

Thanks also go to Evelyn Olson, Linda Bayma, and many others at Merrill/Prentice Hall. I am indebted to Sue Dolter, whose eye for detail and copy-editing ability have made this a more readable book. I also appreciate the fine work of Emily Hatteberg of Carlisle Publishers Services throughout the production process.

Finally, I am most grateful for the wisdom, advice, support, and kindness of my editor, Linda Montgomery. Thank you, Linda, for the gentle pushes and the many caring words.

J. L. S.

Contents

How to Use This Book

Begin by examining the Reading Diagnosis Chart (see p. xiii), which lists 29 reading or reading-related skills. Because these skills are keyed to specific chapters in the book, they are numbered from 1 to 29. Next, you may wish to skim the book from beginning to end to develop familiarity with the contents. Each of the 29 chapters on reading or reading-related skills is organized in the same way. First, an explanation about how to recognize the difficulty with the specific skill is presented. A brief discussion explains any pertinent problems. Although this section is relatively brief, it is important because it provides a framework for the techniques and procedures that follow. Specific recommendations for correcting the targeted weakness follow the discussion. Finally, in some chapters, a list of games and exercises is presented to help correct these reading difficulties. In most cases, you will not be able to attempt everything listed as a recommendation; however, you can choose the techniques that seem most appropriate for your situation.

The Reading Diagnosis Chart is constructed to give you an opportunity to check each of the 29 skills three times during the year. The time period between checks will depend on the intensity of the help or the normal teaching program: it could be as often as once a month or once during each semester of the school year. You should attempt to locate student difficulties as early in the year as possible. The "Recognized By" section in each chapter will be helpful in determining whether certain skills are deficient. After determining which skills are weak, tally the total number of students who are weak in each area. If possible, group the students who need reading instruction in similar areas. In some cases, you may base your instruction on those areas in which the class as a whole is weakest. Then turn to the "Recommendations" and the "Games and Exercises" sections to use the suggestions given there.

Before initiating actual instruction, read the section titled "Principles of Effective Instruction" in Part 1. The information in Part 1 is based on the authors' reading and research and more than 60 years of combined experience in helping students learn how to read. It is hoped that these suggestions will guide you in selecting the most appropriate recommendations in each chapter for your student or students.

The Reading Diagnosis Chart does not categorize reading difficulties by the severity of the problem. Be aware, however, that some of the items listed are more serious than others. Each discussion section explains how to determine whether the difficulty needs treatment or is only a symptom of a more serious problem. For example, word-by-word reading, improper phrasing, and repetitions usually are symptoms of more serious problems such as difficulty in decoding, fluency skills, or comprehension. In this situation, treatment for these larger problems probably would cause the symptoms of word-by-word reading, improper phrasing, and repetitions to disappear automatically. Read each discussion section carefully to ensure adequate diagnosis and to determine the proper techniques for instruction.

After noting on the Reading Diagnosis Chart the skills in which your students are weak, consult the table of contents to quickly locate corrective procedures for each of the problems listed. The numbers on the Reading Diagnosis Chart correspond to the chapter numbers for each difficulty noted. For example, students who have difficulty with basic sight words can be helped by using the corrective procedures in chapter 3, while those who are unable to skim or scan can be helped by using the procedures in chapter 26, and so on.

Following the Reading Diagnosis Chart is a section titled "Making Your Own Diagnostic Kit From the Appendices." Become familiar with this section, so you can create your own diagnostic kit as you review the various appendices (A-1 through A-11) for testing or assessing reading difficulties. After becoming familiar with the text, you may wish to reproduce copies of the Reading Diagnosis Chart so you will have a record for each member of the class, or for each student with whom you are working. It will be easier to locate certain difficulties if you use the code for marking in oral diagnosis that is described in Appendix A-1. This code will enable you to find exactly what type of mistakes students make in their reading. With a little practice, you will become adept at transcribing the student's oral reading. You will, of course, need a set of graded reading passages to mark as the student reads. These can be in the form of an informal reading inventory, or a copy of what the student is reading (preferably double-spaced). You will also find this marked or coded copy useful in rechecking a student's reading to record progress in overcoming earlier difficulties. If you are selecting the passages for the student to read, try to find material that will cause the student to make 5 to 10 errors per page. If the material is too easy and the student is able to read it without error, you obviously will be unable to determine the nature of his reading difficulties. On the other hand, if the student makes more than about 10 errors per page, the material may be so difficult and frustrating that he will guess wildly and lose his ability to apply the reading skills he does possess. This guideline applies to the selection of reading material *for testing/diagnosis purposes* only. The difficulty of other reading material will vary according to the purpose for which it is used. The student should be able to decode at least 95% of the words in material you use for instructing him and at least 98% of the words in material that he reads independently.

Sometimes a particular suggestion will be appropriate for a younger child but inappropriate for an older student. We have not listed the various suggestions as appropriate for certain grades or age levels. Exercise your own judgment based on the severity of the problem and the age and attitude of the child. We have, however, noted that some problems are beyond the beginning reading stage.

If you are relatively new to the area of reading instruction, you may encounter some unfamiliar terms in this book related to the field of reading. Many of these terms will be bold-faced the first time they appear in the text. Each of the bold-faced terms is defined in the Glossary near the end of the book. You may wish to skim through this section to acquaint yourself with these terms before you read the book.

Reading Diagnosis Chart

NAME ——————   GRADE ——————   TEACHER ——————   SCHOOL ——————

	1st Check	2nd Check	3rd Check		
1				Phonemic Awareness	Emergent Literacy Skills
2				Alphabet Knowledge	
3				Basic Sight Words Not Known	Decoding Skills
4				General Sight Vocabulary Not Up to Grade Level	
5				Phonics Difficulties: Consonants	
6				Phonics Difficulties: Vowels	
7				Phonics Difficulties: Blends, Digraphs, or Diphthongs	
8				Structural Analysis Difficulties	
9				Contractions Not Known	
10				Inadequate Ability to Use Context Clues	
11				Poor Pronunciation	Specific Oral Reading Difficulties
12				Omissions	
13				Repetitions	
14				Inversions or Reversals	
15				Insertions	
16				Substitutions	
17				Guesses at Words	
18				Word-by-Word Reading	
19				Incorrect Phrasing	
20				Voicing, Lip Movements, Finger Pointing, and Head Movements	
21				Word Meaning / Vocabulary Knowledge Inadequate	Comprehension Skills
22				Comprehension Inadequate	
23				Low Rate of Speed	Study Skills and Other Abilities
24				Inability to Adjust Reading Rate	
25				High Rate of Reading at the Expense of Accuracy	
26				Inability to Skim or Scan	
27				Inability to Locate Information	
28				Undeveloped Dictionary Skills	
29				Written Recall Limited by Spelling Skill	

The items listed here represent the most common difficulties encountered by students in the reading program. Following each numbered item are spaces for notation of that specific difficulty. This may be done at intervals of several months. One might use a check to indicate difficulty recognized or the following letters to represent an even more accurate appraisal:

D—Difficulty recognized
P—Student progressing
N—No longer has difficulty

Making Your Own Diagnostic Kit From the Appendices

Materials are included in Appendices A-1 through A-11 for developing your own diagnostic kit for use in locating students' reading difficulties. Most of these appendices are organized as follows.

Preparing for the test. In this section, you will find instructions for preparing the material in this book for use in testing. In most cases, the directions include removing an answer sheet, which is to be duplicated. Directions are also included for removing and laminating a stimulus sheet. We suggest that you file the materials from each of these appendices so that you may easily retrieve them. You may wish to file each test or assessment device in a large manila envelope and then label each envelope like a file folder. These may then be kept in a portable file box, and easily transported from place to place as needed in various testing situations.

Specific directions for administering each test or assessment device. In this section, you will find specific directions for administering each test or assessment device.

Important points to remember. In administering any test or assessment device, there are certain techniques that you will find helpful and others that should be avoided. This section, found in each appendix, includes this information.

Following is a list of appendices and testing or assessment devices that you should have in your kit when it is completed.

Appendix A-1: Code for Marking in Oral Diagnosis

Appendix A-2: Preparation and Use of Materials for Testing Phonemic Awareness

Appendix A-3: Preparation and Use of Materials for Testing Letter Knowledge

Appendix A-4: Preparation and Use of Materials for the Quick Check for Basic Sight Words

Appendix A-5: Preparation and Use of Materials for Testing Basic Sight Words and Phrases

Appendix A-6: Preparation and Use of Materials for the Phonics Assessment

Appendix A-7: Preparation and Use of Materials for the Structural Analysis Assessment

Appendix A-8: Preparation and Use of Materials for Testing Knowledge of Contractions

Appendix A-9: Preparation and Use of Materials for the Quick Survey Word List

Appendix A-10: Preparation and Use of Materials for Testing Ability to Use Context Clues

Appendix A-11: Preparation and Use of Materials for the Reading Interest Surveys

It will *never* be appropriate to give all of these tests or assessment devices to any one child. Which tests you use with a particular student will depend on the student's current reading level and the amount of information you wish to obtain. With some experience in conducting individual diagnostic testing, most examiners can do a thorough evaluation in 20 to 60 minutes.

PART ONE

INTRODUCTION

Introduction: Important Principles and Useful Methods for Teaching Students With Reading Difficulties

In this chapter, you will find information about principles of effective instruction for students who have reading difficulties. It is important to apply these principles when you are organizing your instruction and selecting techniques to use from various chapters in this book. Next, you will find information about the use of several techniques or approaches that are especially helpful with students with reading difficulties. In this section, several highly effective oral reading techniques are described. These techniques are among the most powerful available because, when properly chosen, they provide students with authentic practice in the act of reading at a level where they can read successfully. Effective oral reading activities are included in this introductory chapter because they enhance students' reading abilities in virtually all areas of reading difficulty.

Next, the language-experience approach is described. Although many primary-grade teachers use this approach as a part of their regular classroom reading program, certain procedures emphasized in this section are particularly appropriate for disabled readers of any age.

PRINCIPLES OF EFFECTIVE INSTRUCTION

This book is designed to help teachers, reading or learning disabilities specialists, tutors, or others help students overcome reading difficulties. Students may have problems learning to read for a number of reasons. These include some combination of physical, psychological, socioeconomic, and educational factors. In this book, we focus on educational/instructional issues and provide you, the reader, with specific tools for locating and correcting reading difficulties.

Students often fail to learn to read because large class sizes and multiple demands on the time of classroom teachers make it difficult or impossible for them to give students the concentrated instruction they need. Many teachers also lack adequate knowledge and sufficient experience to assist students who struggle with literacy tasks. By understanding a few key principles and applying some highly effective teaching strategies, you will help students improve their reading abilities more quickly and easily.

Our reading of the considerable literature in the field of reading instruction and our experience in the roles of classroom teacher, reading specialist, school administrator, college teacher, and director of university reading clinics have persuaded us that, with reasonable conditions and appropriate instruction over time, nearly every disabled reader can make significant progress. The teaching of reading is not a mystical process. Although much remains to be learned about how we can best help those who are failing, we do know which practices succeed most often. The recommendations provided in this book will be most effective if you are mindful of the following principles.

1. Most students require a certain amount of systematic, sequential skill instruction to learn how to decode or pronounce unknown words fluently. The amount of this type of instruction required varies considerably from student to student.

2. Nearly all remedial readers require **direct instruction,** in which the teacher clearly presents information to the student in small increments of learning, guides the instruction, and monitors the pace of student learning of new material.

3. All students should be taught, and should practice, reading at an appropriate level of difficulty so that they can experience frequent success. All too often, disabled readers are expected to read material that is much too difficult for them. From this experience they learn only frustration, instead of how to read successfully.

4. All students need substantial amounts of practice in the act of reading to ensure that important skills are learned and utilized and to promote an appreciation for the value and joy of reading. Far too many struggling readers spend too little time actually **engaged** in the act of reading.

You will notice that some of the recommendations in this book require the teacher to interact with students in order to guide them in developing strategies to improve their reading abilities. These techniques may require the teacher to describe or model a strategy, assist the students in using it, and then provide the students with opportunities to use the strategy on their own. These recommendations are usually the most important and most effective. Other recommendations, while valuable, are less critical. For example, in most chapters you will find suggestions for worksheets, games, or other activities that will give students independent practice in certain skills. These activities may be motivating and may give students beneficial practice when they are working alone or in small groups without the teacher present, but they cannot replace the direct instruction provided initially by the teacher.

For students to benefit most from their reading instruction and practice, activities must be presented at the appropriate level of difficulty. When reading independently, students should be able to decode at least 98% of the words on their own. (A simple procedure for helping students determine whether reading material is too difficult is presented in Chapter 22 under "Procedures for Improving Overall Comprehension," item A.) If the level of instruction is too high or the material is too difficult, students will become frustrated. If such frustration occurs frequently, then the "assistance" provided to students may actually do more harm than good. When in doubt, have students read easier material. Even if it is too easy, they will benefit from the practice in reading it.

For new learning to transfer and become permanent reading ability, it is essential that students have abundant opportunities for practice in the authentic act of reading. Such practice is **holistic** in nature, consisting of the reading of whole, contextual material, not merely flash cards, word lists, or items on a worksheet. This practice should occur both in and out of school and may include both oral and silent reading of magazines, stories, books (fiction and nonfiction), poems, instructions, recipes, newspapers, child-authored books, manuals, and so forth. As a teacher of reading, you should make every effort to motivate students to read for information and pleasure. While engaged in the act of reading, students put the "pieces" of reading instruction together and gradually develop the fluency that makes reading an automatic process. Such fluency is also required for adequate reading **comprehension**.

Several unusually effective techniques or approaches are presented in the following sections of this chapter. Each of these techniques or approaches embodies the principles we have described.

EFFECTIVE ORAL READING TECHNIQUES

A number of oral reading techniques or methods may be used to help students begin the process of decoding, to improve their decoding ability, and to correct various fluency problems such as reading rate, accuracy, phrasing, or expression. Among the best known of these techniques are the neurological-impress method, echo reading or imitative reading, repeated readings, and precision reading. Each of these, and a number of other techniques, will be described in the following sections. We recommend these methods not because oral reading is the goal, but because these techniques help students with a wide variety of specific reading difficulties.

Oral reading is most effective when it is done in a one-to-one fashion or with very small groups, so students participate as much as possible. Pairing students is a common and effective practice to facilitate oral reading in the classroom. In using these methods, it is important for the teacher to stress to students that oral reading is only one way of reading and that this practice will ultimately lead the student to greater ability in silent reading. Also, oral reading practice is not substituted for silent reading. Rather, it is presented to give students additional experience with the printed word.

The Neurological-Impress Method

The **neurological-impress method (NIM)** was explained some years ago by R. G. Heckelman (1966). It has been extremely successful with many students with reading difficulties and it is easy to use. In fact, NIM is so easy to use that teachers are often hesitant to try it. A procedure for using NIM follows:

1. Seat the student slightly in front of you, so you can point to the material the student is reading and read directly into the student's ear.

2. Begin with material that is at the student's instructional or independent reading level. As you continue to work with the student, you can increase the level of difficulty of the material.

3. Tell the student that you are going to read the material and that she is to read along with you as you point to the words. Then begin to read at a slightly slower-than-normal rate for you. While reading, be sure to point to each word as you read it. *This part of the procedure is extremely important.* The student may complain, at first, that she is unable to keep up with you. This should not, however, prevent you from using the procedure. Explain to the student that she will become a better reader and will probably soon be able to keep up with you.

4. As you work with the student, you are likely to notice a sharp improvement in her ability to read. Begin to increase your rate of reading as the student's reading improves.

5. Read for periods of 5 to 15 minutes two to four times per day. Heckelman suggests that it is common to cover from 10 to 20 pages of material in one session.

6. Heckelman suggests that if periods of approximately 15 minutes are used, then the procedure should be continued until the student has read for an accumulated total of 8 to 12 hours. However, if the student fails to make progress after 4 hours, the method should be discontinued.

Heckelman has emphasized that, in using this method, you will probably see a great increase in the student's ability to read. He cautions that one of the teacher's most frequent mistakes is to spend too much time reading material written at low levels of difficulty because the teacher does not expect the student to learn so rapidly. For example, Heckelman says that if a student is started at the first-grade level, she might be expected to be reading materials at the third-grade level after an accumulated total of 2 hours. After an accumulated total of 6 hours, the student might be reading materials at the fifth- or sixth-grade level of difficulty.

Heckelman suggests that one of the reasons for the remarkable success that students often experience with NIM is that the student is exposed to many words, many times, in a relatively short period of time. For example, a student reading for approximately 15 minutes may be exposed to from 1,000 to 2,000 words.

A teacher using NIM seldom, if ever, offers specific correction, nor does the teacher ask questions or test students on the content of the material. As the student's ability improves, she may take over the finger movements and the teacher may select more challenging material to be read.

Studies have been conducted in which teachers have tried to duplicate NIM using tape-recorded materials and having students follow along with the tape-recorded reading. However, this has not produced results comparable to those obtained when working with a student in a one-to-one setting. This is probably because when a student is reading in conjunction with a tape recorder, the teacher has no way of ensuring that the student is actually looking at the words being read. If the student is not actually looking at the words being read, then she is not likely to benefit any more than if she were only listening to the passage.

Dyad Reading

Eldredge and Butterfield (1986) adapted the neurological-impress method so that it could be used in the classroom by pairs of students; this is known as the **dyad reading** method. The teacher should identify both proficient and struggling readers and then pair them. The capable reader (known as the *lead reader* or *team leader*) assists the less able student (called the *assisted reader* or *team member*). In this method, the difficulty level of the material is not as important as the interest level to the students. The student pairs are encouraged to read extensively from both narrative (stories) and expository (text) materials.

The two students share one book and sit next to each other while reading. The lead reader sets the pace of oral reading and points to each word with her finger while reading, as the assisted reader reads along orally. The reading should be done in a fluent, natural style, not word by word. As the assisted reader's reading ability improves, the lead reader can begin reading silently, allowing the assisted reader to be more assertive. Even in this phase, however, the lead reader should assist the less capable reader with unknown words when necessary.

Group-Assisted Reading

Eldredge (1990) modified the dyad reading method so that it could be used with groups of struggling readers in the classroom. He called this technique **group-assisted reading.** To implement this approach, you should follow three steps.

1. The material to be read must be seen by all students who are participating. This can be accomplished by using big books or chart paper, presenting the material on an overhead transparency, having at least one book available for every two students, or having the material printed and duplicated for each child.
2. The teacher and the students read the material out loud together. In this method, the teacher assumes the role of lead reader, while all of the participating students become assisted readers. The teacher should read orally at a slightly slow pace and in a fluent, expressive manner.
3. The teacher touches each word with her finger as it is read. If using this method with big books, a chart, or an overhead transparency, the teacher should be sure that all students can see the simultaneous reading and touching of the words. If one book is used for every two students, they can take turns touching the words as they are read. If each child has a copy of the material being read, each child can read and touch along with the teacher.

Echo Reading or Imitative Reading

In **echo reading,** or **imitative reading,** the teacher reads first and the student repeats what the teacher read. Material can be read in either phrases or sentences; finger pointing is used in this method also. A common variation uses recorded texts; students first listen straight through while following the written text and then read along with the recording. An advantage of this method is that a teacher need not be present. On the other hand, this variation lacks the immediacy and psychological force of the teacher's presence. A number of high-interest, low-vocabulary read-along materials are available in varying formats with accompanying records, tapes, or slides. Students seem to enjoy these, and, if used properly, they can be beneficial. The teacher must be sure that students *can* read the materials and that they stay on task and *do* read when they are supposed to. Whenever possible, encourage students to point to each word as it is read.

Repeated Readings

Repeated readings is a method suggested by S. Jay Samuels (1979). The student is given a selection that consists of 50 to 200 words. The student is instructed to practice her selection and then is timed, after which her reading rate and number of errors are recorded on a chart. (See Appendix B-10 for a blank repeated readings chart and an example of a completed chart.)

While the teacher is checking other students, the student rereads the material along with a recording of the text. The rereading may be done over and over. When the student feels ready, she is given another test. Comprehension checks may also take place. Graphing the student's results serves as a motivator for continued progress.

We believe that the repeated-readings method is excellent, but we would add one caution. Our experience has led us to conclude that a primary cause of fluency difficulties is that disabled readers often try to read too fast. For most students, it is helpful to encourage them first to read accurately and later to work to improve their speed.

Paired Repeated Reading

Koskinen and Blum (1986) created **paired repeated readings (PRR)** so that students could work in pairs to achieve the goals of Samuels' method. Each pair of students chooses easy, interesting material that is about 50 words long. Then each student reads the material silently. Next, the students decide who will begin reading orally. The first reader reads the selection out loud three times while the other student listens and provides assistance, if necessary. After each reading, the reader evaluates her effort; after the second and third readings, the student who was listening uses a check sheet to offer positive feedback to the oral reader. Then the roles and the responsibilities that go with them are reversed, so that each student has an opportunity to read orally, self-evaluate, and critique the other reader. The teacher's role is to demonstrate and facilitate the activity, provide a model of fluent reading, and offer support and encouragement for the students' efforts.

Precision Reading

Precision reading is an oral reading technique that emphasizes accuracy first, then speed. While the student reads, the teacher records the student's accuracy sentence by sentence on the precision reading form. (See Appendix B-11 for a blank precision reading form and instructions for its use.) The form has spaces to indicate the beginning and ending page numbers of the material read, the total number of sentences read, the number of sentences read perfectly, and the number of sentences read with one or more errors. At the beginning, the student is given relatively easy material and reads a set number of sentences, such as 25. The teacher records the student's accuracy on each sentence, so that on completion a fraction of correct sentences out of the total is derived—for example, 20/25. This indicates that the student read 20 sentences perfectly and made one or more errors on 5 of the sentences. The fraction is then changed to a percentage—in this case, 80% accuracy—and the percentage figure is graphed daily. (Appendix B-11 also includes a sample accuracy graph.) Students enjoy seeing their performance graphed, and this serves as a powerful motivator for continued progress.

The material selected should not cause the student's accuracy rate to drop below 75%. Also, the teacher may select different material for the student to read each day. However, it is helpful if the passage is chosen at least one day in advance so that the student can begin practicing the material in advance as part of her homework. As the student improves and begins to read consistently at or near 100% accuracy, the teacher may provide more difficult material or add the factor of speed. To do the latter, you may have the student read as many sentences as possible within a prescribed time, as long as the accuracy does not drop below, say, 90%. Then the *number* of sentences read perfectly is graphed daily. (An example of this type of graph is also presented in Appendix B-11.)

Reader's Theater

Reader's theater is a strategy that is very popular with most students. It provides students a safe way to read out loud and perform before a group. Unlike a play in which students must memorize a script, reader's theater allows students to read their parts from a script while standing or seated (often on step stools) in front of the group. Of course, students have ample opportunity to practice reading their parts; this enables them to read fluently and confidently. Minimal or no props are required. Sometimes teachers will have students wear hats or masks or use stick figures.

The selection of material to be read for reader's theater is critical. The material should not be too difficult for the students doing the reading and should be highly motivating. Students enjoy selections with a number of characters and lots of dialogue. They also enjoy reading poems and rhymes. In either case, some of the reading can be performed in unison, while other parts are read by individual students. Few rules apply, and teachers should feel free to experiment.

Listed here are some typical steps to be followed in preparing a reader's theater performance:

1. Select the material to be read.
2. Discuss the topic to be read and draw on students' own experiences with the topic, story, or characters.

3. Have students read the selection silently, or, if this is too difficult, read the script to students while they follow along.

4. Have all students read the script out loud together (**choral reading**).

5. Have students select parts or assign them. It may be helpful to mark or have students mark their own parts on the script.

6. Conduct more oral rereadings, this time with students reading their own parts and the unison parts.

7. Perform the material in front of other class members or another audience. Give multiple performances, if students wish.

8. Discuss the performance with the participating students. This is a good opportunity to reward students with praise and encouragement.

Shared Book Experience

The **shared book experience,** often called **shared reading,** was derived from whole-language theory and is designed for beginning readers. It was developed by Holdaway (1979) to extend to the classroom many of the nurturing aspects of the "lap method" provided by parents to their young children. Big books are especially appropriate for this method because they provide big, colorful pictures along with large print, both of which can be seen by many children at once. Charts may also be used, and teachers may add illustrations or rebuses to such charts. It is helpful to have a big book stand or easel to hold the book while it is being read to and by the class. In some cases, teachers also provide small, personal copies of the story for children to use in reading along with the big book or for later reading on their own in school or at home.

In the shared book experience, teachers can model many aspects of reading in front of their students. For example, they can point to or move their hands under the words as they are read aloud. By watching and following along, children will begin to identify specific words and discern that reading is a process of identifying symbols from left to right. Teachers can use this method to help children learn many other concepts about print, including word boundaries, reading from top to bottom, the return sweep at the end of each line of print, upper- and lowercase letters, and so forth. When students are ready, teachers can also begin providing specific instruction on aspects of decoding, such as phonics, sight words, or context clues.

Often, books are chosen that contain repetitive rhymes, predictable patterns, or other easy-to-learn structures. Students enjoy having favorite books read over and over. As students begin to memorize or recognize words or phrases, they can read out loud along with the teacher. Extension activities include writing language-experience charts or class books, drama, art, or movement activities.

Other Oral Reading Techniques

The following oral reading activities are also effective and provide variety for students:

1. The teacher and student (or pairs of students) take turns reading the material out loud by alternating paragraphs, sentences, or lines.

2. The student prereads silently first, notes difficult vocabulary, and reviews the vocabulary with the teacher or other helper; then the student and teacher or helper read together.

3. The teacher provides choral reading activities for small groups of students.

4. The teacher provides plays for students to read. A number of kits are available with simple two-, three-, or four-person plays; or teachers and students can write their own plays.

5. Many students enjoy relaxed paired reading. A student and a friend select two copies of a good book and then take turns reading it out loud together.

6. Younger students read selections using puppets.

7. Older remedial readers can be assigned as tutors to help younger students. In the process of assisting the younger student, the older student often learns more about words and reading than the student she is helping.

8. The teacher may provide a reinforcer, such as clicking a counter or putting a chip in a bank, each time the student reads a sentence perfectly.

9. The teacher may use favorite games such as tic-tac-toe, hangman, and dots to score reading accuracy. For example, one student reads while another draws part of the hangman if the student who is reading makes an error. (Items 8 and 9 are variations of the precision reading method described earlier.)

10. A number of suggestions for using an audio tape recorder to help students practice oral reading are presented in Chapter 18 under item L.

THE LANGUAGE-EXPERIENCE APPROACH

The **language-experience approach (LEA)** combines all of the language arts: listening, speaking, reading, and writing. When using the language-experience approach, one need not be concerned about whether the material being read is in the learner's background and will be too difficult to comprehend or whether the student will be interested in the subject. One also need not be concerned about whether the reading material will appear too "babyish" for the student. This is because in the language-experience approach the reading material is generated by the student.

The language-experience approach can be used with a single student or with a group of students. Much has been written about the use of the language-experience approach, and varying procedures for its use have been suggested. The material presented here indicates how it might be used with an individual and with a group. Certain procedures are also stressed that may seem unimportant at first. However, certain aspects of the language-experience approach are extremely important to its success, and we recommend little variation from these specific procedures. The material that follows is divided into five sections: (1) the theory behind the success of the language-experience approach; (2) using the language-experience approach with individual students; (3) using the language-experience approach with small groups of students; (4) important procedures and information about the use of the language-experience approach; and (5) a description of a number of highly motivating language-experience activities.

The Theory Behind the Success of the Language-Experience Approach

The language-experience approach uses the language of the students as the basis for writing materials that will later be read by those same students. When a student dictates something to the teacher or writes something herself, it will naturally be something in which the student is interested and will also be something that the student will understand with no difficulty. Furthermore, it will be written at a reading level appropriate to the student, and its content will not insult the student, regardless of her age.

Using the Language-Experience Approach With Individual Students

In using the language-experience approach with individual students, the teacher should follow this general procedure:

1. Tell the student that you would like her to dictate a story to you, so she will have something to read immediately. Spend some time discussing topics about which she would like to talk or write.

2. When she has chosen a subject, ask the student what she would like to use as a title for the story. You may wish to make suggestions; however, it is much better to get the student to use her own language. The student may wish to write about some experience that she has had lately, or she may wish to write about a favorite pet or a brother or sister. There are often hands-on experiences that have taken place in the classroom setting about which the student may wish to write, such as a science experiment or something the student is making as an art project or social studies assignment.

3. When the student has decided on an appropriate title, begin to write. Use either manuscript or cursive writing, depending on the age/grade level of the student and what she has previously been taught. If the student has done very little writing of any kind, or if you are in doubt, then you should use manuscript writing. As you write each word, make sure the student is watching. Say each word as you write it. As soon as you have finished writing the title or any sentence, stop and bring your finger down on each word and read it back to the student. It is important to bring your finger down on each word for two reasons. First, it will help the student understand that each set of letters stands for a particular word; second, it will set a pattern for the student to follow when she begins to read. It is also important that you read the material first, so that the words will again be emphasized. This will give the student a second chance to learn each written word.

4. Ask the student to read the title to you. Make sure that the student brings her finger down on each word as she reads it. This will ensure that the student again notes each word carefully and sees each word as a part of the overall title or sentence. In most cases, the student will be able to read the title or a sentence back to you without carefully looking at what has been written. Having the student

bring her finger down on each word will also ensure that she is actually looking at the word she is pronouncing and not saying one word while looking at another. If you allow the student to slide her finger under the words as she reads, she may have a tendency to read ahead of or behind where her finger is pointing. Students are hesitant to do this at times; they may have had a teacher who told them not to point to words as they were reading. A student may also resist raising her finger up and bringing it down on each word. Insist that it be done this way and you will, in most cases, find that any initial resistance is quickly overcome.

5. Proceed through the rest of the story as you did the title. Stop after you have written each sentence and point to each word as you reread the sentence. Bring your finger down on the word and say it at exactly the same time your finger comes down on it. After you have read the sentence, have the student read it in the same manner. Add a sentence at a time until you have finished the story.

6. After finishing the story, point to each word and read the entire story. Then have the student do the same. If she miscalls a word, quickly correct her and continue. Depending on the student and her ability to remember, it may be advisable to read the story several times.

7. The length of each story will depend on the characteristics of the student who is dictating it. However, in the beginning stages, be careful not to allow stories to become too long. The student will lose accuracy in rereading a particularly lengthy story, thus defeating the purpose of having her create her own material. As students continue to improve their reading, you are likely to find that they begin to dictate longer stories.

8. At this point, you may let the student illustrate the story or apply stickers or appropriate pictures from other sources.

9. Next, type or print the story using a word processor. If you use a typewriter, use primary or pica type, whichever is appropriate to the age/grade level of the student. If you use a word processor, you should be able to select from a number of fonts and sizes. The student should have the ability to transfer knowledge of words from manuscript or cursive writing to printed type.

10. After a period of time, such as would elapse after doing another activity, have the student reread the original story and then the typewritten or printed copy. You may wish to have the student take the original illustrated story home and practice reading it to someone in her family. Some students may lose their stories; saving them on a word processor will ensure that all stories remain intact.

11. At the next meeting with the student, ask her to read the story written in the previous session. If she reads it without errors, write another story, using the same procedure. Continue this sequence, that is, rereading all previous stories and writing another one each time you meet.

12. After the student has written a number of stories, bind them into a booklet and let the student create a cover.

13. After the student has built up a considerable sight vocabulary and has developed some beginning word-attack skills, you may have her gradually begin to read basal readers or general books.

Using the Language-Experience Approach With Small Groups of Students

In using the language-experience approach with small groups of students, you may wish to follow a sequence such as the following:

1. Brainstorm events or subjects of interest with the group, and tell students that you would like to help them write a story about one of these events or subjects.

2. Ask students to decide on a title for the story. When they have agreed on a title, write it using the exact words given by the students. As you write it, say each word. After finishing the title, direct students to watch carefully as you read it. Point to each word as you read it. Be careful to bring your finger down on each word and read it only as your finger touches the word. Then ask the students to read the title as you point to each word. You may have several students read it individually.

3. When writing the story, use the following general guidelines:
   A. Use the type of writing to which the students are accustomed, that is, either manuscript or cursive.
   B. Use the language that the students suggest and make very few, if any, changes.
   C. Write on something that can be saved for future use. Use 24″ × 36″ lined chart paper if it is available.
   D. Use a felt-tip pen or marker that will make broad, readable lines.
   E. In the beginning stages, use one-line sentences and gradually increase the length of the line as students' reading improves.
   F. Emphasize a left-to-right movement.
   G. Make sure students see all words as they are written.

4. After the story has been finished, read it to the class, being careful to point to each word as you read it. Be sure to read the story with enthusiasm.

5. Have the students read the story as a choral exercise as you point to each word.

6. Have individual students come to the chart and read the story. The chosen student should point to each word as she reads it, exactly as you have been doing. While this student points and reads, the rest of the students should read the story quietly as a choral exercise. (Although this may seem like a lot of reading of the same story, you will find that it is excellent practice and the students will enjoy participating.)

7. Use a typewriter or word processor to prepare a printed copy of the story after it is finished. Also, have students copy the chart in its exact form.

8. If possible, duplicate the story and give each student a copy to take home to practice reading to someone in her family.

9. After a period of time, ask students to reread the story. You may have students take turns reading a sentence at a time.

10. After students have practiced reading the story a number of times, you may also duplicate the story on a large piece of tagboard. The tagboard may then be cut into strips with one sentence on each strip. Either you or the students may then place the strips in a pocket chart to re-create the original story. At this time, make sure each student can read each sentence in isolation. After you have done this, you may cut the strips of sentences into phrase strips and re-create the original story by placing each phrase in the pocket chart. Have students practice reading these phrases to build fluency. Then the phrases may be cut into individual words and used once again to reconstruct the story. Students may manipulate the word cards to create new sentences, experiment with sorting the individual words into various categories, and select several words to add to their personal word banks.

11. Each time you meet with the group, read the previously written story and then write another one. Continue this process until stories have been read many times and students know all, or nearly all, of the words as sight words.

12. As students grow in their ability to read, let them begin to write and illustrate their own stories. Then bind these into booklets and let the students create the covers. Have students exchange booklets and read each other's stories.

13. Have students begin to read commercially written materials as their sight vo-cabulary and word-attack skills permit.

Important Procedures and Information About the Use of the Language-Experience Approach

1. Teachers should remember the following important procedures about the lan-guage-experience approach:

   A. When students dictate stories, attempt to use the exact language of the students. However, if you are concerned about students' incorrect usage or inappropriate language, you may modify the transcription of the dicta-tion slightly and tell the students, "That's a good thought; another way we might say this is . . ." (See item 4.)

   B. Make sure that both you and the students point to each word as it is being read. Doing this in the beginning stages of using the language-experience approach ensures that each word is memorized as a separate entity as well as a part of an entire story.

   C. Keep words clearly spaced, so students will recognize the difference be-tween *words* and *letters*.

   D. In the beginning stages, be sure to use only one-line sentences. Then grad-ually expand the length of the sentences as the students become more adept at reading.

   E. Emphasize a series of events, if possible, so students will see the devel-opment of the story.

   F. If possible, use 24″ × 36″ chart paper, so capital letters are 2″ high and low-ercase letters are 1″ high.

G. Make sure students see the words as they are being written.

H. Duplicate the chart so students can take the materials home to be practiced with another member of the family.

I. Emphasize left-to-right direction and the return sweep in writing and reading the stories.

2. Keep in mind that the language-experience approach has certain limitations. For example, a teacher using this approach almost exclusively is not likely to follow a sequential program in teaching word-attack skills. Many studies have shown that structured programs tend to produce better overall achievement from students. For this reason, you would probably want to use the language-experience approach in conjunction with a **basal reader** or other skills program or as a supplemental program for students with reading difficulties.

3. Different types of charts may be written in essentially the same manner as has been described in the preceding material. Some types of charts and their uses are the following:

A. *Summarizing chart.*   This chart shows a series of events on a field trip or a step-by-step procedure for doing an experiment in science.

B. *Story chart.*   This chart describes an event in the life of a group or an individual.

C. *Planning chart.*   This chart lists plans for such things as an anticipated trip or some other event in which the entire class will participate.

D. *Direction chart.*   This chart gives specific directions, such as for the assembly of a toy or paper-folding exercises.

E. *Dictionary chart.*   This chart lists new words that students have learned in science, social studies, or other subject areas.

4. Considerable controversy exists with regard to the shaping of the language of students who are using the language-experience approach. For immature speakers and students whose language is somewhat divergent from what might be considered standard English, the question sometimes arises as to whether the teacher should correct certain usage errors made by these students. It is probably true that more fuss is made over this issue than is necessary. If the teacher chooses to modify the students' language slightly, as indicated in the preceding directions, and if this is done gently, then no damage to either the children's self-esteem or their reading progress need occur.

5. It should be remembered that unless students begin to read trade books and other types of materials as they develop their sight vocabularies, their reading vocabularies will, of course, be limited to only those words in their speaking vocabularies. Therefore, students using the language-experience approach should be encouraged to read other materials along with their language-experience charts and books.

Twenty Language-Experience Activities

Listed here are a number of language-experience materials created by students. Most of the items in the list are examples of individual descriptions of illustrations done in a group setting. With this approach, the teacher motivates the students and leads a brief discussion on the topic. The children then draw pictures of the topic. Some sample topics for this type of activity for beginning readers include the following:

1. Happiness is. . . .
2. Sadness is. . . .
3. A friend is. . . .
4. I feel afraid when. . . .
5. If I were the teacher I would. . . .
6. If I had a million dollars I would. . . .

Students decide how they will finish the sentence and begin their illustrations. (These are sometimes called *model sentences.*) The teacher (and other adults, if available) circulates quickly about the room and writes down the students' words, such as "A friend is my Daddy," or "A friend is someone who rides bikes with you," or "A friend is a big yellow zebra." The teacher writes down the exact words the student says. With practice, the teacher can catch all the students' responses while they illustrate. Then, the teacher collects the pictures and binds them and the sentences into a book that students can read later.

A collection of these student books often becomes the single most popular item in the classroom. The students eagerly read them many times and learn to recognize not only their own words but also the words dictated by their peers. Variations on these examples can be created for virtually any grade level.

Student books can be made from simple materials. The most common type uses a fabric cover around construction paper pages. Here are the directions for making this type of book.

Materials: A piece of fabric, approximately 22″ × 16″
Sheets of 12″ × 18″ construction paper (one sheet for every four pages of the book, plus one sheet to attach to the cover)
One sheet of 12″ × 18″ tagboard for the cover
Needle and thread
Rubber cement or equivalent

Procedure:

For pages:

Fold construction paper pages in half.
Sew pages in the middle from bottom to top.
Do not sew through the tagboard cover.

For cover:

Put rubber cement around inside edge of tagboard.
Put fabric around cover; cement overlap on inside edges of cover.
Fold cover in half.

To attach pages to cover:

Put rubber cement on outside of front and back pages.
Cement outside of pages to cover.

Some Ideas for the Beginning of the Year

1. *Our Class:* You will need one page for each student. The student selects a pre-cut circle of the appropriate color for her face, then draws in the face and the body around it. The student dictates a couplet, which the teacher copies along with the student's name. If one is available, the teacher adds the child's actual picture from a class composite. Examples: "My name is Russell and I have a big muscle," "My name is Brenda Lee and I got stung by a bee," "My name is Ted and I fell out of bed."

2. *All About Us:* Originally these were individual projects that were placed on bulletin boards or around the room. Later they were put together in a large class book. Each student creates her face, arms, and legs out of construction paper that is pasted to a large tagboard sheet. Each student also makes hair out of yarn. The body is $9'' \times 12''$ construction paper with writing paper on the inside. The construction paper is folded to make the body, then unfolded to read the dictated story.

3. *All About Me:* In this case, each student makes her *own* book, consisting of many pages. Pages may be completed one per day and then bound into an individual student book when finished. Example pages: Page 1—All About Me. The student colors the page and writes her name. Page 2—My name is _____. This is me. The student draws a picture of herself, writes her name, and learns to read a few words. Other pages may include: This is my house; This is my family; I like _____; I would like to be a _____; My best friend is _____; I like to eat _____; I don't like to eat _____; I like to play _____; I am afraid of _____; and so on.

4. *My Favorite Things:* This activity is the same as item 3. Pages for individual books like these are sometimes available commercially in teacher supply stores. Typical pages: My favorite pet is _____; My favorite color is _____; My best friend's name is _____; If you want to phone me, call this number _____; If you want to send me a letter, here's my name and address _____; My teeth—I've counted them, I have _____ up top and I have _____ downstairs; My hair looks like this; My nose looks like this; My eyes look like this; My favorite song is _____; My favorite sport is _____; My favorite instrument is _____; I go to bed at _____; I get up at _____; When I grow up, I want to be _____.

5. *Let's Pretend:* This activity is similar to items 3 and 4; the teacher makes an individual book for each student. Example pages: If I were invisible I would _____; If I had a magic carpet I would _____; If I had one million dollars I would _____; If I were the teacher I would _____; If I could have only one wish it would be _____; If I met Jack Frost I would _____; If I lived under the sea I would _____; Once upon a time there lived an ugly princess who _____; A long,

long time ago there lived a tiny mouse who _____; The wicked witch waved her magic wand and turned the boy into a _____.

More Ideas

6. *Happiness and Sadness:* This is a two-part book. For the first part, each student draws a picture and then dictates a statement about "Happiness Is." The second part is "Sadness Is." Examples: Happiness is: "Holding a cat and eating ice cream," "Looking at your muscle." Sadness is: "Getting picked on by someone bigger."

7. *A Friend Is:* This is another sentence completer. The student finishes the thought "A friend is _____," and draws a picture. The teacher or other adult takes dictation, collects the pictures, and binds them into a class book. Examples: "A friend is someone who rides bikes with you"; "A friend is someone who celebrates your birthday in a tent with you"; "A friend is my Daddy."

Holiday Specials

8. *Secret Recipe for Witches' Brew:* The teacher writes the word *cauldron* on the chalkboard and discusses it with the students. Each student has a page shaped like a cauldron and draws on it pictures of items to go into the witches' brew. The teacher or other adult then writes down the words that describe the pictures, collects the pages, and binds them into a book. Examples from a kindergarten version: *skeleton, fairy godmother, spider, bloodsucker,* and *spider web.*

9. *The Turkey Book:* This is similar to item 8. The students' pages are shaped like a turkey, and the students draw items related to Thanksgiving.

Still More Ideas

10. *Round Is:* This is a concept book. Each student has a circle on which she draws a picture of something that is round. The teacher or other adult writes down each student's words to describe the picture.

11. *Class Fortunes:* An inscription on the first page describes the book: "Before we made this book, we pretended that we were fortune tellers. We said some magic words and then looked into our make-believe crystal balls and concentrated very hard. We each drew the name of another person in the class. These are the people whose fortunes we wrote." (Warning: Students must be prohibited from making unpleasant fortunes for their classmates!) Examples (written by second and third graders): (1) "In my crystal ball I see Darcella. She is an astronaut, but works in a hospital and at Sir Pizza in her spare time. She lives in Hawaii and is married to a bachelor." (2) "In my crystal ball I see Ricardo. He is a truck driver. He lives in Arizona. He is a bachelor and is playing around." (*Bachelor* must have been a popular word that week!)

12. *Riddles From A to Z:* Each student is given a letter of the alphabet. The student writes a riddle, the answer to which begins with the letter. Example: For the letter *F*—It runs around the house, yet never moves. (A fence.)

13. *Words With Feeling:* Each page in this book has pasted on it an item that students can see or feel. The pages consist of a listing of words that come to mind when students think of the item. For example, a piece of aluminum foil is pasted on page 1. The page has written on it: "*Shiny* makes me think of: diamonds, gold, silver, sun, rings, and clean hair." Other examples: "*Velvety* makes me think of my mother's rug, shag carpets, and green moss." "*Stretchy* makes me think of rubber bands, elastic, waking up, spaghetti, gum, and silly putty." Other key words are: *silky, striped, rough, wavy, furry, bumpy, smooth, spotted, spongy,* and *bright.*

14. *Moody Me:* The inscription on the first page describes the book: "We had a lot of fun writing this book! First, we acted out all the different moods and talked about them. All of the things in the book have happened or could easily happen to us. These are our real joys, sorrows, dreams, and fears." Each student picks one mood or emotion, draws a picture of herself expressing that emotion, and dictates to the teacher or other adult. Examples: "I feel sad because I don't have any friends." "I feel nervous because I saw a ghost." Other key words: *silly, embarrassed, relieved, happy, awful, excited, confused, proud, mean, overjoyed, itchy, pretty, sick, kind, anxious, mad, hot, worried, cold,* and *scared.*

15. *Ridiculous Rhymes:* Each student dictates a couplet and draws a picture that the couplet describes. Examples: "I saw an ant who had no pants." "I saw a turtle who wore a girdle."

16. *Whose Eyes:* The all-time favorite. The inscription on the first page describes the book: "One night, as I lay in my bed almost asleep, I heard a loud knock at my door. The door opened slowly and in the doorway I could see two eyes staring in at me. I have never been so scared in all my life! Who or what could those strange eyes be?" On each page, the student sees a door made of black construction paper, with a yellow self-sticking dot for the doorknob. When the door is opened, the student sees two more yellow dots, which are the eyes. The student then draws a picture around the eyes and dictates to the teacher or other adult what the picture is about. Examples: (1) "It was my mother. She came to bring me a glass of water." (2) "It was a vampire. It wanted to suck my blood." (3) "It was my cat. It came to get tuna fish." (4) "It was my Mom. She came to take my money." (5) "It was a ghost. He was looking for potato chips."

17. *How the Elephant Got Its Trunk:* Inspired by the *Just So Stories,* students dictate or write their own versions of how the elephant got its trunk.

18. *Our Monsters:* This book combines an art activity with language experience. The students make watercolor monsters and dictate stories about them.

19. *Did You Ever See. . . ?* Based on the book of the same name, this is a collection of illustrated couplets. The illustration on the front side of the page corresponds to the first rhyming word of the couplet; the illustration on the back side of the page corresponds to the second rhyming word. Examples: (1) "Did you ever see a lion—" "—Cryin'?" (2) "Did you ever see a pig—" "—Wear a wig?" (3) "Did you ever see a rabbit—" "—Kick the habit?"

20. *Interviews:* This is a series of language-experience books created by a small group of students. (1) The students interview each other in pairs. (2) Each stu-

dent introduces her partner to the members of the small group. (3) Members of the small group write a page about each student in the group. (4) Each student draws a picture about herself. (5) The teacher makes copies of the books for all members of the group. (6) Students then read each other's books.

REFERENCES

Eldredge, J. L. (1990). Increasing the performance of poor readers in the third grade with a group-assisted strategy. *Journal of Educational Research, 84,* 69–77.

Eldredge, J. L., & Butterfield, D. D. (1986). Alternatives to traditional reading instruction. *Reading Teacher, 40,* 32–37.

Heckelman, R. G. (1966). Using the neurological-impress remedial reading technique. *Academic Therapy Quarterly, 1,* 235–239.

Holdaway, D. (1979). *The foundations of literacy.* Sydney, Australia: Ashton Scholastic.

Koskinen, P. S., & Blum, I. H. (1986). Paired repeated reading: A classroom strategy for developing fluent reading. *Reading Teacher, 40,* 70–75.

Samuels, S. J. (1979). The method of repeated readings. *Reading Teacher, 32,* 403–406.

PART TWO

EMERGENT LITERACY SKILLS

CHAPTER 1

Phonemic Awareness

RECOGNIZED BY

While the student may not have difficulty in speaking or understanding English, he is unable to recognize, identify, and manipulate individual speech sounds.

DISCUSSION

Phonemic awareness, sometimes called *phoneme awareness* or *oral phonemic* **segmentation,** is the understanding of, and the ability to manipulate, the smallest units of sound (**phonemes**) that make up spoken words. There are approximately 40 different phonemes in English, which are represented by one or more of the 26 letters in our alphabet. For example, in the word *dog*, there are three phonemes, the sounds of which are represented as follows: /d/, /o/, and /g/. While phonemic awareness is not necessary for understanding and speaking the language, research has shown that it is critical to reading success. In fact, phonemic awareness is more highly related to learning to read than are other well-known measures such as alphabet knowledge, intelligence, other emergent literacy skills, and listening comprehension. Phonemic awareness has been shown to be the most important causal factor that distinguishes successful from disabled readers. Youngsters who lack phonemic awareness tend to have difficulty in understanding the alphabetical system of English required for changing print into meaningful sound. Phonemic awareness skills are prerequisites for benefiting from phonics instruction. They are also an important factor in learning how to spell.

Experts do not agree on all of the components of phonemic awareness. Some authorities believe that some of the higher-level phonemic awareness skills are more a consequence of reading acquisition than a cause.

Students with strong phonemic awareness skills understand about the individual *sounds* in spoken words, not written words. They know that individual words are made up of different sounds, and they know how to manipulate these sounds to make different words. Once students add another key emergent literacy skill, alphabet knowledge, they have two key prerequisites for successful decoding. Next they learn how the letters and sounds correspond (which is called **phonics**), and active reading begins.

One helpful sequence of phonemic awareness skills follows. These three examples can be used to quickly assess a student's level of phonemic awareness. You can also test for these important phonemic awareness tasks more thoroughly by following the specific instructions on the phonemic awareness tests that appear in Appendix A-2. Such testing will enable you to determine each child's abilities prior to providing instruction in the areas where weaknesses are exhibited. The tests in Appendix A-2 provide scoring sheets you can use to keep track of each child's performance.

    A. *Rhyming Abilities*
        1. *Rhyme production.*   Say the words *rat* and *sat*. Ask the student to tell you another word that rhymes with *rat* and *sat*. Let the child know it does not have to be a real word. (Answer: *cat* or *fat* or similar word.) If the child is unable to produce a rhyming word, then assess rhyme recognition.
        2. *Rhyme recognition.*   Demonstrate pairs of rhyming words by saying *big, pig, rain, pain,* and *tree, see.* Then ask the child to hold his thumb up if the next two words you say also rhyme. Then say *hope, rope* and see if the child puts his thumb up. Next, say some pairs of words that rhyme and do not rhyme to determine if the student can recognize rhyming words or if he is merely guessing.
    B. *Initial sound recognition.* Say the word *box*. Ask the student to tell you the beginning sound of the word. (Answer: /b/.)
    C. *Phoneme blending.* Slowly pronounce the three phonemes /m/, /a/, /n/. Ask the student to tell you what the word is. (Answer: *man.*)
    D. *Phoneme segmentation.* Say the word *cat*. Ask the student to say each of the three phonemes in the word. (Answer: /k/, /a/, /t/.)

Eldredge (1995) recommends assessment of two additional areas of phonemic awareness as follows.

    E. *Recognizing the number of sounds.* Say the word *back*. Ask the student to tell you how many sounds can be heard in that word. (Answer: three.)
    F. *Ending sound recognition.* Say the word *toss*. Ask the student to tell you the ending sound of the word. (Answer: /s/.)

Students' phonemic awareness ability should be assessed by mid-kindergarten. Students who are not progressing adequately should be provided with intensive phonemic awareness training.

RECOMMENDATIONS

Informal Language Activities

Phonemic awareness can be fostered both through informal language activities that encourage students to explore and manipulate the sounds in words and through formal, systematic instruction. Phonemic awareness activities should begin prior to kindergarten and may include the activities listed here.

To provide informal language activities that encourage students to explore and manipulate the sounds in words, the teacher might do the following:

A. Read to students throughout the day and engage them in discussions and explanations to enhance oral language development. Use pictures and objects to demonstrate word meanings and associations.

B. Point out to students the separate words as they appear in sentences on charts or in big books. Pronounce the words clearly while doing this.

C. Help young students to hear the syllables in words by clapping them out and pronouncing them in exaggerated ways.

D. Use alliterative literature to help students develop the concept of beginning sounds. Ask students to identify words that start with the same sounds in the text. After reading a book, have students generate more words that have the same beginning sounds. Using the pattern of the text, have students create alliterative sentences for a class book. Each student can illustrate a sentence. You will find a list of trade books to assist in teaching alliteration in Appendix B-1.

E. Provide other activities that encourage children to identify and manipulate phonemes, such as these:
   1. "What is the beginning sound of _____?"
   2. "What is the ending sound of _____?"
   3. "Do *dog* and *cat* rhyme?"
   4. "How is *bat* different from *sat?*"
   5. "Listen to the word *time.* Can you change that word by giving it a beginning sound of /d/?"
   6. "What are all of the sounds you hear in *feet?*"

Each of these suggestions can be expanded into activities that may consume several instructional sessions. Do not attempt to teach these concepts too quickly; do not expect all students to learn them at the same time.

Direct Instruction

To provide direct instruction in phonemic awareness, the teacher might key the instructional activities to the skills described in the "Discussion" section of this chapter. The first four instructional activities below match the specific areas tested in the Phonemic Awareness Tests (Appendix A-2). The final two sections offer techniques for teaching the two additional areas of phonemic awareness recommended by Eldredge.

A. *Rhyming abilities.* Teach and practice rhyming skills using songs, poems, nursery rhymes, and chants. Read the rhyme aloud, pointing to each word. Reread the text and engage the students in a variety of responses.
   1. Have students hold up colorful objects or clap each time they hear a rhyming word.
   2. Ask students to identify the rhyming words in the text, then highlight the words on chart paper.

3. When students know the text well, pause before each rhyming word to allow students an opportunity to supply the word.
4. Select rhyming words from the text and ask students to generate additional rhyming words.
5. Cover up rhyming words in the text and have students provide different rhyming words.

Refer to Appendix B-1 for a list of rhyming books.

B. *Initial sound recognition.* Begin with the following one-syllable words: *top, dog, bus, sit,* and *cup.*

1. Say: "I want to see if you can listen very carefully and tell me the sound you hear at the beginning of the word I say. Listen. /t/ /o/ /p/. Were you listening for the /t/ sound at the beginning of the word? Good for you. Let's try /d/ /o/ /g/. What was the first sound? /d/. Good."
2. Continue with the rest of the words. Expect that some children may have difficulty with the concept of "beginning sound." You may need to demonstrate several times. It may be helpful to use a hand signal, such as raising your hand, while you are pronouncing the first phoneme.

C. *Phoneme blending.* Select a number of easily discriminated one-syllable words, such as *bat, sit, red, top,* and *cup.* (It is better initially to use words with single consonants at the beginning and end, rather than consonant blends.)

1. Begin with the first word, *bat.*
2. Slowly pronounce each of the phonemes, being careful to clearly separate them from each other initially. Say: "I'm going to tell you a word by first saying each of its parts very slowly. Listen carefully. /b/ (pause) /a/ (pause) /t/. Now, I'm going to blend those parts of the word together. Listen. /b/ (brief pause) /a/ (brief pause) /t/. Now, listen one more time while I put the whole word together." Say the whole word *bat,* slowly enunciating each phoneme. "Who can tell me what the word is? Good. What is a bat?"
3. Repeat the previous step with the other one-syllable words.
4. As students begin to catch on, you can speed up the process of pronouncing each word as described in step 2.

D. *Phoneme segmentation.* Choose more words. This time ask students to listen to and identify (repeat) each of the phonemes as you pronounce them.

1. Say: "This time I am going to say a word and I want you to tell me all of the sounds you hear in the word. Let's try one. Listen. /p/ /a/ /t/. Did you hear all three sounds? Good. Let's say them again together: /p/ /a/ /t/. Very good."
2. Continue with other two- and three-phoneme words.

E. *Recognizing the number of sounds.* Choose more words, such as *fun, rap, me, is,* and *I.*

1. Begin with the word *fun.*
2. Say: "This time I want to see what good counters you are." Slowly pronounce the three separate phonemes of the word *fun.* Say: "Listen. /f/ /u/ /n/. How many sounds did you hear in that word? Three? Good for you."

3. Say: "Now listen for the next word and count again: /r/ /a/ /p/. How many sounds did you hear? Three? Very good!"

4. When you get to the word *me*, expect that some students will guess "three" again. Those who, in fact, are developing phonemic awareness should arrive at the correct answer, two.

5. Alternate between one-, two-, and three-phoneme words (all only one syllable) to make sure students are listening and telling you how many sounds they are actually hearing rather than guessing.

F. *Ending sound recognition.* Repeat the process in step B, but this time have students listen for and identify the ending sound of the words you pronounce. This task may be considerably more difficult than beginning sound recognition for some students.

In using this approach, do not expect young students to go through all five areas at one sitting. How fast they are able to progress will depend on your skill in providing instruction, the number of students present (the fewer the better), the literacy backgrounds of the students, and other factors. Do remember that your goal is to *teach* the students to enhance their phonemic awareness, not merely to test them. Therefore you will need to modify your instruction as necessary to help your students understand these concepts. That may mean moving more slowly, providing more repetition, or presenting smaller increments of learning.

GAMES AND EXERCISES

Find Your Buddy

Purpose: To practice identifying rhymes; can be modified to provide practice in identifying beginning or ending sounds

Materials: Large index cards featuring pairs of pictures that rhyme, such as *car* and *star*. Make one picture for each student.

Procedure:

Hand each student a picture. Have students circulate and find a buddy whose picture rhymes with the picture they are holding. The game can also be played to practice matching objects with the same beginning or ending sounds.

Guess the Sounds

Purpose: To practice phoneme blending

Materials: A bag full of unrelated objects or objects related to a classroom theme

Procedure:

Begin with objects that have three sounds. Grab an object without removing it from the bag. Create simple riddles to provide practice in oral blending by stretching out the sounds of the objects. For example, "I am holding something that likes to chase mice. It is a /c/ /a/ /t/. (Emphasize and distinctly separate each of the sounds, but do not distort the sound.) Call on students to first repeat the sounds as you said them, then blend the sounds together and pronounce the word, to identify the object. Remove the object from the bag to confirm the answers to the riddle. As students become more skilled at this activity, you may omit the riddle so they focus exclusively on blending and pronouncing the segmented sounds.

Elkonin Boxes

Purpose: To practice segmenting sounds

Materials: Objects such as chips, pennies, or buttons for each student;
            A paper with three connected boxes for each student—The boxes must be large enough to accommodate the objects being used (see illustration below.)

Procedure:

Elkonin (1973) developed sound boxes to assist students in the difficult task of segmenting words into sounds. Select a group of familiar words, each of which consists of three sounds (phonemes). Say one of the words. Then say the word again, stretching out each sound. Have students pronounce the sounds, pushing an object into each box as they pronounce each phoneme. When students demonstrate sufficient skill, select words with four phonemes. To extend the activity, give students picture cards illustrating three- and four-phoneme objects. Have them select a card, then determine the number of sounds in the object illustrated. Finally, have students place their picture cards on a graph to show how many of the objects consisted of three versus four phonemes.

Variation:

Use color tiles instead of the sound boxes. As students say the sounds, have them line up a color tile, from left to right, for each sound they hear.

REFERENCES

Eldredge, J. L. (1995). *Teaching decoding in holistic classrooms.* Upper Saddle River, NJ: Merrill/Prentice Hall.

Elkonin, D. B. (1973). In J. Downing (Ed.), *Comparative reading* (pp. 551–579). New York: Macmillan.

CHAPTER 2

Alphabet Knowledge

RECOGNIZED BY

The child is unable to recognize the letters of the alphabet when shown the letters, is unable to point to the letters of the alphabet, is unable to match uppercase and lowercase letters, or is unable to match one uppercase or lowercase letter with another letter that looks exactly the same.

DISCUSSION

Alphabet knowledge, the ability to recognize and name the letters of the alphabet, appears to be the second most important instructional factor in learning to read. Research has consistently shown that alphabet knowledge is highly correlated with, and usually predictive of, later reading success.

Students who, when administered an informal reading inventory, know very few words, or students who appear to be severely disabled in reading should be given a test for **letter knowledge**. Keep in mind that there are various levels of difficulty in testing for letter knowledge. The materials listed in Appendix A-3 will enable you to determine whether the student has difficulty with the alphabet and, if so, the *level* of difficulty at which the student is weak. For example, it is more difficult for a student to name letters in random order than it is to point to the letters named by the teacher.

RECOMMENDATIONS

A. Use a wide variety of alphabet books to help students recognize the letters and learn the sequence of the alphabet. Such books also help students build vocabulary and learn letter-sound associations, especially beginning sounds. Appendix B-1 provides a list of 20 alphabet books, giving the book title, author, publisher, and publication date. Also included in that appendix is a list of eight additional alphabet books written in alliterative language.

B. Create a collection of non-book materials to encourage students to explore the alphabet, including magnetic letters, letter stamps, flashcards, and dry-erase boards. Also include items such as cereal boxes, catalogs, magazines, and newspapers. Provide opportunities for students to freely explore the alphabet.

C. Teach students the alphabet song. Then present a copy of the alphabet (in alphabetical order), and as students sing the song, ask them to point to each letter.

D. Present a letter and discuss its characteristic shape; for example, that it has an ascender, such as the letter *h*, or a descender, such as the letter *p*. The speed at which students learn letters is highly variable. Some can learn several letters at a time, while others can learn only one letter per week. Some letters are easily confused and should not be taught closely together, such as *p-d*, *b-d*, *p-q*, *q-b*, *m-n*, and *i-j*. (If students have difficulty with letters that are easily confused, refer to the recommendations in items H and I.)

E. Prepare a blank book and label the pages with the letters of the alphabet. Have students cut out letters from cereal boxes, catalogs, magazines, and newspapers, and then paste the letters in the book. To help students learn that letters appear in a variety of styles, point out the different fonts that appear in text and encourage them to collect many styles for each letter.

F. Make a tape recording of the letters of the alphabet to accompany an alphabet book such as *Animalia* by Graeme Base. Students will find this entertaining, and it provides a way for them to learn the letters in context.

G. When teaching the alphabet, be sure that it appears on a chart where students can see it constantly. Using just a few letters at a time, work with students until they can instantly tell you which letter comes before or after any other letter. For example, if you say, "Which letter comes before *G?*" and point to a child, he should instantly say "*F.*" Most adults can instantly give the letter that immediately *follows* another; however, they usually pause a few seconds before they tell which letter *precedes* another. Knowing the order of the letters will save time later when students are using the dictionary.

H. If some letters are reversed, or if a student seems to have a difficult time learning them, prepare letters cut from fine sandpaper and have him feel the letters as he pronounces them. This can also be done with three-dimensional letters made of felt or similar material. (Do not become overly concerned if children tend to reverse letters. This is a normal part of the learning process with emergent readers and almost always disappears gradually as letter knowledge increases.)

I. Place a thin layer of salt or fine sand in the bottom of a shoebox lid and have students trace letters with their fingers in the sand or salt.

J. Make a list of the first third of the alphabet.

1. A		5. E	
2. B		6. F	
3. C		7. G	
4. D		8. H	

Then make a recording for students to take home or work with in the classroom. The tape-recorded script can be as follows: "Look at the letter by number one. This letter is *A*. Point to it and say '*A*.' Look at it very carefully and say '*A*' again. The next letter by number two is *B*. Point to it and say '*B*.' Look at it very carefully and say it again." Continue through the list. You may wish to modify this script to have students also write the letter. In this case, the script would be as follows: "Look at the letter by number one. This letter is *A*. Point to it and say '*A*.' Look at it very carefully and say it again. Now write the letter and say '*A*' as you write it," and so on. Note: This presentation will be successful only with students who are able to learn letters easily and rapidly. For other students, the presentation can be simplified by presenting only one or two letters at a time. Also, you must observe students when they are learning in this way. Some students, especially younger ones, cannot stay on task without direct participation or instruction from the teacher. For these youngsters, this technique will not be effective.

GAMES AND EXERCISES

Alphabet Hunt

Purpose: To practice knowledge of the alphabet

Materials: A pointer for each student

Procedure:

The teacher calls out a letter and students hunt for the letter in the room, using their pointers to identify the letter. The teacher can make the game more challenging by specifying uppercase and lowercase letters, provided students are able to recognize both forms of the letters.

Alphabet Concentration

Purpose: To practice knowledge of the alphabet

Materials: A set of 10 to 12 letters, with two cards for each letter; pairs can be lowercase only, uppercase only, or a combination of the two

Procedure:

The players lay the cards facedown and alternate turning the cards over two at a time. If the letters on the cards match, the player keeps them and takes another turn. The game is over when all of the cards are taken.

Newspaper Search

Purpose: To practice knowledge of the alphabet

Materials: A newspaper page and a crayon or marker for each student

Procedure:

The teacher or a student names a letter. The remaining students search their newspaper pages to find the letter and circle it with their crayon or marker. Students then hunt for another letter, and the game continues in this manner. To provide additional practice, have the children search for both uppercase and lowercase examples of the letter named.

Letter Bingo

Purpose: To practice knowledge of the alphabet

Materials: A bingo card filled with alphabet letters (each card should contain the same letters, but in different positions)
Markers for each student

Procedure:

The caller names a letter and holds up the matching card while players search for and cover the named letter on their cards. The first player to cover a row calls "Bingo!"

PART THREE

DECODING SKILLS

CHAPTER 3

Basic Sight Words Not Known

RECOGNIZED BY

The student is unable to read some or all of the **basic sight words,** those words of high utility that make up from 50% to 70% of the words in most reading material. The percentage is, of course, higher in materials written at a lower reading level.

DISCUSSION

There are several lists of the common or basic sight words. One is provided in Appendix A-5. Because, by definition, these are the words that appear most frequently, it is essential that students recognize them instantly. If students do not have these words in their sight vocabulary, or cannot recognize them instantly, they cannot become fluent readers. Students often confuse certain basic sight words, especially those with similar beginnings, such as *when, where,* and *what,* or *this, that,* and *those.*

If you observe your students when they read orally, you can determine whether they usually pronounce basic sight words accurately. With some experience, you will have little difficulty recognizing which words are basic sight words. (Just by glancing at the words listed in Appendix A-5, you will see that most of the words you would think of as most common do, in fact, appear on the basic sight word list.)

A first grader is generally expected to master about one-third of the basic sight word list by the end of the year, a second grader is expected to master another third, and a third grader should master the final third of the list by the end of the school year. *Mastery* means that the student can pronounce the basic sight words instantly on viewing them. Also, the student should pronounce the words correctly *each time* they appear. If a student mispronounces or even hesitates on the pronunciation of a basic sight word, or if the student pronounces the word correctly only some of the time, then the student has not mastered this basic sight word.

Many older students and most illiterate adults have significant problems with basic sight words. These individuals, along with primary-grade children who are not progressing satisfactorily, need systematic and thorough instruction on basic sight words.

A test of the basic sight words often is given by having the student look at four or five different words on a page while the teacher pronounces one of the words and asks the student to circle or underline the word pronounced. The cognitive process required to *distinguish* a word from a choice of four or five words is not, however, the same as the process required to *pronounce* the word after seeing it in print. You frequently will find that students can score 100% on a basic sight word test if it is given in the manner described, but these same students may not be able to pronounce the same words when they are asked to read them.

When you are testing for students' knowledge of basic sight words, you should present each word for approximately one-half to one second. If you give the student more time than this to look at the word, then, to some extent, the test becomes a measure of word-analysis skills rather than of knowledge of sight words. You can have the student read words from a list; however, it is difficult to control the time each word is exposed to the student. If you do have the student read basic sight words from a list, remember to count as wrong any word at which the student pauses for more than about one second. Having students read the basic sight words from a list is a quick way to check those students who you think, but are not quite sure, know most of the words. The Quick Check for Basic Sight Words, which appears in Appendix A-4, may be used for this purpose.

The best way to test basic sight words is to use flash cards with a tape recorder. Specific instructions for doing this are presented along with the lists of basic sight words and phrases that appear in Appendix A-5. This procedure should be used to test both the individual basic sight words and the **basic sight word phrases**. Each sight word test takes approximately 6 minutes per student to administer and score.

When testing is completed, you can examine the prepared lists and determine specifically which basic sight words and phrases the student has not mastered. These can then be taught without having to misuse instructional time teaching words or phrases that are already known.

RECOMMENDATIONS

The suggestions listed in items A through J and the games and exercises will be helpful in teaching basic sight words. Most students will learn basic sight words quickly and easily when they are simply shown the word, hear it used in a sentence, repeat it, and practice reading it. Immediate reinforcement (lots of practice) is essential for students to *master* new words. The best way to provide this reinforcement is to have students read over and over simple student- or teacher-constructed sentences or stories that contain the new words and to do lots of reading in easy books. It is very important to provide students with ample practice in authentic reading. It is not enough to simply have students read these words off of lists or flash cards. Remember: the goal is to permanently implant these words in students' minds so they can *instantly* retrieve them *when reading*.

The suggestions listed in items A through F and the games and exercises in this chapter can be used to have students learn and practice sight word *phrases* as well as individual sight words. Direct instruction of the words, followed by focused practice in reading the words in isolation, phrases, sentences, and stories is the most effective way to help students master basic sight words. Games and exercises should be used only to motivate students and provide additional practice.

Many teachers will have students practice the phrases after a set number, say 20, of the words have been mastered. The sight word phrases that appear on the list in Appendix A-5 are compiled so that each word from the isolated word list is presented in a phrase without adding a lot of new words for the student to master. In addition, a list of prepositional phrases is provided in Appendix B-7. You may wish to have students practice reading these phrases after all the basic sight words have been learned. A list of basic sight word *sentences* is provided in Appendix B-2. These sentences are derived from the basic sight word phrases presented in Appendix A-5.

It is important to provide a variety of easy readers so students can practice reading basic sight words while engaged in the act of reading. The language-experience approach and the various oral reading procedures presented in the introductory chapter are also effective. In using these methods, you will not be focusing on any particular basic sight word. However, because the words appear so often, most students will be successful in learning them because of their repeated appearance in the stories that the students write using the language-experience approach and in the passages they read during oral reading.

When teaching students individually or in small groups, introduce the words a few at a time. The number of words to be learned per week will vary from student to student. Success, however, is critical. *It is better to learn fewer words well.* Students should see mastery as a challenging goal. Often the students themselves can best determine the number of new words to be learned at a time. If in doubt, begin with five words.

When presenting sight words, always be sure that the student is looking *at the word*, not at you. If possible, try to spend a few minutes with the student individually when presenting the words for the first time.

A. The following dialogue presents a thorough approach to the initial teaching of basic sight words. Usually not all of the steps noted are necessary.

Teacher:	(*holds up a flash card*) "Look at this word. The word is *the*." (*uses it in a sentence*) "I am *the* teacher. Say the word."
Student:	"The."
T:	"Good. Now say it five times."
S:	"The, the, the, the, the."
T:	"Outstanding. Now say it really loud."
S:	"The."
T:	"No, that's not loud enough. Let me hear you say it really loud."
S:	"The."
T:	"Here, I'll show you. THE!"
S:	(chuckles) "THE!"
T:	"Fantastic. Now let me hear you whisper it."
S:	(whispers) "The."
T:	"Excellent. Now close your eyes. Can you see the word on your eyelids?"
S:	"Yup."
T:	"Spell it."
S:	"T-h-e."

> **T:** "Good. Now describe the word. What does it look like?"
> **S:** "Well, it's kinda small."
> **T:** "How are you going to remember it?"
> **S:** "Uh, it has two letters that stick up."
> **T:** "Terrific!"

Present each new word using the "overlearning" procedure: 1, 2; 1, 2, 3; 1, 2, 3, 4; 1, 2, 3, 4, 5. For example: *the, to; the, to, and; the, to, and, he;* and so on. If, after all the new words have been presented, the student still has difficulty pronouncing them quickly, you may take the following steps:

1. Have the student trace the word, write it on paper, or use chalk or a magic slate.
2. Have the student repeat the word each time he writes it.
3. Have the student write the word without looking at the flash card then compare the two.

B. Arrange "study buddies." Match learners in the classroom with fellow students who have mastered the words. Take time to teach the "tutors" how to reinforce new words. Provide a reward to both tutor and learner once the learner has attained the goal.

C. Provide charts, graphs, and other devices for students to display their progress. These serve as excellent motivators, especially because students are competing with themselves rather than with one another.

D. Pass out a few basic sight words on cards to students. Each student, in turn, goes to the board and writes her word. The other students participating should try to say it aloud. After it is pronounced correctly, have them write it in a notebook. On some days, have students select words from their notebooks and write them on the chalkboard. Then ask various members of the group to say these words.

E. Have students use the words from their notebooks to create simple sentences or stories. It is fine for these stories to be silly; students can also be encouraged to include their own names and names of fellow students in the stories. During free time, students may illustrate or decorate these sentences and stories. As often as possible, students can practice reading their own and fellow students' sentences and stories over and over again.

F. Have the student read the entire sentence, look at the beginning and end of the word, and then try to pronounce it on the basis of its context and configuration.

G. Have the student write troublesome words on cards. Use the cards to form sentences. Also, provide sentences with the sight words omitted. Have the student fill in the blanks with the appropriate word from her cards.

H. Use the sight words that cause difficulty in sentences. Underline the words that cause difficulty, as in the following examples:

1. I *thought* it was you.
2. I could not go even *though* I have time.
3. She ran right *through* the stop sign.

A list of basic sight word sentences, derived from the sight word phrases, is provided in Appendix B-2.

I. Use commercially prepared games or computer software designed for teaching basic sight words.

J. Provide reinforcement games for students to use on their own or with their study buddies. (See the suggestions under "Games and Exercises" later in this chapter.)

Students who have particular difficulty with certain words may benefit from one or both of the following activities:

K. Cut letters from fine sandpaper or velvet so that the student can "feel" the word as she pronounces it. For certain students, it may be helpful to put a thin layer of salt or fine sand in a shoebox lid and let them practice writing the word in the salt or sand.

L. Place a piece of paper over a piece of screen wire (such as the wire used for screen doors). It is a good idea to cover the edges of the screen wire with bookbinding tape, so the rough edges do not cut anyone. Writing on the paper over the screen with a crayon will leave a series of raised dots. Have the student write basic sight words in this manner, and then have her trace over the words, saying them as she traces.

GAMES AND EXERCISES

Note: For these games and exercises to be most effective, students must receive lots of practice in *looking at* and *quickly saying* the sight words. (See also the games and exercises in Chapter 4, "General Sight Vocabulary Not Up to Grade Level." Many of these are appropriate for improving knowledge of basic sight words.)

Guess the Word

Purpose: To provide practice in recognizing basic sight words

Materials: Basic sight words written on an overhead transparency, large flashcards, or sentence strips, OR flashcards placed in a pocket chart, as shown in the examples in Figure 3.1.

FIGURE 3.1

that	
what	that
which	
- - - - - - - - - - - - -	
there	
where	where
were	

Procedure:

Show only the three words on the left to students while you cover the word on the right. Have students pronounce each of the exposed words while you point to them one at a time. Give students a moment to guess which one of the three words will appear when you reveal the word on the right. Then uncover the mystery word so students can see if they guessed correctly. Before going on to the next set of words, have students again pronounce all four words while you point to them in varying order. (Note that the examples shown for this activity require students to pronounce easily confused basic sight words. For many students, such words are especially challenging and require considerable practice, using both isolated activities such as this one and frequent practice in the act of reading easy contextual materials.)

Dominoes

Purpose: To provide practice in word discrimination

Materials: Flash cards, divided in half by a line, with a different word on each side of the line; make sure words are repeated several times on different cards (Figure 3.2).

FIGURE 3.2

the	what
a	and

and	the
go	a

Procedure:

After mixing the cards, the game proceeds the same as dominoes. The student pronounces the word as she matches it.

Word Order

Purpose: To provide practice with basic sight words, general sight words, or with phonic elements

Materials: Photocopied lists of words arranged in the same manner as shown here

A. why   _____   B. c _____
    what   _____   d _____
    when   _____   g _____
    where _____   b _____
    which _____   f _____

C. cat   _____   D. sound   _____
   mule   _____   frog   _____
   cage   _____   wolf   _____
   pill   _____   rabbit   _____
   duck   _____   pass   _____

Procedure:

Play a recording or read words or sounds to students who have the photocopied lists. Each set of words should, however, concentrate on practice in only one area. The directions for the preceding sets would be similar to the following example:

Set A: Number the words in the order in which they are read.

Set B: Number the letters that match the beginning sound that you hear in the following words (in the order they are given): *book, food, good, can, dog.*

Set C: Put numeral *1* in front of the word with a long /a/ sound.
         Put *2* in front of the word with a short /u/ sound.
         Put *3* in front of the word with a short /a/ sound.
         Put *4* in front of the word with a long /u/ sound.
         Put *5* in front of the word with a short /i/ sound.

Set D: Number the words, in the order they are given, that have ending letter sounds. Give the following sounds: /f/, /t/, /g/, /d/, /s/.

Passport

Purpose: To provide practice with basic sight words or general sight words

Materials: Group-size (6″ × 3″) or individual-size cards (3″ × 1½″)
            One set is given to the group of students and one is kept by the captain, who is usually a student who knows the words well

Procedure:

Each student is given one or several words (passports). In order to get aboard the boat, she must show her passports to the captain. When the captain calls the port (the word or words) from her deck of cards, the person who has a card matching the captain's must show it to her to get off the boat.

Variation:

The same game can be played with the sounds of the consonants and vowels to practice phonics skills. In this case, the captain has word cards, and the student who has a letter matching the sound of the first letter in the word called by the captain shows her passport (letter) and is allowed to leave the boat.

Word in the Box

Purpose: To provide review and reinforcement of words that present problems to students

Materials: A large box
              Word cards with words on them that have given the students trouble in
                  their reading

Procedure:

Students sit in a circle around the box. You either read or play a tape recording of a
story. Before hearing the story, each student is given a card on which there is a word
from the story. When that word is read in the story, the student says, "_____ goes in
the box," and throws the word in the box. The student then is given another word,
so she may continue in the game.

Word Football

Purpose: To provide practice in recognizing basic sight words or general sight words

Materials: A large sheet of drawing paper
              A small replica of a football
              Word cards

Procedure:

Draw a football field on a large piece of paper. The game begins at the 50-yard line,
where the football is placed. The word cards are placed face up on the table, and
two students, or two teams, take turns reading them. If a student reads a word correctly, she moves the ball 10 yards toward the opponent's goal. If she reads the word
incorrectly, it is considered a fumble, and the ball goes 10 yards toward her own
goal. Each time the ball crosses into the end zone, 6 points are scored. The scoring
side then gets to read one more word to try for the extra point.

Word Checkers

Purpose: To provide practice in word recognition or phonic sounds

Materials: Checkerboard
              Small squares of paper with sight words or phonic sounds on them

Procedure:

You or the student covers the black squares with the words. The game is played the
same as regular checkers, but the player must say the word that appears on the
square before a checker is placed on that space. (To give the students extra practice, have them say the words three times before moving the checkers.)

Variation:

Phonic sounds may be used instead of words.

Pack of Trouble

Purpose: To discover which children do not know certain sight words and to pro-
              vide special help in such cases

Materials: Word cards using the vocabulary currently being studied
Blank cards on which you can print words

Procedure:

You flash word cards to individual students and ask them to pronounce the words as quickly as possible. Whenever a student misses a word, she is given that word and makes a copy of it to keep. The student then can give the original back to you. Each student develops her own pack of trouble, which she can use for study with another individual or with a small group. As soon as the student masters a word, she may give it back to you. The idea is, of course, for students to keep their packs of trouble as small as possible.

Climbing the Word Ladder

Purpose: To provide practice with basic sight words, with general sight words, or with sight phrases

Materials: A number of card packs of 10 words (basic sight words, other sight words, or sight phrases)
A small ladder that will hold 10 cards (the rungs of the ladder may be made from wooden dowels ¾" round and the vertical poles from wood of 1" × 2"); see Figure 3.3.

FIGURE 3.3

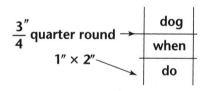

Procedure:

Each student receives a pack of cards and tries to climb the ladder with them. Cards are laid on each rung of the ladder. The student then tries to climb it by saying the words. After the student has mastered her own words, she exchanges packs and begins again with new words.

Hands Up (Words)

Purpose: To provide practice in recognition of basic sight words or general sight words

Materials: Group-size cards (6" × 3")

Procedure:

Quickly flash a word card around the group, allowing each student to see it. The student whose turn it is to pronounce the word then has a chance to do so. If the student pronounces the word correctly, she is given the word card. If the student does not pronounce the word correctly, she is required to raise her hand. When the next card is flashed, the second student has a chance to say it. If, however, the student who has her hand up can pronounce the word before the second student, she gets the card and may put her hand down. The second student then receives a chance at another word. If she misses that word, then that student must hold up her hand, and so on. The object is to get the most cards. There may also be a number of children with their hands up at any one time. If this is the case, the one who pronounces the word first gets the card.

Surprise Words

Purpose: To reinforce knowledge of the basic sight words or general sight words

Materials: Word cards to fit a pocket chart
             Pocket chart

Procedure:

Fill the pocket chart with words that are currently being studied. Turn the cards so only the backs are showing. Students take turns coming up to the chart and taking a surprise word. If they can pronounce the word, they get to keep it; if they cannot, they must leave it in the chart. The student with the most words at the end of a certain time period wins the game.

Gamble for Words

Purpose: To provide practice with either basic sight words or general sight words

Materials: Pocket chart
             Cards with either the basic sight words or any sight word on them
             A die

Procedure:

Place the words to be worked on in the pocket chart. One student then rolls a die. She may pick up the same number of cards from the chart as the number indicated on the die. She must, however, be able to say each word as she picks it up. The turn then passes to another student. The object is to see who can get the most words. This game may be played using either a student-versus-student approach or a team-versus-team approach. You may set a time limit for the game or limit the game to a certain number of refills of the pocket chart.

Word Match

Purpose: To provide practice in word recognition

Materials: A pack of word cards in which every card has a word on it that is duplicated; that is, there should be two cards for each word to be used. The number of cards will depend on the number of players involved.

Procedure:

Players are each dealt four cards, which are placed face up in front of each player. Five cards are then placed face up in the middle of the table. The remainder of the pack is placed face down in the middle of the table. If the first player has a card that matches any of the five face-up cards in the middle of the table, she picks it up, pronounces the word, and keeps the pair, placing them face down in front of her. The student may continue playing until she can make no more pairs. The student then draws to fill her hand to four cards and replaces the five face-up cards on the table. If, in this process, cards that match are drawn and placed on the table, they are left for the individual who has the next turn. Play continues to the first player on the left. If a player can match a card in the middle of the table but cannot pronounce the word, she must place her card in the middle and leave it. If the following player can pronounce the word, she receives the pair. The winner is the person with the most cards when all of the cards are paired.

Rolling for Words

Purpose: To teach and provide practice with basic sight words

Materials: Three colors of construction paper
A die
Three small boxes

Procedure:

Cut the colored construction paper into 1″ squares. Print a basic sight word on each square. Put the squares into separate boxes according to the color of the paper. Players throw the die to see who starts the game. The student with the highest number starts by selecting as many words from any one box as the number on the die. If she fails to say any one of the words, she loses all the words from that turn. After being told the missed word by the teacher, the student returns the words to the appropriate box. Play continues to the first player's left. The winner is the one with the most words when all three boxes are empty, and the game ends.

Finding Rhyming Words

Purpose: To teach and reinforce basic sight words

Materials: Flash cards of basic sight words from which rhyming words can be made
Pocket chart

Procedure:

Place the flash cards in the pocket chart. Then say, "I want a word that rhymes with *fat.*" Students take turns looking for a word to rhyme with the one you give. If the student cannot find the word, she is given a word to hold by you or by another student who knows it. The winners are those students who are holding no words at the end of the game.

Finding Phrases

Purpose: To reinforce knowledge of the basic sight words

Materials: Pocket chart
Basic sight word cards (3″ × 8½″)

Procedure:

Place the words in the pocket chart to make four or five phrases (for example, *is in* and *wants to go*). Say a sentence such as, "The boy wants to go." Students take turns going to the pocket chart and placing their hands on the phrase from the sentence and reading it. If a student fails to read it correctly, she must take the cards from that phrase to be studied. The object is to have no cards at the end of the game.

The Password

Purpose: To provide practice with especially difficult basic sight words

Materials: Straight or safety pins
3″ × 8½″ cards

Procedure:

Group students who are having trouble with the same basic sight words. Write one of the basic sight words on each card, and go over the words thoroughly with the students. Then pin one card on each student. Throughout the day, whenever one student must deal with another or whenever you wish to get a response from that student, call the basic sight word written on the student's card rather than her name before that student is to respond. This can be done daily with different groups of words and students.

Concentration

Purpose: To develop the ability to recognize basic sight words

Materials: Basic sight word flash cards in which each card has a duplicate

Procedure:

Find 10 to 12 cards and their duplicate cards (for a total of 20 to 24). Shuffle the cards and lay them face down on the table. The first student turns up a card and says the word. She then turns up another card, trying to find the duplicate of the first one turned up. If the second card is not a duplicate of the first or if the student does not know the word, she turns them face down, and the next student takes her turn. If a student is able to turn up one card, say the word, and then turn up the duplicate of that card, she gets to keep the pair. As play continues, students will, of course, find it easier to find matching pairs. The person with the most pairs at the end of the game wins. (*Note:* Be sure to have each student *pronounce* each word as it is turned over. This is where the practice and learning takes place. Often, in a game of Concentration, students are interested only in matching pairs quickly and will prefer not to say each word.)

CHAPTER 4

General Sight Vocabulary Not Up to Grade Level

RECOGNIZED BY

The student fails to instantly recognize words thought to be common at or below his grade level. (Failure is not limited to basic sight words.)

DISCUSSION

In advancing from grade to grade, students should increase their sight vocabularies at each grade level. Students' sight vocabularies are not up to grade level unless they can correctly pronounce 95% of the words in books written at their grade level. Students who have not mastered an adequate number of sight words are greatly handicapped because they must analyze many more words than normal readers. These students are more likely to encounter reading material at their frustration level.

You should not determine whether a book is at a certain grade level using the publisher's recommendation unless that recommendation is based on one of the better readability formulas. Unfortunately, many of the popular readers are prepared with stories at a variety of levels. That is, you cannot be sure that all stories in a book that is designated at, say, a fourth-grade level are actually written at that level.

RECOMMENDATIONS

The first and most important recommendation to help students increase the size of their **general sight vocabulary** is to have them read widely about many subjects. If students have adequate word-attack skills and are pronouncing the words correctly, they will automatically learn many new sight words by seeing them a number of times. However, if students do not have adequate word-attack skills for their grade level, then the appropriate procedures in Chapters 3 through 10 should be used as needed to improve students' abilities with phonics, structural analysis, or context clues. The various methods described in the introductory chapter will also improve students' overall sight vocabulary.

    A. Have students read as widely as possible at their independent or low-instructional level. In doing so, they will learn new words from such practice in the act of reading.

B. Teach the word-attack strategy described in Chapter 10, item A.

C. Once students have learned to use the word-attack strategy, allow them to ask you or others for assistance with difficult words during silent reading but only after they have worked through the first three steps of the strategy on their own. Remember: if students ask for help on more than 10% of the words, the material is too difficult and should be replaced with easier material.

D. Encourage students to preread material silently before asking them to read it orally.

E. Build on students' background of experience as much as possible. Use discussions, demonstrations, computer software, videotapes, tape recordings, or anything that will build their listening/speaking vocabulary. This will make it easier for students to acquire new words through context clues.

F. Have students start a card file of new words. Write the word (or have the student write the word) and the definition on the front of the card. On the back, write the word in its proper context in a sentence. (Never write just the word and the dictionary definition alone.)

G. Use picture word cards on which the unknown word appears under a picture illustrating that word. When making these, it is important to use the word in a sentence as well as by itself. Have students work in pairs or small groups to learn these new words from the word cards. Have students work cooperatively to build a file of pictures representing scenes, action events, and so forth in stories. Before students begin to read the new stories, discuss these picture files with them. Pictures may also be put in scrapbooks, and pages may be divided into sections (represented by letters) on numbered pages. You can then make a tape recording to go along with the scrapbook. The script for the tape recording might read as follows:

> On page 3 of the scrapbook, in picture A, you see a picture of a waterfall. In the story you are going to read today, a man goes over a waterfall in a boat. The boat probably looks like the one in picture B. The men have been camping in the woods and probably look like the men in picture C.

Assign students to listening stations and have them prepare for reading a story by listening to these tapes and looking at the scrapbooks.

H. Have students pantomime certain words such as *write, hear,* and *walk.* Make sure students see the words immediately before, during, and after the pantomime.

GAMES AND EXERCISES

Sight Words in Context

Purpose: To provide practice in recognizing sight words and context clues

Materials: Pocket chart
Group-size word cards
Tape recorder

Procedure:

Place 8 to 10 words in the bottom pockets of the pocket chart. These should be new words on which you wish to provide practice. Play a tape recording of a short story that uses the words in the bottom rows of the pocket chart. Say the word and at the same time ring a bell or sound a buzzer. At the signal, the student picks the correct card from the 8 to 10 choices in the bottom rows and places it in the top row of the pocket chart. Be sure to pause briefly after the word to give the student a chance to look for it. You will need to allow for longer pauses at the beginning of the story when there are more words at the bottom of the pocket chart. The cards should be placed in order from left to right beginning with row 1. When the top row is full, the cards begin the left-to-right sequence in row 2, and so on until all cards have been transferred from the bottom to the top of the chart. After all the words are transferred from the bottom to the top of the chart, you can check the words with the students in the following manner: "In row 1, the first word is _____, the next word is _____," and so on. This makes the exercise self-correcting when it is programmed on the tape along with the rest of the exercise.

Variation:

Instead of saying the word as a bell or buzzer rings, ring the buzzer and let the student find the word from context.

Zingo

Purpose: To provide practice in recognizing basic sight words or general sight words

Materials: A number of word cards (7″ × 7″) with 25 squares, each of which has a different sight word on it
A list of each of the sight words
A number of kernels of corn, buttons, or beans

Procedure:

This game is played like bingo. Read a word from the word list and ask students to hunt for that word on their word (zingo) cards. When they find the word pronounced, they place a kernel of corn or some other marker on it. The first student to get five spaces filled in any direction is the winner. After a student has won, he should pronounce the words covered by the markers. This will ensure that students not only recognize words by sight but that they also can say them.

Construct your word list so that you can allow various individuals to win if you so desire, e.g., zingo card 3 may win by saying words 2, 8, 10, 12, and 15. Although this is a prearranged game, it will enable you to allow the students who need motivation to win.

Racetrack

Purpose: To provide practice in recognizing basic sight words or general sight words

Materials: A large sheet of drawing paper
Two duplicate sets of individual-size word cards (3″ × 1½″)
Two toy automobiles

Procedure:

Draw an oval track on the drawing paper to resemble a racetrack, as shown in Figure 4.1. Be sure to put in a start and finish line. Divide the track into sections in which there are printed drill words. Each of the two players has a toy automobile, placed on the starting line of the track. Each player has a set of small word cards that are duplicates of those of the opposing player and are the same as the words on the racetrack. Each player places his pile of cards face up. One player then reads the word on his top card. If the word is the same as the one in the first space of the racetrack, he moves his auto to that space. If it is not the same, he may not move. His card is placed on the bottom of the deck, and the other player takes a turn. The winner is the first player to go around the racetrack to the finish line. Be sure cards are shuffled well before each game.

FIGURE 4.1

Treasure Hunt

Purpose: To provide practice in recognizing basic sight words or general sight words.

Materials: Sight word cards with a word on one side and a direction on the back such as "Go to a word that starts with *c*," or "Go to a word that starts with *w*."

Procedure:

A number of word cards are placed on the top of students' desks with sight words showing. To begin the hunt, give two or three students different cards with the directions face up. Students immediately start to hunt for words with the beginning letters as indicated. When they find a word that starts with one of the letters, they say it. They may then turn the card over and get directions for the next step in the treasure hunt. The last card should have a picture of a treasure chest on the back of it instead of directions to look further. You will need to arrange the card sets so that each student goes through the same number of steps.

Donkey

Purpose: To provide practice in recognizing basic sight words or general sight words

Materials: Make a deck of cards using one new word causing difficulty on each card. You may use any number of players. In the deck you should include three to five cards with the word *donkey* written on them.

Procedure:

Deal all cards to the players face down. The players then take turns turning up a card, pronouncing it, and placing it in a pool in the middle of the table. When the donkey card appears, the player drawing it says "donkey" and throws it in the center of the table. All the players try to grab the donkey card. The one who gets it may keep it and all cards that have been thrown into the pool. The winner of the game is the player who ends up with all of the cards or the most cards when all donkey cards have been drawn.

The Head Chair

Purpose: To provide practice in recognizing basic sight words or general sight words

Materials: Group-size word cards (6″ × 3″)

Procedure:

Arrange students' chairs in a circle and mark one as the head chair. Begin play by flashing a card to the person in the head chair. If the student says the word correctly, he stays in his chair. If the student misses the word, he goes to the end chair, and all students from this student to the end move over one chair. Continue around the circle from the head chair to the end chair. The object is to try to end up in the head chair.

Variation:

If you are working with a relatively small group, have all of the chairs facing you. This will enable all of the students to see all of the words.

Cops and Robbers

Purpose: To provide practice in recognizing basic sight words or general sight words

Materials: Tagboard
Word cards

Procedure:

On a piece of tagboard, construct an irregular course of dots and then connect the dots with lines. At points along the course place hideouts, dried-up water holes, deserts, and so on. The game is played with two students—one a bank robber, one a police officer. The bank robber will place his marker on the course as far from the officer's marker as possible. The game begins with each player turning over a word card from a pack placed face down on the table. The student reads the word on the card and then moves the number of dots denoted by a number appearing in one of the corners of the word card. The robber tries to avoid the officer. The game ends when the robber is captured (that is, when the police officer catches up with the robber). A more difficult game can be made by increasing the number of moves allowed according to the difficulty of the word given.

Team Sight Word Race

Purpose: To provide drill on basic sight words or general sight words

Materials: A group-size (6″ × 3″) set of basic sight word cards or sight words on which you want to provide practice

Procedure:

The students are divided into two teams. Each team member takes a turn attempting to pronounce a word turned up from a pile of sight words. If one team member misses, the opposite team then receives a chance to pronounce that word, in addition to the team member's regular turn. Score is kept on the number of words each team pronounces correctly. Do not have members sit down when they miss a word, but have each team member go to the back of the line after each try, whether successful or not. This enables all members of each team to gain equal practice and does not eliminate those students who need practice most.

Variation:

Instead of using single or isolated words, use phrase cards or sentence cards in which the word being emphasized is underlined. Allow students to make the cards with a final check by you. You can use a number of smaller teams and have several races going at one time.

Stand Up

Purpose: To provide practice in recognizing the basic sight words or general sight words

Materials: Group-size word cards (6″ × 3″)

Procedure:

The students are seated in a group around you. One student stands behind the chair of another student who is sitting with his chair facing you. You then flash a card. If the student who is standing pronounces the word before the student in the chair, then the student who was sitting must stand up behind someone else.

Word Hunt

Purpose: To provide practice in recognizing basic sight words or general sight words

Materials: Blindfolds
Group-size word cards (6″ × 3″)

Procedure:

Have several students cover their eyes. The rest of the group hides the cards where they can be found easily. When all the cards are hidden, the students who are "it" are given a signal to immediately take off their blindfolds and begin hunting for the cards. A student may pick up a card if he knows the word on it. No cards may be picked up unless the word is known. The student who finds the most words is the winner.

Seven Up

Purpose: To provide practice in word recognition and word meaning

Materials: Group-size word cards (6″ × 3″). Be sure there are seven times as many cards as students playing.

Procedure:

The students sit in a circle, with the flash cards in a pile face down in the center of the group. Each student takes a turn by turning over a card and reading it. If the student reads it correctly, he keeps it. When a student has seven correct cards, he stands up. The game continues until all players are standing. Students then sit down and see how fast they can make a sentence with some or all of their seven cards. Be sure both nouns and verbs are included in the stack. As soon as a student has made a sentence, he stands. Play continues until all students who can make sentences of their words have done so.

Noun Label

Purpose: To teach nouns to non- or limited-English-speaking students and to improve the vocabulary of those students who have insufficient vocabulary knowledge. It may, of course, be used in the early stages of reading in the regular developmental program.

Materials: Group-size word cards (6″ × 3″) with the names of common nouns written on them

8½″ × 11″ tagboard sheets with a picture of one of the common nouns on the top half of the sheet

Chalkboard

Procedure:

The pictures on the tagboard sheets are placed on the tray of the chalkboard. The students are then given words that correspond to the pictures. They come up to the chalkboard and place their words under the appropriate pictures. See the example in Figure 4.2.

FIGURE 4.2

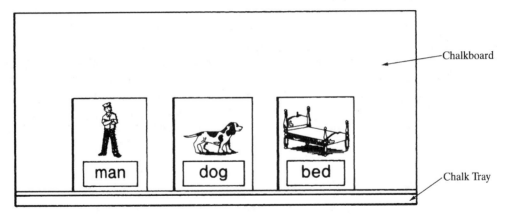

Word Golf

Purpose: To provide practice in recognizing basic sight words or general sight words

Materials: Nine packs of word cards, each with 10 sight words in it

A player and a scorekeeper

Procedure:

The player takes the first pack, shuffles the cards, and places them face down in front of him. He takes a card from the top of the pack, turns it face up, and reads it. If he misses a word, the scorekeeper makes one mark on the scoring sheet. The number incorrect for the first pack is the player's score for the first hole. The student continues in this manner through the nine packs, trying to receive as low a score as possible.

What Word Am I?

Purpose: To provide practice in recognizing sight words

Materials: Two duplicate sets of cards with sight words printed on them

Procedure:

Divide the class into two groups. Each student has a word card pinned on his back. The duplicates of the cards are spread out on a table. The object of the game is to see which group can guess all their words first. The students take turns going to the table, picking up a word card, and asking, "Am I _____?" saying the word on the card. If the student chooses the card that matches the word on his back and pronounces it correctly, he keeps the card. If the student selects a card that doesn't match, he puts the card down on the table and takes his seat. The game continues until one group guesses all its words.

Jumping the Fence

Purpose: To provide practice in recognizing basic sight words or general sight words

Materials: Flash cards with sight words on them
             White tape

Procedure:

Place the flash cards on the floor in a row leading to the fence (white tape on the floor). A student who reads a word correctly jumps over the card and advances toward the fence. He may jump the fence when he reaches it. If he misses a word, he sits down and another student has a turn.

The Witch

Purpose: To provide practice in recognizing sight words. This game works well with four players if 20 cards are used.

Materials: Use a deck containing about 20 cards with one additional card that has a witch on it. Print one set of words on half of the cards. Duplicate the first set of words on the other half of the cards.

Procedure:

One person deals out all the cards; players pick them up and look at them. Beginning with the person at the dealer's left, players take turns drawing cards—each player draws from the person on his right. As students form pairs, they pronounce the words and place their cards on the table. Play continues until all cards are matched. The player left with the witch is the loser and receives a *w*. The next time he loses, he has *wi*, and so on. The object is to try to avoid losing enough times to spell *witch*.

Silly Sentences

Purpose: To teach or reinforce recognition of sight words

Materials: Plain flash cards and a pocket chart, OR flash cards with flannel backing and a flannel board

Procedure:

Lay out sentences in mixed-up order on the pocket chart or flannel board. Have students take turns coming up and unscrambling the sentences and reading them after they are placed in a sensible order. Make sure all students get a chance to read each logically ordered sentence.

CHAPTER 5

Phonics Difficulties: Consonants

RECOGNIZED BY

The student is unable to use consonants to decode one-syllable words because she is unable to give the correct sounds and the variant sounds of the consonants. The **letter-sound correspondences** for the consonants are presented in Appendix B-3.

DISCUSSION

An enormous body of research over many years has clearly established that effective phonics instruction can be a crucial aid in unlocking the puzzle of reading for the beginning reader. However, phonics is only *one* of the tools that readers use in **decoding.** Millions of people have learned to read English without receiving instruction in phonics. These include most of the population of American public schools in the middle decades of the twentieth century, who learned to read using the Look-Say approach of the famous Dick and Jane series, published by Scott-Foresman and Company. These youngsters learned to decode by relying on a substantial sight vocabulary combined with skill in using context clues. Indeed, the reading progress of many students may be hampered by too much emphasis on phonics, particularly if the focus is on the **phonic elements** that are least critical for successful decoding.

We certainly do not recommend a return to reading instruction as it occurred in 1950. Appropriate phonics instruction is required for most young children to learn to read English. Such instruction should be balanced, research-based, and presented using the best instructional practices.

Phonics instruction tends to be most helpful to students reading at or below the second-grade reading level. Students who can read at or above a third-grade reading level rarely profit from an emphasis on phonics. That is because phonics is a useful tool for decoding one-syllable words that happen to be phonetically regular. Non-phonetic words (such as many of the words on basic sight vocabulary lists) should be learned as sight words—that is, by memorizing them. Words of more than one syllable are decoded most efficiently through the combined use of structural analysis and context clues.

For the student who is unable to decode regular, one-syllable words, some phonics skills are more helpful than others. Research and experience have shown that

FIGURE 5.1

Phonics

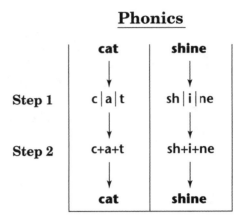

Step 1: Identify and separate
phonemes.

Step 2: Pronounce and blend
letter sounds.

beginning letter sounds are most useful. Generalizations about ending sounds and vowel sounds are less helpful. Students who struggle to read materials written at or below the second-grade level should be taught to recognize and apply the letter-sound associations for single consonants, **consonant blends,** and consonant **digraphs.** In addition, instruction on vowels should be provided as described in Chapter 6.

The application of phonics skills is really quite simple. The beginning reader is taught to do the following when she encounters an unfamiliar one-syllable word: first, identify and separate the letters; then, pronounce and blend the individual letter sounds, or phonemes, to decode the word. For example, in the word *cat,* the reader identifies and separates the three letters *c, a,* and *t.* Then she thinks of the sound that each letter represents, and pronounces and blends the three sounds together to make the whole word. (When reading in context, the student is encouraged to use other words in the sentence to assist with decoding unknown words.) Not all one-syllable words are composed of three letters, of course; however, the process remains the same. To decode the word *shine,* for example, the reader identifies and separates the letters— *sh, i, ne,*—then pronounces and blends the three letter sounds together to make the whole word. These examples are illustrated in Figure 5.1.

Note that the decoding of these words requires a considerable amount of phonics knowledge for a young student. In the word *cat,* the reader must know the hard *c* sound, the short *a* sound, and the *t* sound. To decode the word *shine,* the reader must know the sound of the consonant digraph *sh,* the long *i* sound, and the *n* sound.

Before beginning phonics instruction, you should determine whether the student needs instruction in some or all areas of phonics. To do this, administer a phonics test such as the Phonics Assessment found in Appendix A-6. If a student is deficient in nearly all areas—initial consonants, consonant blends and digraphs, and so on—you may need to start from the beginning with the teaching of phonics. In this case, you will find that, for many disabled readers, instruction using the phonogram lists as described in Appendix B-4 will enable the students to quickly learn a great many initial consonants, consonant blends, and consonant digraphs in a relatively short time.

RECOMMENDATIONS

Many of these suggestions provide effective ways to teach students to recognize and pronounce consonants in isolation or in single words. However, for phonics instruction to be effective, students must transfer their knowledge of consonant letter sounds to the act of decoding. The best way to help students do this is to first provide direct instruction in the consonant letter sounds to be learned, then give the student substantial practice in the act of reading. As each consonant sound is taught, you should provide short, easy sentences and/or stories for students to read. You may create these sentences or stories yourself, have the students assist you in their development through language-experience activities (see the introductory chapter), or use commercial materials that have been designed for this purpose. Students may need to read these sentences and stories over and over to master their phonics skills. The use of contextual material is essential because you want students to use context clues to assist them as they are learning phonics. You also want to be sure that students understand that the purpose of your instruction is to aid them in decoding so that they can obtain *meaning* from printed words.

There are many methods of teaching phonic elements. One typical procedure for teaching a consonant letter sound follows:

1. Develop awareness of hearing the sound.

    Say, "Listen to these words. Each of them begins with the *b* sound. Circle the *b* on each word on your paper as you hear the sound. *Ball … bat … base … banana. . . .*"

2. Develop awareness of seeing the **grapheme** (letter or letters) that stands for the sound.

    Tell students to circle all of the words in a passage that begin with *b*.

3. Provide practice in saying words with the *b* sound.

    Pronounce each word and have students pronounce it after you: "*Big, bad, baseball, basket, beach. . . .*"

4. Provide practice in blending the *b* sound with common word families or phonograms.

    Teach or use several phonograms with which students are already familiar, such as -*ake* and -*and*. Put the *b* in one column, the phonogram in a second column, and the two combined in a third column as follows:

b	ake	bake
b	and	band
b	at	bat
b	ig	big
b	ike	bike

and so on. Instruct students to say *b* (either the letter name or the sound /b/), then the phonogram (the sound represented by the letters in the phonogram, such as /at/), and then the word formed by the two, /bat/.

5. Ask students to help you make a list of some words that begin with *b*. Ask students to say each word with you as you write it. You may then have the students themselves write the same words (on paper, small chalkboards, white boards, or magic slates) and say them as they write them.

6. Provide practice in reading *b* words. Present sentences, paragraphs, or simple stories that have a number of *b* words in them for the students to read. If the students are able to read only a few words, you can use illustrations (or rebuses) if necessary instead of the other words.

The following activities will also assist students in learning the consonant sounds:

A. If the student does not know a great many of the initial consonants, **consonant clusters,** vowels, vowel teams, and special letter combinations, use the phonogram list as described in Appendix B-4.

B. Construct flash cards on which the consonant is shown along with a picture illustrating a word that uses that consonant, such as *b* in *b*all, or *c* in *c*at. On the opposite side of the flash card, print the letter only. This can be used as the student progresses in ability. See Figure 5.2.

FIGURE 5.2

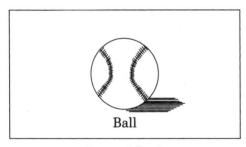

Ball

Front of Card

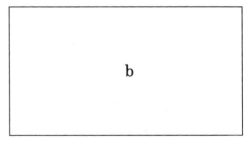

b

Back of Card

C. Put the consonant letters on 3″ × 3″ cards. Divide these cards into groups of 10 each. Lay out separate groups of letters, so the student can see all 10 at once. As you call the sounds of letters, or as they are played from a tape recording, have the student pick up the correct card to match the sound of the letter. As there are fewer words to observe—that is, after some have already been picked up—you will need to speed up the rate at which you pronounce the remaining words. The following timing seems to work well: pronounce the first word, wait 7 seconds; pronounce the second word and wait 7 seconds again; then 6, 6, 5, 5, 4, 4, and 3 seconds. Many students are unable to manipulate the cards in less time than this.

D. Tape-record words and have the students write the letter that stands for the beginning, ending, or both beginning and ending sounds of these words. See the following example:

Directions: As you hear a word called on the tape, write the letter that begins the word. (Tape script says, "Number one is *come*, number two is *dog*," and so on.)

   1. c
   2. d
   3.
   4.
   5.

E. Use the same system as in item D. Instead of having students write letters they hear, have them pick up the card that matches the beginning or ending letter they hear in the words.

F. Put various consonant letters on the board or in a pocket chart and have the students make lists of words that begin with these letters.

G. Record the consonant letters with their sounds and let students hear these as many times as is necessary. They should, however, have a chart they can follow to see the letters as they hear the sound.

H. Use charts that are available commercially for teaching consonants. Tapes that give the proper pronunciation of the consonant sounds are also available.

I. Use commercially prepared games or computer software designed to teach consonants and the application of consonant sounds in decoding.

GAMES AND EXERCISES

Phonics Posters

Purpose: To develop an awareness of related sounds

Materials: Tagboard
Old magazines or old textbooks

Procedure:

At the top of a piece of tagboard, place a letter or combination of letters. Have the students find pictures of objects in the old magazines or textbooks that start with the sound or sounds displayed in the heading. These object pictures should be cut out and mounted on the tagboard to provide practice for individuals who need special help.

Poet Play

Purpose: To help students develop an awareness of sound similarities through the use of rhyming words

Materials: Pocket chart
Word cards
Envelopes

Procedure:

Give students envelopes containing a number of word cards. Place a master word in the pocket chart and have students locate in their envelopes a word that rhymes with the one posted. Number the envelopes and allow students to exchange them after each round, so they will become familiar with a great many words and their sound similarities.

Line Up

Purpose: To provide practice in discriminating between like and unlike sounds

Procedure:

When there is extra time before lunch or dismissal, you might use this game. It is both interesting and beneficial. You call, "All those whose names start like *meat* may line up and get their coats." Repeat as many times as needed to dismiss the students. As a variation, use letters that are in the middle or end of students' names. Students also might use this method to choose groups or sides in other games.

Rhyme Time

Purpose: To discover which students are having auditory discrimination problems and to provide practice through the use of related phonic sounds

Materials: Tagboard
Word cards

Procedure:

Write sentences on the tagboard. On the word cards print a variety of words that will rhyme with selected words given in the sentences. Have students locate and match their cards with the rhyming words in the sentences. Place each set of cards in an envelope and number the envelopes, so students can keep a record of the sets on which they have worked. See the following example:

1. The <u>dog</u> bit the mailperson. (log, hog)
2. The candy tasted <u>sweet.</u> (treat, beat)

3. <u>Look</u> out the window. (took, book)
4. The wall had a large <u>crack</u>. (back, sack)
5. She cut down the apple <u>tree</u>. (see, flee)

Making and Exchanging Picture Dictionaries

Purpose: To learn initial consonant sounds

Materials: Old notebooks or paper to be bound together
             Crayons and/or paints
             Magazines and other materials containing pictures

Procedure:

Have students cut out or draw pictures representing various initial consonant sounds. Under the picture, write the letter or letters of the initial sound and the word that stands for the picture. Under each picture, use the word in a sentence. After the students have finished their books, have them exchange dictionaries, so each student learns to read every other student's dictionary.

I'm Thinking of a Word

Purpose: To provide practice in auditory discrimination and the recognition of beginning, ending, or both beginning and ending sounds

Materials: Pocket chart
             Cards with words that begin with various consonants
             Cards with words that end with various consonants

Procedure:

Fill the pocket chart with about 10 cards, each of which has a different beginning sound. The first student says, "I'm thinking of a word that begins like /d/." (The student says the *d* sound.) The student draws a card, trying to get the word beginning with that sound. She gets to keep the card as long as she matches a sound and word. She may thus take all of the cards from the pocket chart. If the student gives a sound and draws a word that does not begin with that sound, play then passes to the next student. If the student gets all of the cards, another student then follows the same procedure. The same procedure can also be used with ending sounds.

Variation:

There are many possible variations of this game. You may have students come to the front and say, "I'm thinking. . .," and call on someone to guess the word. Another game might have a student put letters in the pocket chart and say, "My word is *dog*." The other students then have to find a *d* or *g* depending on whether you are working with beginning or ending sounds. The students also may play the same game and be required to find both the beginning and ending sounds.

Catch the Stick

Purpose: To improve auditory discrimination and to improve students' ability to make the connection between sounds and letters

Materials: A number of group-size cards (6″ × 3″) with the beginning consonant sounds on them
A yardstick

Procedure:

Seat the students in as small a circle as possible for the number of students you wish to have play the game. Ten to 12 students are optimum. Students are all given a different beginning consonant sound on a group-size card. One student stands in the center of the circle and holds the yardstick in an upright position, with one end on the floor and the top end held in place by the tip of her finger. The student in the center then pronounces a word that begins with a consonant. At the same time the student pronounces the word, she takes the tip of her finger off the top of the yardstick. The student who has the beginning letter of the word named by the student in the center of the circle must catch the yardstick before it falls to the floor. If the student who had the consonant letter catches the stick, she returns to her seat and the person in the center must say another word. However, if she does not catch the stick, then she must change places with the student in the center and give her card to the student she is replacing.

Phonic Rummy

Purpose: To provide practice in various phonic elements. This game works well with two to four players when using 36 cards, or up to six players when using 48 or 52 cards.

Materials: A deck of cards with phonic elements that you wish to teach. On each card will appear one phonic element and four words that use that particular phonic element. One of the four words will be underlined. The deck may consist of 36, 40, 44, 48, or 52 cards. For each phonic element there will be 4 cards, each of which has a different word underlined. A deck of 36 cards would involve 9 phonic elements; 40 cards would involve 10 phonic elements. See the following example:

i	*ay*	*gr*
did	stay	green
pit	may	grass
if	play	grow
fish	clay	grab

Procedure:

The dealer shuffles the cards and deals eight cards face down to each player. The rest of the cards are placed face down in the center of the table. The first player to the left of the dealer calls for a word using a certain phonic element on which she wishes to build. (See the examples.) For example, the student might say, "I want Sam to give me *fish* from the *i* group" and would pronounce the short /i/ sound. If Sam had that card, she would give it to the caller. The player (caller) then continues to call for certain cards from specific people. If the person called upon does not have the card, the caller takes a card from the center pile, and the next player to the left takes her turn. When a player completes a "book" (that is, when she has all four cards from a certain phonic element), she lays it down. Players can only lay down books when it is their turn to draw. The object is to get the most books before someone empties her hand.

Think

Purpose: To provide practice with initial vowels, consonants, and initial consonant blends. This game works well with four players.

Materials: Enough small cards so that each letter of the alphabet and each initial blend can be printed on a separate card. There may be more than one card for each vowel.

Procedure:

Place the cards face down on the table. Players take turns selecting a card and naming a word that begins with the same letter or blend. If someone cannot name a word within 5 seconds, she puts the card back. The winner is the person who has the greatest number of cards after the entire pile has been drawn.

Word Trail

Purpose: To provide practice in mastering consonants, consonant blends, vowels, digraphs, and diphthongs

Materials: A piece of tagboard
A list of phonic elements to be taught
A die

Procedure:

Draw a margin (approximately 2″) around the sheet of tagboard. Divide the margin into spaces large enough for inserting the phonic elements for practice. On the corners and in several spaces between corners, insert penalties and rewards, such as "Take another turn" or "Move back three spaces." Players then take turns rolling the die and moving their markers along the spaces, saying each phonic element as they move. If they cannot say a certain phonic element, they must stop on the space behind it and wait for another turn. The first player around the word trail is the winner.

Any Card

Purpose: To provide practice with consonants, consonant digraphs, consonant blends, and rhyming sounds. This game can be played with two to four players.

Materials: A deck of 36–52 cards with words such as the following:

pan	fun	sock	mill	call	harm
man	bun	knock	still	fall	charm
can	run	shock	kill	ball	farm

Also include four cards with "any card" written on them.

Procedure:

A player deals out five cards. The player to the left of the dealer plays any one of her cards and names it. The next player plays a card that either rhymes with or begins with the same letter as the first card. For example, if *sun* has been played, *bun* (rhyming with *sun*) or *sock* (with the same first letter) could be played. If a student cannot play, she draws from the pile in the center until she can play or has drawn three times. If the student has the card with "any card" written on it, she may play this card and name any appropriate word. The first player who runs out of cards wins the game.

Blending Wheel

Purpose: To provide practice in blending beginning consonants, consonant blends, or beginning consonant digraphs

Materials: Two cardboard circles, one of which is approximately 2″ smaller in diameter (convenient sizes are 8″ and 10″)

Procedure:

Fasten the two circles together with a paper fastener, as shown in Figure 5.3. The outside circle should have word roots or major parts of a word on it, and the inside circle should have a specific consonant, consonant blend, or consonant digraph for

FIGURE 5.3

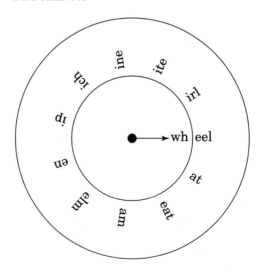

which you wish to provide practice. Have the student rotate one of the circles and practice blending the root or word part with the consonant, consonant blend, or consonant digraph.

Word Puzzles

Purpose: To provide practice in recognizing blend sounds and to provide practice in blending

Materials: Envelopes
             Word cards

Procedure:

Cut out a few word cards of equal size. Print a word containing a blend that has been taught—for example, *gl*ad or *st*and—on each card. Cut each word in two between the blend and the remainder of the word. Place 8 to 10 of these in each envelope and pass out the envelopes to the students. Students then assemble the blends and word parts to make words. After you check them, have students exchange the envelopes so that each student eventually assembles the words in each envelope.

Hard and Soft C and G

Purpose: To teach the rules for hard and soft *c* and *g*

Materials: Rule chart with pockets
             Flash cards with various *c* and *g* words on them

Procedure:

Construct a large chart about 8½″ × 11″, like the chart shown in Figure 5.4. The bottom half should contain two large pockets marked as shown. The top half should contain the rule for soft and hard *c* and *g*. Students are then given a number of flash cards with soft and hard *g* words on them. They put each card into the appropriate pocket according to the rule stated on the chart. Students may check their own work if the words *hard* or *soft* are written on the back of each flash card. (Do the same for *c*.)

FIGURE 5.4

G followed by *e*, *i*, or *y* usually has a soft sound. If *g* is followed by any other letter, it usually has a hard sound.	
Hard *g* (game)	Soft *g* (gentle)

CHAPTER 6

Phonics Difficulties: Vowels

RECOGNIZED BY

The student is unable to use vowels to decode one-syllable words because he is unable to give the correct sounds and variant sounds of the vowels and vowel teams. The letter-sound associations for the various vowels and vowel teams are presented in Appendix B-3.

DISCUSSION

To check the student's knowledge of vowels, use the Phonics Assessment in Appendix A-6.

In the past, students who were learning phonics were often taught a great many rules that would supposedly help them to decode. Some programs taught students well over 100 different symbol-sound correspondences. However, research studies over many years have shown that some of the rules formerly taught had little utility. Most of the unreliable rules related to the teaching of vowel sounds. Listed here are 10 generalizations that appear to be the most reliable of the vowel rules. However, even these rules are not helpful to many struggling readers:

1. If there is only one vowel letter and it appears at the end of a word, the letter usually has a long sound. Note that this is true only for one-syllable words. (Examples: *go* and *be.*)
2. A single vowel in a syllable usually has a short sound if it is not the last letter in a syllable or is not followed by *r.* (Examples: *cat* and *sit.*)
3. A vowel followed by *r* usually has a sound that is neither long nor short. (Examples: *star* and *work.*)
4. When *y* is preceded by a consonant in a one-syllable word, the *y* usually has the sound of long *i.* (Examples include: *by* and *my.*) But in words of two or more syllables, the final *y* usually has the sound of long *e.* (Examples: *baby* and *funny.*)
5. In words ending in vowel-consonant-*e*, the *e* is silent, and the vowel may be either long or short. Try the long sound first. (Examples: *cave* or *have* and *dome* and *come.*) As you can see, this generalization has a lot of exceptions. Fortunately, many of the exceptions are basic sight words, which should be memorized by students and thus should not cause undue confusion.

6. In *ai*, *ay*, *ea*, *oa*, and *ee*, the first vowel is usually long and the second is silent. A common mnemonic that is used to help students remember this generalization is: "M*ai*ds m*ay* *ea*t *oa*k tr*ee*s." (Note, however, that *ea* has many exceptions, including *head*, *great*, and *heard*.)

7. The vowel pair *ow* may have either the long *o* sound as in *low* or the diphthong heard in *owl*. (In a **diphthong,** the two vowel letters, in this case *o* and *w*, are both heard and make a gliding sound.)

8. In *au*, *aw*, *ou*, *oi*, and *oy*, the vowels usually blend or form a diphthong.

9. The *oo* sound is either long as in *moon* or short as in *book*.

10. If *a* is the only vowel in a syllable and it is followed by *l* or *w*, then the *a* will usually be neither long nor short, but will have the *aw* sound heard in *ball* and *awl*. (When one of the letters *r*, *w*, or *l* comes immediately after a vowel, it usually distorts the sound of the previous vowel, making it neither long nor short. *R*eally *W*eird *L*etters is a good mnemonic to help students remember this.)

If you study these rules for a while, you will have little difficulty coming up with exceptions to all of them. In fact, every one of these so-called "reliable" rules uses words such as *either*, *or*, *usually*, or *may*, and many of the rules also include alternative examples. It is important to recognize that the vowel rules are the *least* consistent phonics generalizations in English. It would probably be accurate to say that those students who least need them—the students who are already capable decoders—best understand these rules. Thus, forcing students with reading difficulties to learn many inconsistent phonics rules often proves fruitless.

For students who have difficulty learning the symbol-sound association for vowels, the phonogram approach is often more effective. A **phonogram,** as defined here, is a common word family beginning with a vowel or vowel pair followed by a consonant or consonants, and sometimes ending in *e*. Examples of phonograms are: *ake*, *at*, *ed*, *ime*, *old*, and *up*. These word endings, and many others, almost always are pronounced the same way in the many different words in which they appear. Because of this consistency in pronunciation, students often find it much easier to learn to decode when they are taught using phonograms.

RECOMMENDATIONS

A. It is helpful to teach the most common vowel sounds (long and short) using the following types of phonograms: words that end with the vowel-consonant-*e* configuration (as in *cake*) for long vowel sounds and words that have the CVC configuration (as in *hit*) or the CVCC configuration (as in *mask*) for the short vowel sounds. The complete procedure for using the phonogram approach presented in this book appears in Appendix B-5. A brief review of this method is presented here.

If you wish to teach the long and short vowel sounds for *a*, choose the following words:

mat   hat   rat   fat

Discuss the sound represented by short *a*. Then present the previously listed words. If the student cannot pronounce them, help him to do so. Then present the following words:

mate   hate   rate   fate

Discuss the fact that when the *e* is added, the first vowel takes on its long sound; when the *e* is removed, the vowel takes on its short sound. Review the long vowel sound as you did the short vowel sound. Then present other words, such as those that follow, from Appendix B-5. Cover up the final *e* in each word and ask the student to pronounce the word. Then expose the final *e* and ask him to say the word with the long sound.

pale   gale

Use the words in Appendix B-5 to teach each of the short and long vowel sounds in the same manner. The advantage of this method of teaching the vowel sounds is that students learn these two fundamental rules at the same time.

B. Construct flash cards in which the vowel is shown along with both the word and a picture illustrating a word that uses that vowel, for example, short *a* in *hat* or long *a* in *rake*. On the opposite side, print only the vowel letter, marked long or short, to be used as the student progresses in ability. When using this method with a large group, you can substitute transparencies for the overhead projector for flash cards. See Figure 6.1.

FIGURE 6.1

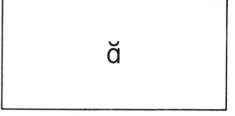

<table>
<tr><td align="center">Front of Card</td><td align="center">Back of Card</td></tr>
</table>

C. Have students circle or underline the words that have vowels with the same sound as the first word in the line. See the following examples:
1. lot   lone, dog, of, to
2. rat   car, bear, sad, same
3. line   with, win, bike, is

D. Record the vowel letters with their sounds and variant sounds and play them to students as many times as necessary to learn them. They should, however, have a chart they can follow to see the letter as they hear the sound. Many commercial programs exist to achieve this objective in fun or clever ways.

E. Put the vowel letters on cards (3″ × 3″). Use the breve (˘) and the macron (¯) to indicate the short and long sounds. Divide these cards into groups of 10 each. Lay out separate groups of letters so the student can see 10 at once. As you call the sounds of the vowel letters, or as they are played from a tape recording, have the student pick up the correct card to match the sound of the letter. (See Chapter 5, "Phonics Difficulties: Consonants," under "Recommendations," item C.)

F. Use the same system as in item E. Instead of having the students match letters they hear, have them write the letter matching the letter sound (phoneme) they hear in words.

G. Use commercial charts that are available for teaching vowels. Audio tapes to accompany the sounds are also available.

H. Use commercially prepared games or computer software designed for teaching the vowels and the application of vowel sounds in decoding.

GAMES AND EXERCISES

Note: Much of the material listed under "Games and Exercises" in Chapter 5 can also be adapted for teaching the vowel sounds.

Game Board for Sorting Vowel Sounds

Purpose: To learn to hear various vowel sounds

Materials: Word cards containing pictures or words with various vowel sounds in them
Tagboard

Procedure:

Construct a board as shown in Figure 6.2. Have students sort the pictures or words into the correct intersecting squares (pictures must be used with beginning read-

FIGURE 6.2

	A	E	I	O	U
Long					
Short					
R-Controlled					

ers) according to the sound in the name of the object in the picture. For example, *hen* would go under the square under the *e* column and the row across from *short*. The pictures from some commercially sold games such as Vowel Lotto work well with this game board.

Vowel Tic-Tac-Toe

Purpose: To learn vowel sounds

Materials: Flash cards with the following written on them:

Short *a*	Long *a*	R-controlled *a*
Short *e*	Long *e*	R-controlled *e*
Short *i*	Long *i*	R-controlled *i*
Short *o*	Long *o*	R-controlled *o*
Short *u*	Long *u*	R-controlled *u*

Procedure:

Have the two students who are playing tic-tac-toe draw a vowel card. Then, instead of marking each square with *X* or *O*, the student writes words that have the sound on his card. If, for example, one student gets short *o* and the other gets long *a*, then each person must write a word with that sound when it is his turn to play instead of making the traditional *X* or *O*. An example of a partially finished game is shown in Figure 6.3.

FIGURE 6.3

Variation:

This is also a good learning device if the two participants have to draw a new card before each move. When playing the game this way, use two different colors of chalk or pencil to help remember which words belong to each player.

Sorting Pictures According to Matching Vowel Sounds

Purpose: To teach short and long vowel sounds

FIGURE 6.4

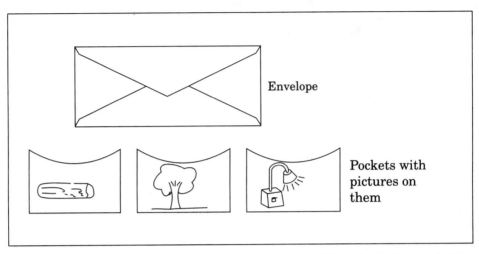

NOTE: This illustration shows only 3 pictures: a log, a tree, and a light. There should, of course, be 10 pictures, each representing a short or long vowel sound.

Materials: Use a pocket chart OR construct a large chart using all 10 of the short and long vowel sounds on pictures placed on pockets as shown in Figure 6.4. On the top half of the chart, glue a large envelope in place. Find many pictures representing various short and long vowel sounds and place them in the large envelope.

Procedure:

Have students take pictures from the large envelope and say the word related to the picture. Remind them to listen for the vowel sound they hear in that word. Then have them find the corresponding vowel sound from the picture on the pockets below and place the picture from the large envelope in the proper pocket. This activity can be made self-checking by numbering the pockets and the backs of the pictures from the large envelope to correspond with the small pocket in which they should go. After students have placed all of the pictures from the large envelope in the small pockets, they can turn the pictures over to see if they match the numbers on the small pockets.

Sorting Vowel Sounds

Purpose: To learn to hear various vowel sounds

Materials: Ten shoeboxes for each group
About 100 word cards, each using the sound of only one vowel

Procedure:

The team captain draws a card. Students read it and listen for a specific vowel sound. They then analyze the word and place it into the correctly marked short or long *a*, *e*, *i*, *o*, or *u* shoebox.

Vowel Relay

Purpose: To give practice in blending and learning sight words

Materials: Chalkboard
Flash cards with various sounds (graphemes) such as the following

Long *a*	Short *a*	R-controlled *a*	L-controlled *a*
Long *e*	Short *e*	R-controlled *e*	W-controlled *a*
Long *i*	Short *i*	R-controlled *i*	W-controlled *o*
Long *o*	Short *o*	R-controlled *o*	W-controlled *e*
Long *u*	Short *u*	R-controlled *u*	

Procedure:

Divide students into two groups and the chalkboard into two parts. Each group lines up in front of its half of the chalkboard. The pile of cards is divided in half and placed in the chalk tray below each of the two divisions of the chalkboard. When you say "Go," the two front players each move up and turn over a card. Each player must write a word using his designated vowel sound in a period of 10 seconds. However, new players cannot move up until you again say "Go" in 10 seconds. If the student cannot think of a word, he draws a line. The next player moves up and turns over another card when you say "Go." The team that has all of its cards turned over with the most correct words is the winner.

CHAPTER 7

Phonics Difficulties: Blends, Digraphs, or Diphthongs

RECOGNIZED BY

The student is unable to give the correct sounds of the blends, digraphs, or diphthongs (see Appendix B-3), is unable to use these phonic elements to decode, or both.

DISCUSSION

As with the consonant and vowel sounds, it is important that the student know the consonant blends and consonant digraphs to analyze certain words. The vowel digraphs and diphthong sounds, however, are much less important. If the student has mastered phonics in the areas of single consonants, consonant blends, consonant digraphs, and long and short vowels, then it may not be necessary to teach the vowel digraphs and diphthongs. Instead, remediation efforts to assist decoding might more wisely be spent on the areas of structural analysis, context clues, and basic sight words.

The Phonics Assessment in Appendix A-6 will help you determine which phonics areas are causing the most difficulty for the student. Administer the test before beginning a program of help in this area.

RECOMMENDATIONS

A. As with the initial consonant sounds, if a student does not know a number of consonant blends, use the phonogram lists as explained in Appendix B-4. You are likely to find that the student learns most of these in a relatively short time. You can then retest the student and teach those that are still not mastered.

B. For teaching vowel digraphs and diphthongs, use the phonogram lists to find words with the digraphs or diphthongs not mastered. Use the tape recorder to provide practice with those combinations, as explained in Appendix B-4. For example, give students who do not know the *ai* (long a) sound words such as *aid, braid, laid, maid,* and *paid,* as well as *ail, hail, nail, pail, quail,* and so on.

C. Construct flash cards in which the blend, digraph, or diphthong is shown along with a picture that illustrates a word using that letter combination. See

Appendix B-3 for suggested words. On the opposite side of the card, print only the blend, digraph, or diphthong to be used as the student progresses in ability. When using this method with a large group of students, you can substitute $2'' \times 2''$ slides or transparencies for the overhead projector instead of flash cards. (See the illustration of a sample card in Chapter 6, Figure 6.1.)

D. Record the letter combinations with their sounds and let students hear these as many times as necessary to learn them. They should, however, have a chart they can follow to see the letter combinations as they hear the sounds. Ask each student to point to the letters as she hears them on the tape.

E. Put diphthongs, digraphs, and blends on $3'' \times 3''$ cards. Divide these cards into groups of 10 each. Lay out separate groups of diphthongs, digraphs, and blends and allow the student to see all 10 at once. As you call the sounds of these various letter combinations, or as they are played from a tape recording, have the student pick up the correct card to match the sound of the letter combinations. (See Chapter 5, "Phonics Difficulties: Consonants," under "Recommendations," item C.)

F. Use the same system described in item E, only tape-record words and have the student pick up the letter combinations she hears in these words.

G. Use charts that are commercially available for teaching various letter combinations. Recordings to accompany these sounds are also available.

H. Use commercially prepared games or computer software designed for teaching blends, digraphs, and diphthongs. Often students can use such materials either individually or in small groups.

I. Immediately after using any of these procedures to teach the symbol-sound correspondences (phonics) for blends, digraphs, or diphthongs, it is *extremely important* that students be provided with sentences, passages, or stories that enable them to apply the newly learned phonics skills in the act of reading contextual materials. Many commercially prepared materials are available for this purpose. Also, the teacher, or the teacher and student, may create sentences or stories (including silly ones) that emphasize the blends, digraphs, or diphthongs just taught.

GAMES AND EXERCISES

See "Games and Exercises" in Chapters 5 and 6. Much of the material listed in these two sections can be adapted to the teaching of blends, digraphs, and diphthongs.

CHAPTER 8

Structural Analysis Difficulties

RECOGNIZED BY

The student is unable to pronounce multisyllabic words.

DISCUSSION

Structural analysis, often referred to as **morphology,** is concerned with the study of meaning-bearing units such as root words, prefixes, suffixes, possessives, plurals, and syllables. As a decoding skill, structural analysis is analogous to phonics, but it is used to decode words of more than one syllable. This relationship is illustrated in Figure 8.1. As described in Chapter 5, in using phonics, the reader identifies, separates, pronounces, and blends individual sounds, or phonemes, to decode one-syllable words. In the word *cat*, for example, the reader identifies and separates the three letters *c*, *a*, and *t*. He then thinks of the sound that each letter represents, and pronounces and blends the three sounds together to make the whole word. (Context clues provided by other words in the sentence simultaneously assist the reader in decoding this or any other unknown words.)

Let us assume the student does not immediately recognize the word *refinement*. This word has too many phonemes (eight to be exact) for phonics to be an efficient decoding tool. Instead, the reader uses structural analysis to decode *refinement*. To do so, the reader first identifies and separates the units or parts of the word: *re*, *fine*, and *ment*. He then pronounces each of the parts and blends them together. As you can see from Figure 8.1, phonics and structural analysis are very similar decoding processes. They differ primarily in the size of the parts of the words used in decoding.

For purposes of decoding multisyllable words, it is not necessary for the student to know the meaning of structural parts. In our example word, *refinement*, the student may not know that the prefix *re-* means "back" or "again," and that the suffix *-ment* means "the act, fact, process, art, state, condition, or degree." Usually the context of the passage provides better clues to the meaning of the word than the meanings of the small structural parts. In this case, the context clues provided in the following sentence will likely assist the student in understanding the meaning of *refinement:* "She was a woman of refinement; always polite, gentle, and elegant." One of the reasons we teach students to use context clues along with the other decoding skills (basic sight words, phonics, and structural analysis) is that they are helpful in both decoding and obtaining word meanings.

FIGURE 8.1

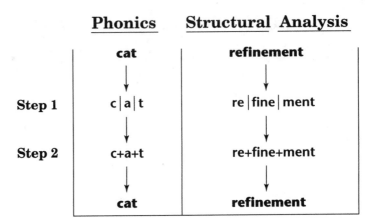

Phonics | Structural Analysis

cat | refinement

Step 1 | c|a|t | re|fine|ment

Step 2 | c+a+t | re+fine+ment

cat | refinement

Step 1: Identify and separate
phonemes or morphemes.

Step 2: Pronounce and blend
letter sounds or word parts.

Structural analysis begins when the student is able to recognize the root word in words with *-s*, *-ed*, or similar endings—for example, *run* in *runs* and *look* in *looked*. From this beginning, the student learns to recognize the parts that make up compound words, such as *tooth* and *ache* in *toothache*, and *green* and *house* in *greenhouse*. He should also begin to recognize common roots, suffixes, and prefixes. Most authorities in the field of reading believe it is not good, however, to look for little words within bigger words because the smaller words may not have their usual pronunciation. For example, the words *go*, *over*, and *me* are not helpful in decoding the word *government*.

One of the best ways to determine whether a student is having difficulty with structural analysis is to ask him to read orally. While the student reads orally, you can note the types of errors he makes. The student with structural analysis difficulties will often decode basic sight words and most one-syllable words successfully but fail to pronounce accurately words of more than one syllable. This is a common and serious problem among students with reading difficulties. Such students are often unable to read materials with readability levels above grade 3 or 4. As the difficulty of the material increases, the student's ability to read it decreases. Another way to determine whether a student is having difficulty with structural analysis is to administer the Structural Analysis Assessment, which may be found in Appendix A-7. This series of tests measures the student's ability to use structural analysis skills both in isolation and in context and provides a blueprint for instruction in the specific aspects of structural analysis in which the student is weak.

Fortunately, structural analysis difficulties can be overcome if several conditions are present. First, the student must master the prerequisite decoding skills (basic sight vocabulary, phonics, and context clues) required to read up to about the third-grade level. (See Chapters 3–7 and 10.) Second, the teacher must provide adequate direct instruction designed to teach the student strategic ways to decode multisyllable words. Third, the student must receive sufficient practice decoding multisyllable words both in isolation and in context.

Students are often taught five or six syllabication rules or generalizations to assist them in dividing long words. This approach is *not* helpful to most remedial readers for two reasons: (1) the rules are not very reliable—that is, there are many exceptions to these rules; and (2) some of the rules or generalizations are quite complicated and difficult to remember. Fortunately, it is not necessary for a student to memorize the syllabication principles if he is taught how to attack multisyllable words as described under "Recommendations."

RECOMMENDATIONS

A. Teach the students to apply the five-step strategy to decode multisyllabic words shown in Figure 8.2. (This strategy is similar to the word-attack strategy presented in Chapter 10.)

FIGURE 8.2

WHEN YOU COME TO A HARD WORD

1. Look for prefixes or suffixes.

2. Look for a base or root word that you know.

3. Read to the end of the sentence. Think of a word with those parts (from steps 1 and 2) that makes sense.

4. Try other sounds, syllables, and accents until you can form a word that makes sense.

5. If you still cannot figure the word out, skip it, ask someone, or use the dictionary.

To teach the strategy, you should model its use, then provide the students with guided and independent practice as follows:

1. Present the steps, using a written chart that students can remember and to which they can refer.
2. Choose a difficult word and put it into a sentence.

3. Demonstrate how you would use the steps, one at a time, to figure out the hard word.
4. Use enough examples to show how a student may use a different number of steps each time to get the correct pronunciation. (Always go through the steps in order.)
5. Provide students with sentences that they may use to apply the steps as you provide guidance.
6. Assure students that the strategy works and encourage them to read a lot until the strategy becomes automatic.

Listed here are 10 sentences that you may use to teach and give students practice in the five-step strategy. They are difficult because most include more than one long word. If they seem too difficult for your students at first, prepare more sentences like numbers 1 and 2.

1. The amplifier made the music louder.
2. Sara is a kind, compassionate person.
3. The archaeologist studied the bones of the dinosaur and the other artifacts found near the caves.
4. The twelve contributors contributed five hundred dollars to the charity.
5. That delicatessen has delicious potato salad.
6. After the explosion there was an evacuation of the building.
7. The horizontal lines on the television screen make it impossible to see the picture.
8. The intricate puzzle is very frustrating.
9. The hurricane did substantial damage to our neighborhood.
10. The barometric pressure is falling rapidly.

B. Refer to Appendix B-6, "Words, Sentences, and Stories for Teaching Structural Analysis." These materials will be helpful to you in teaching and having students practice structural analysis skills.

C. Make lists of common word endings and have the students underline and pronounce these endings.

D. Use multiple-choice questions that require the student to put the proper endings on words. See the following examples:
   1. The boy was (looked, looks, looking) in the window.
   2. That is (John, John's, Johns) ball and bat.
   3. The boys came (early, earlier, earliest) than the girls.

E. Make lists or flash cards of the common roots and **affixes** (prefixes and suffixes). Use these in forming new words. You may have students practice these sounds, but do not require memorization of the meanings of affixes. (See Appendix B-8 for a list of prefixes and suffixes.)

F. Make lists or flash cards of common letter combinations such as *tion* and *ult*. Practice with these may be helpful; however, avoid listing letter combinations that have sounds that may vary according to the word in which they are used. Make lists on transparencies for the overhead projector or on large pieces of cardboard.

G. Make lists of and discuss compound words as the student encounters them in his reading lessons.

H. Make lists of all the words that can be made from certain roots. For example:
   1. work—works, working, worked
   2. carry—carrying, carrier, carried, carries
   3. faith—faithful, faithless
   4. lodge—lodger, lodging, lodged

GAMES AND EXERCISES

Prefix and Suffix Baseball

Purpose: To provide practice in recognizing prefixes, suffixes, and their meanings

Materials: Cards with a prefix such as *un* or a suffix such as *ly* on them; be sure to include the line to indicate whether it is a prefix or a suffix

Procedure:

This game is not to be used until considerable work has been done with affixes. Native English-speaking students have less trouble with the game than non-native speakers because they already have a large vocabulary and need only to realize that these words contain prefixes and suffixes.

Each of the two teams chooses a pitcher who will "pitch" a word to the "batter." The batter will think of a word to go with the prefix or suffix and then pronounce it. If the student does this much but cannot use it in a sentence, he has hit a single. If the student can think of a word, pronounce it, and use it in a sentence, he hits a double. After students become more adept at the game, you may wish to confine the hits to singles to slow down the game.

Caution: Remember that only a few suffix and prefix meanings are consistent enough to warrant memorizing their meanings.

Dig Up the Root

Purpose: To develop recognition of word roots and attached affixes

Materials: Pocket chart
Word cards

Procedure:

Divide the pocket chart into two columns. In the left-hand column list a number of root words. In the right-hand column, randomly list words composed of the root words plus an affix. Have the students match the root word in the first column with the root and its affix in the second column.

1. finish   undecided
2. reach   finishing
3. determine   replace
4. decided   nationality
5. place   reached
6. nation   predetermine

Prefix and Suffix Chart

Purpose: To teach the meanings and uses of suffixes and prefixes

Materials: Chart similar to the one shown in Figure 8.3

FIGURE 8.3

Prefix	Prefix Meaning	Root	Whole Word	Suffix	Suffix Meaning
un	—	do	undo	x	x
x	x	soft	softly	—	in a way
x	x	play	playful	ful	—
—	from	port	—	x	x
pre	—	—	—	x	x
x	x	care	—	—	without
re	—	gain	—	x	x

Procedure:

Have students fill in the blank spaces in the chart. Place an *X* in the spaces that are not applicable.

Spinning for Suffixes

Purpose: To give practice in recognizing and attaching suffixes. This game will also help the student to learn the meanings of certain suffixes. This game is intended for small groups of two to five students.

Materials: A heavy piece of cardboard or a piece of plywood cut in a circle about 2–3 feet in diameter. Around the edge of the board, write a few suffixes, so they occupy the same positions as the numbers on the face of a clock. (You don't need 12 suffixes. See Figure 8.4).

FIGURE 8.4

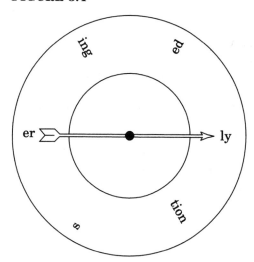

Extra overlays of paper to attach to the face of the circle. These overlays will enable you to readily change the suffixes with which you are working.

A pointer in the center of the circle that can be spun

A number of word cards that can be used with each overlay. For example, for the suffixes *-ed*, *-ing*, and *-tion* on the overlay, you might use the word *direct* on a word card.

A shoebox

Procedure:

Pass out an equal number of word cards to each member of the group. Spin the pointer, which stops on a certain suffix. Call on each member of the group, and ask him to take his top card and try to attach the suffix at which the pointer stopped. The student may be asked to spell and pronounce the word. When a student has done this correctly, he puts his card in the box. The student who has all his cards in the box first is the winner.

Variation:

Make overlays that contain prefixes to fit on the face of the circle and play the game in the same manner as with the suffixes.

Endings

Purpose: To provide practice in structural analysis

Materials: A number of cards with suffixes or word endings printed on them

Procedure:

Divide the class into two equal teams. On the chalkboard, list a number of familiar root words such as *run, sleep, help, rain, ask,* and *splash.* In a circle on the floor, place cards of suffixes such as *-ed, -d, -ing,* and *-y.* In the center of the circle, a blind-folded team member is turned around. The student points to a card and the blind-fold is removed. He goes to the chalkboard, chooses a word, and adds the ending to it, writing the new word on the board. He then pronounces the word. If the word is written correctly, he scores a point. If the word is pronounced correctly, he scores another point. If the word is written incorrectly, the next member of the rival team gets a chance to write and pronounce the word. If he writes it correctly, the rival team scores a point. The first team to receive 25 points wins.

CHAPTER 9

Contractions Not Known

RECOGNIZED BY

The student is unable to pronounce contractions when she encounters them in print. For comprehension and writing purposes, it is also useful to know what two words each contraction stands for and to be able to make contractions from various words. A test for students' knowledge of contractions can be found in Appendix A-8.

DISCUSSION

For some students, a part of poor oral reading is the lack of knowledge of contractions. This is usually a minor reading problem.

When testing for a student's knowledge of contractions, you should show the student the contraction and ask her to pronounce it. If she can pronounce the word, it will suffice for decoding purposes. For example, the student pronounces the word *can't;* for decoding purposes, she does not need to know that it means "cannot." Have the student tell what two words the contraction stands for, so you know if she understands the meaning of the contraction and will be able to recognize it for comprehension purposes and use it in her written work. Refer to the list of 47 common contractions (see Figure 9.1) that are used for testing knowledge of contractions in Appendix A-8.

RECOMMENDATIONS

A. For any contraction not known, write the two words it stands for and then the contraction on the chalkboard. Have students make up sentences using both the contracted and noncontracted form. See the example.

      let us   let's

    1. Let us go with Mother and Father.
    2. Let's go with Mother and Father.

B. Give students a matching exercise by placing a few contractions on slips of paper in an envelope. Number each contraction. In the same envelope, place slips that name the two words each contraction stands for and write the matching number of the contraction on the back. Students then try to match

FIGURE 9.1

anybody'd	I'd	weren't
aren't	I'll	we'd
can't	I'm	we'll
couldn't	I've	we're
didn't	let's	we've
doesn't	she'd	what's
don't	she'll	where's
hadn't	she's	who'd
hasn't	that's	who'll
haven't	there'll	won't
he'd	there's	wouldn't
he'll	they'd	you'd
he's	they'll	you'll
here's	they're	you're
isn't	they've	you've
it's	wasn't	

FIGURE 9.2

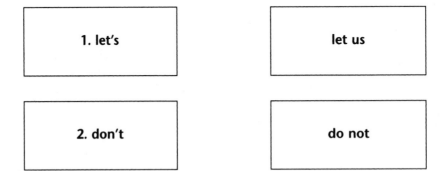

the contractions with the correct words by placing them side by side, as illustrated in Figure 9.2.

After the student has completed the exercise, she can turn the cards in the right-hand column over to see if the numbers on the back match the numbers on the slips in the left-hand column. (Be aware that whenever you use a self-checking format as described here, some students may not be able to prevent themselves from peeking at the answers on the back of the cards. Because of this, some teachers do not prepare games or exercises that are self-checking in this manner.)

C. Give students paragraphs to read in which several words could be contracted. Underline these words. Direct students to change these words to contractions as they read. See the following example:

> Kareem said to Miguel, "We have only two days before you are going to leave."
>
> "Yes," said Miguel, "I am waiting to go, and I have already packed my suitcase."

After doing this type of exercise, discuss why contractions are used and which form — long or short — sounds more natural in common speech.

D. Conduct contraction races between two students. Tell the students two words and see who can call out the contraction first. Also give contractions and have students call out the words that are contracted.

E. Give students newspaper articles and have them underline all contractions and words that could have been contracted.

F. As students talk, call attention to the contractions they use by writing them down. Discuss why they used the contracted form.

CHAPTER 10

Inadequate Ability to Use Context Clues

RECOGNIZED BY

The student is unable to derive meaning or pronunciation of a word from the way it is used in a sentence.

DISCUSSION

The use of **context clues** can be one of the student's greatest helps in determining the pronunciation and meaning of unfamiliar words. It is not a difficult reading skill to teach; however, many teachers incorrectly assume that all students will learn to use context clues on their own. Capable readers usually do, but disabled readers often need a considerable amount of instruction and a great deal of practice to learn this skill.

A test for determining whether a student is able to use context clues effectively is found in Appendix A-10. When using this test, it is important that the student read at his **independent reading level** or at an easy **instructional reading level.** Do not expect students who are reading at a difficult instructional level or at their **frustration reading level** to be able to use context clues effectively. (An explanation of each of these three levels is found in the glossary at the end of this book.)

You can also determine whether a student is having difficulty using context clues by listening to him read orally from material on which he will make 5 to 10 errors per page. (This material could well be at the student's frustration level, but such reading is justified because you will not have the student read such difficult material for long and because you are doing this for diagnostic purposes.) While the student reads, note whether miscalled words are logical replacements; that is, does the student rely on context clues when other decoding skills are inadequate? You may also question the student about the meaning of certain words where that meaning is evident from the context.

Bear in mind that students' difficulties with context clues may be reflected in two opposite behaviors. Many students fail to use context clues adequately and appear to read word by word. A classic example of this type of problem is the student who reads the sentence *The boy went into the house* as *The ... boy ... went ... into the ... horse.* This student apparently overrelied on graphic information at the expense of meaning clues, thus substituting the word *horse* for *house*. The two words are similar in appearance but quite dissimilar in meaning. At the other extreme are students who overrely on context. These students may appear to be reading fluently, but what they read may not be what was written. Such a student might read the sample sentence as: *The boy went into the garage.* While the first type of problem is more common and often more difficult to remediate, both forms of context-clue difficulties are detrimental to reading ability.

RECOMMENDATIONS

A. The best way to teach students to use context clues when they are reading independently is to teach them the word-attack strategy shown in Figure 10.1.

FIGURE 10.1

WHEN YOU COME TO A WORD YOU DON'T KNOW:

1. Say the beginning sound.

2. Read the rest of the sentence. THINK.

3. Say the parts that you know. GUESS.

4. Ask someone or skip it and go on.

When encountering an unknown word, step 1, "Say the beginning sound" (phonics), is the one most students will do automatically if they have had any phonics training at all. This is fortunate because beginning sounds are often the most helpful clue in decoding an unknown word. (Students who have had no phonics training at all may guess wildly and insert any word that might make sense.)

Step 2, "Read the rest of the sentence," requires the student to use context clues before applying additional phonics or structural analysis. In most cases the combination of initial letter sounds and context will result in correct identification of the unknown word. Step 2 requires the student to read to the end of the sentence to take advantage of the context clues that may come after the unknown word. (Words that come *after* are often more helpful than those that come *before* unknown words.) If the student still has not decoded the word, step 3, "Say the parts that you know," has him use other word-analysis clues, such as ending sounds, vowel sounds, and structural analysis. The student is encouraged to guess, if necessary, so as not to spend too much time trying to decode a single unknown word. The last step, "Ask someone or skip it and go on," encourages the student to ask for help or continue reading if all else fails. It is quite possible that context clues picked up in reading further will permit the student to identify the unknown word.

If students must resort to step 4 often, they should be given easier material to read. Similarly, if students encounter more than one unknown word in a single sentence, this word-attack strategy is likely to break down, indicating that the material is too difficult.

To teach the strategy, you should use the following steps:

1. Present the steps, using a written chart that students can remember and to which they can refer.
2. Model use of the steps yourself with sample sentences.
3. Assure students that the strategy works.
4. Provide students with sentences that they may use to apply the steps as you provide guidance.
5. Ensure that students use the steps as they practice in the act of reading.

At the end of this paragraph is a list of sentences that you may use to teach and give students practice in the four-step word-attack strategy. The numbers after each sentence indicate which steps are likely to assist students. It is not possible to determine exactly which steps will help students. Some students will recognize unknown words at sight. Others will use only one or two steps. Some may not succeed at all. You will need to provide other examples for students based on their specific needs.

1. The *light* is red. (1, 2)
2. I will *take* you there. (1, 2)
3. I cannot *remember* your name. (1, 2, 3)
4. I like *chocolate* cake. (1, 2, 3)
5. The *cat* is my pet. (1, 2)
6. The *hamster* is my pet. (1, 2, 3)
7. The *armadillo* is my pet. (1, 2, 3, 4?)

B. Encourage practice in the act of reading. Such practice is essential for students to learn to read for meaning. Provide time, appropriate (easy!) materials, the proper setting, and encouragement for sustained silent reading.

C. Show (demonstrate to) the student that it is possible to derive the meaning of words from their context. Provide specific examples.

1. The careless boy did his work in a *haphazard* manner.
2. He felt that although his work was *imperfect*, it was still good.
3. When he tried to *insert* the letter in the mailbox, the mailbox was too full.
4. They called in a *mediator* to help settle the problems between labor and management.

D. Have students preread material silently before reading orally. Discuss troublesome vocabulary.

E. Set purposes for reading. Stress accuracy in reading, not speed.

F. Use short, easy selections. Have students stop frequently to explain what they have read in their own words.

G. Use high-interest material, including student-authored language-experience stories.

H. Have students scan for important words. Have them guess the content and then read to see if the guess was accurate.

I. Construct sentences or short paragraphs, omitting selected words that students should be able to determine by their context. In place of each key word, insert an initial consonant and then x's for the rest of the letters in the words. See the following example:

When Jack <u>ix</u> in a hurry, he always <u>rxxx</u> home from school.

When students have become proficient at this, advance to the next step, which is to replace key words with x's for *each* letter.

When Jack <u>xx</u> in a hurry, he always <u>xxxx</u> home from school.

After students are able to get most of the omitted words by replacing the x's with letters, leave blank lines to replace entire omitted words.

When Jack _____ in a hurry, he always _____ home from school.

J. Use multiple-choice questions in which the student fills in blanks: "Jack _____ a black pony (rock, rode, rod)." Using words that look alike also will give the student practice in phonic and structural analysis.

K. Make tape recordings in which key words are omitted. Give the student a copy of the script and have him fill in the blank spaces as the tape is played.

L. Create a series of sentences using words that are spelled alike but may have different pronunciations or meanings, such as *read* and *lead*. Have the student read sentences using these words in proper context.

He read the book.
He will read the story.
It was made out of lead.
He had the lead in the play.

PART FOUR

SPECIFIC ORAL READING DIFFICULTIES

CHAPTER 11

Poor Pronunciation

RECOGNIZED BY

The student fails to pronounce a word correctly.

DISCUSSION

Mispronunciation of words is one of the most serious reading problems of disabled readers. The problem may be caused by one or a combination of the following factors: (1) the student lacks the ability to use phonics when decoding;[1] (2) the student lacks the ability to use structural analysis when decoding; (3) the student has poor **fluency** skills; or (4) the student has a hearing, speech, or language difficulty. In any case, a careful **diagnosis** is needed before a program of correction is started. The following paragraphs suggest ways to diagnose the various causes of poor pronunciation.

Cause #1: The student lacks the ability to use phonics when decoding. If the student fails to correctly pronounce one-syllable words that are not basic sight words, then this student probably lacks the ability to use phonics to decode unknown words. The Phonics Assessment found in Appendix A-6 can be used to quickly spot those areas of weakness in the student's knowledge of phonics. Teachers should be especially careful in selecting a phonics test to use. Research has shown that group phonics tests simply do not measure what a student actually does in applying phonic word-attack skills in the act of reading. Therefore, such tests do not aid diagnostic teaching. This inadequacy is also true of some individual phonics tests. The Phonics Assessment in Appendix A-6 includes test situations that require the student to respond in a way that is similar to or the same as the application of these skills in the act of reading.

Cause #2: The student lacks the ability to use structural analysis when decoding. If the student fails to correctly pronounce words of more than one syllable, then this student probably lacks the ability to use structural analysis to decode unknown words. The Structural Analysis Assessment found in Appendix A-7 will enable you to identify the student's specific weaknesses in this area. The teacher may want to supplement test results by observing the ways in which the student attacks or fails to attack words of one or more syllables.

Cause #3: The student has poor fluency skills. You should stop the reader at a mispronounced word and ask for the correct pronunciation. If the student usually says it correctly, she may lack reading fluency (poor fluency skills). This would still not exclude the possibility that training in various forms of **word analysis** might be beneficial.

Cause #4: The student has a hearing, speech, or language difficulty. An auditory discrimination test is easy to administer and will determine whether a student has difficulty discriminating between somewhat similar sounds. The inability to discriminate between certain sounds can lead to the mispronunciation of words. This knowledge, supplemented with informal hearing tests, such as determining whether the student hears a normal voice at the distance most students hear it, will help you decide whether a hearing defect is contributing to the reading difficulty. A hearing specialist should further examine students indicating difficulty in any of these areas. To determine whether the student has a speech difficulty, ask the student to repeat sentences that are given orally. Use words that were mispronounced in previous reading. Words read incorrectly, but spoken correctly, are not speech problems. Some students may mispronounce words because their first language is not English. This may also occur if the student speaks a nonstandard dialect of English. This need not be cause for concern. If the mispronunciation does not cause loss of meaning (comprehension), then it is not necessary to remediate this difficulty. You can determine whether meaning is affected by using the procedure described in Chapter 19 to check comprehension. Teachers of students who are limited-English speakers or speakers of nonstandard dialects should become familiar with the differences in pronunciations that will occur in the language or dialect spoken. With this knowledge and some experience, you will have little difficulty in determining whether problems in mispronunciation of words affect reading comprehension.

Correcting Poor Pronunciation

If the student lacks the ability to use phonics in decoding, the suggestions listed under "Recommendations" in items A through D and in Appendix B-4 should be beneficial.

If the student lacks the ability to use structural analysis in decoding multisyllable words, consult items E through I and Appendix B-4. If the pronunciation difficulties are caused by poor fluency skills, the suggestions listed in items J and K are appropriate. Finally, if poor pronunciation is caused by hearing, speech, or language differences, consult items L through O.

RECOMMENDATIONS

Students who need help with phonics will benefit from the following interventions:

A. Teach the phonics skills in which a weakness is indicated by the Phonics Assessment in Appendix A-6. Then refer to the appropriate chapters (5 through 7) for corrective procedures.

B. Have students make word cards or lists and build their own file of words that they habitually mispronounce. Allow for periodic independent study of these words. (A shoebox makes an excellent file box for indexing word cards.)

C. Have students make their own lists of common letter combinations that are generally phonetically regular, such as *-tion*, *-ance*, and *-edge*, as they are encountered and learned.

D. Use the phonogram lists in Appendix B-4 as suggested under "Using the Phonogram List to Teach Phonics." If the student continues to have difficulties with phonics, use the phonogram list as follows:

1. Have the student first pronounce *sent;* then give her a number of other words and nonsense words to pronounce that end in *-ent*, such as *dent*, *pent*, and *bent*. This exercise will give the student practice in using various consonant sounds in conjunction with various word endings.

2. Do the same as in item 1, using consonant blends with various combinations; for example, pronounce *slash*, then give a number of other words and nonsense words ending in *-ash*, such as *crash*, *flash*, and *scash*. As the student reads, ask her to try to pronounce difficult words aloud. You should determine which sounds she knows but is not using. Use these sounds to construct exercises similar to the two shown previously or others appropriate for improving the particular phonic elements not being used correctly.

Students who need help with structural analysis will benefit from the following instructional strategies:

E. Teach the structural analysis skills in which a weakness is indicated by the Structural Analysis Assessment found in Appendix A-7. Then refer to Chapter 8 for corrective procedures.

F. Make lists of prefixes and suffixes; however, do not expect students to learn the *meaning* of many of these. Focus only on students' correct pronunciation of these affixes. (See the list of prefixes and suffixes in Appendix B-8.)

G. To help students use their existing decoding skills effectively, teach them to use the word-attack strategy. This strategy and effective ways to teach it are described in Chapter 10, which also presents a number of other recommendations for teaching students to use context clues.

H. For longer, more difficult words, first teach the student to use structural analysis, then teach the student the word-attack strategy, which will enable her to use the various word-attack skills together when she meets unfamiliar words in the act of reading. For structural analysis, the student must learn to identify word parts, visually separate word parts, pronounce word parts, and blend the parts together to form the whole word. Procedures for doing this are presented in Chapter 8.

I. Use the materials in Appendix B-6. These have been designed specifically to remediate difficulties in structural analysis.

Students who have poor fluency skills will benefit from the following approaches:

J. When the student mispronounces a word in oral reading, call attention to the correct pronunciation with as little fuss as possible. Ignoring the mistake tends to reinforce the wrong pronunciation with the student as well as with any other members of the class who are listening. If the student misses the same word more than once, reinforce the student's pronunciation as follows:

1. After you pronounce the word for the student for the second time, ask her to focus her eyes on the word and repeat it five times, then say it loudly.

2. A few minutes later, come back to the word, point to it, and have the student pronounce it. If she says it correctly, reward her with praise. If she has again forgotten the word, have her write it carefully on two flash cards or slips of paper. Have her keep one of the cards or slips of paper to use for practice while you keep the other. Later that day or the next, show her your copy of the flash card or slip of paper. If she says it correctly this time, praise the student emphatically. (This procedure will work with only a few words at a time. If the student is missing more than a few words of the material being read, then the material is probably too difficult and should be replaced by easier reading material.)

K. Use one or more of the oral reading techniques described in detail in the introductory chapter. These procedures are highly effective with a variety of fluency difficulties.

Students whose pronunciation difficulties are caused by hearing, speech, or language differences will benefit from the following interventions:

L. To teach certain sounds with which students are having difficulty:
   1. Set up pairs with only one different sound, such as *hit—heat.*
   2. Make sure students can hear the sound differences.
   3. Make sure students can say the words.
   4. Use each word in a sentence and then have students say the single sound following that sentence.

M. Have students hold their throats with their hands to feel the difference in vibration from one word to another or from one letter to another.

N. Play games that deal with sounds. For example, the first student says, "I am a *ch.*" The rest of the students then guess whether she is a chicken, a chipmunk, and so on. This gives all students many exposures to word beginnings.

O. Consult a speech, hearing, or language specialist, if available, for suggestions or direct services to the student.

ENDNOTE

1. If the student has difficulty pronouncing one-syllable words, then she is likely to have a problem with phonics. If the student has difficulty pronouncing words of two or more syllables, then she is likely to have a problem with structural analysis. These are analogous decoding skills. When using phonics, the student visually divides a one-syllable word into the letters (graphemes) that represent the individual sounds (phonemes), pronounces each sound, and blends the sounds together. When using structural analysis, the student

visually divides a word of two or more syllables into pronounceable parts (morphemes), pronounces each part, and blends the parts together. In using both skills, the student must perform the three acts quickly. A third decoding skill, using context clues, enables the student to use the meaning of other words in a sentence to help in figuring out the unknown word. Skilled readers use all of these skills together, along with sight word recognition, to decode effectively.

CHAPTER 12

Omissions

RECOGNIZED BY

The student omits words, phrases, or both while reading orally.

DISCUSSION

Omissions in reading, the second most common type of **miscue,** are usually caused by inadequate decoding skills. The student encounters a word or phrase he cannot pronounce and skips over it. The student may or may not pause before omitting the word or phrase. Often such a student is fearful of mispronouncing a word when reading orally. In some cases, omissions result from poor fluency skills. The student may read too rapidly or carelessly and omit words for this reason. In either case, the omissions are likely to lead to diminished comprehension, which is a serious problem. Occasionally, omissions result when students purposely skip over unknown words because they have been taught to do so. This is an appropriate decoding strategy in some circumstances. (See the section in Chapter 10 that describes the word-attack strategy.) When students do this, they should return to the omitted word and attempt to decode it using context or other clues.

Before beginning a program of help, you should determine the cause of omissions. To determine whether decoding difficulties or poor fluency skills cause the omission of words, ask the student to pronounce any words omitted after he has read a passage. If the student still does not know the word or words, then the problem is likely to be lack of decoding skills. If the student now knows the word or words, assume that the problem is one of poor fluency skills. You might also have the student read the material at the level in which he is making omissions and note the percentage of words omitted. Then have the student read an easier passage, and note whether omissions still occur. If the percentage of omissions decreases markedly, assume that the student has insufficient decoding skills. If, however, the omissions continue with approximately the same percentage of occurrence, assume that they are a result of poor fluency skills.

The student may lack decoding skills in sight vocabulary, phonics, structural analysis, or context clues, or he may lack comprehension to some extent. If the problem stems from one of these difficulties, the suggestions in items A through I under "Recommendations" will probably be of little or no value, as the omissions are actually only symptoms of a larger problem with decoding or comprehension. It is then necessary to determine in which of these areas the student is deficient. The procedures and suggestions recommended for each area are given in the following chapters:

→ **Sight vocabulary—Chapters 3 and 4**
→ **Phonics—Chapters 5, 6, and 7**
→ **Structural analysis—Chapters 8 and 9**
→ **Context clues—Chapter 10**
→ **Comprehension—Chapter 22**

The word-attack strategy presented in Chapter 10 will prove especially useful to students whose omissions result from inadequate word-analysis skills.

If the student is able to analyze new words but does not have instant recognition of words that, for his grade level, should have become sight words, he probably lacks word-recognition skills. It would then be necessary to help the student build a sight vocabulary. To improve this area, see Chapter 4. If the student's problem is determined to be one of poor fluency skills, the suggestions listed in items A through H should be helpful. Also keep in mind that unless the student's errors are rather frequent and affect comprehension to some extent, they may not be worth addressing.

Some of the recommendations that follow may encourage the student to substitute temporarily one symptom for another. For example, in item D, the student is encouraged to use finger pointing to eliminate omissions. The use of such crutches should not be a problem. As the student's reading ability improves, the new behavior (in this case, finger pointing) will no longer be necessary.

RECOMMENDATIONS

A. Call the reader's attention to omissions when they occur. Making an immediate correction is the first step toward breaking the habit.

B. Allow students to preread material silently before asking them to read it orally. You might allow students to ask you for assistance with difficult words during the silent reading phase. If they ask for help on more than 10% of the words, then the material is too difficult and should be replaced with easier material.

C. Use one or more of the oral reading techniques described in detail in the introductory chapter. These procedures are highly effective with a variety of oral reading difficulties. After calling the student's attention to the problem as mentioned in item A, you may find that these methods are extremely effective.

D. If whole words or phrases are consistently skipped, you might require the student to point to each word as he reads it. It is helpful to ask the student to pick up his finger and then bring it down on each word as it is read. This keeps the student from pointing to words that are ahead of the actual word being read. This technique also should be stopped when the student no longer needs it.

E. Have several students read chorally.

F. Use commercially produced materials that are designed to promote fluent oral reading. Participation in the reading of a play or a reader's theater activity will strongly encourage students to read each word that is written.

G. Ask detailed questions that require thorough reading. Ask about only one sentence or paragraph at a time. Students often will omit adjectives. In this case, it is often helpful to give the student a list of questions such as "Was the bear big or little?" and "What color were the flowers?" The student will be forced to focus on adjectives that could otherwise easily be omitted.

H. To focus attention on words omitted by the reader, tape-record a passage and then give the student a copy of the material as it is played back to him. Have the student follow along and point to each word as it is read. Have him circle all words omitted. After the reading, discuss possible reasons for his omitting the words and the importance of not doing so. Suggestions for additional tape recorder activities appear in Chapter 18 under "Recommendations," item L.

I. As the student reads, ask him to outline the first letter of each word read, as shown in Figure 12.1.

FIGURE 12.1

Sam plays baseball in the park.

This will be helpful for students who make many omissions. You will, of course, want to discontinue this as soon as the student stops making omissions. Another variation of the previous procedure is to have the student underline the first letters of words, as shown in Figure 12.2.

FIGURE 12.2

Mary went with her mother to the store.

Following this, you may wish to have the student draw lines over or below words in phrases or natural linguistic units as he reads, as shown in Figure 12.3.

FIGURE 12.3

Fred has a large brown cat.

CHAPTER 13

Repetitions

RECOGNIZED BY

The student rereads words or phrases.

DISCUSSION

The most common causes of repetitions in a student's reading are similar to the causes of omissions in reading; that is, poor word-recognition skills, poor word-analysis skills, or poor fluency skills. Of these, a problem with **word-recognition skills** (sight vocabulary) occurs most often. It should be pointed out, however, that sometimes a student repeats certain words in order to correct a reading error or to gain time so as to avoid making an error. This may be a stalling tactic the student uses while she mentally works on the upcoming word. If this happens only on certain words that you know are new or difficult for the student, you should, in most cases, ignore it. If the words the student does not recognize are ones that normally should be sight words for that student, you can assume that she is deficient in word-recognition skills. In this case, the recommendations in Chapters 3 and 4 should be beneficial.

The problem of word-analysis difficulties may be in any of the following areas: (1) phonics, (2) structural analysis, or (3) use of context clues. Occasionally the student will need assistance with dictionary skills. If the problem is in one of these areas, some of the recommendations that follow will probably be of little or no value, as the repetitions are only a symptom of the larger problems of word-recognition or word-analysis difficulties. You would need to determine in which area of word analysis the student is deficient. These procedures and the suggestions recommended in each case are given in the following chapters:

➡ **Phonics—Chapters 5, 6, and 7**
➡ **Structural analysis—Chapters 8 and 9**
➡ **Context clues—Chapter 10**
➡ **Dictionary skills—Chapter 28**

The word-attack strategy presented in Chapter 10 will also prove useful to students whose repetitions result from inadequate word-analysis skills.

You can determine, to some extent, whether poor decoding skills are the cause of repetitions by having the student read material at the level in which she is making repetitions. Note the percentage of words or phrases repeated. Then give the student a much easier passage and note whether there is a definite decrease in the percentage of repetitions. If there is, the problem is probably inadequate decoding skills. If, on the other hand, a student continues to make as many repetitions as she did on the more difficult passage, then the problem is probably poor fluency skills.

If you determine that the problem results from poor fluency skills, then the suggestions listed under "Recommendations" in items A through F should prove beneficial. Of these, the simple suggestion given in item A is often all that is needed. Also, the suggestions listed in items G and H are very important and may give the student the confidence she needs to begin reading fluently.

RECOMMENDATIONS

A. Call the repetitions to the student's attention. This is often the most important step in breaking the bad habit.

B. Use one or more of the oral reading techniques described in detail in the introductory chapter. These procedures are highly effective with a variety of oral reading difficulties.

C. Have the student read chorally with other students.

D. Have the student set a certain pace with her hand and keep up with this pace as she reads. Do not let the eyes pace the hand.

E. To focus attention on words repeated by the reader, tape-record a passage that she reads and then give the student a copy of the written material as it is played back to her. Have the student follow along, pointing to each word and underlining any words as they are repeated. After completing the passage, discuss any reasons that the student believes are causing her to repeat words or phrases.

F. Follow the other suggestions for using the tape recorder, as listed in Chapter 18 under "Recommendations," item L.

G. Provide easier or more familiar material in which the vocabulary presents no problem.

H. Let the student read the material silently before she attempts to read orally.

CHAPTER 14

Inversions or Reversals

RECOGNIZED BY

The student appears to read words from right to left instead of the normal left-to-right sequence, for example, *was* for *saw*, or *pot* for *top*.

The student reads letters in reverse, for example, *d* for *b*, or *p* for *g*. The student makes partial reversals in words (the letters within words), for example, *ant* for *nat*.

The student reverses words within sentences, for example, "the *rat* chased the *cat*" instead of "the *cat* chased the *rat*."

DISCUSSION

It is important to recognize that reversals are a normal symptom of poor decoding skills regardless of the age of the reader. An adult who reads at a first-grade level is likely to make the same reversal errors as a 6-year-old reading at a first-grade level, especially when reading words in isolation. As decoding ability improves, reversals almost always disappear.

In nearly all cases, the student has simply not developed a strong enough visual image for the word and miscalls the word because he simply cannot remember what it is. (For an instant the child may ponder: "Is the word *was* or is it *saw?*") When a student is first learning how to decode, the task of correctly pronouncing printed words is quite a struggle and demands most or all of the student's mental energy. At this early stage, the student may pay little or no attention to the context of what he is reading. Gradually, as reading ability develops, context clues help the student pronounce the word correctly. ("The boy *was* the dog" doesn't make sense, but "The boy *saw* the dog" does.) With practice and success over time, the student learns to recognize instantly the many little, easily confusable words in English, such as *on* and *no*, *that* and *what*, *big* and *dig*, *come* and *came*, *went* and *want*, and so on. With this in mind, the teacher should be careful not to fuss too much about these problems with beginning readers. Sometimes too much focus on these errors makes matters worse instead of better.

Some experts claim that reversals occur because the student has failed to develop a left-to-right eye movement or a left-to-right reading pattern. (This problem, if and when it exists, is difficult to determine.) Others believe that a student who reverses letters or words may suffer from some neurological impairment, or he may not realize that the order or position in which letters appear makes a difference.

Regardless of the cause, the recommendations for solving this problem are the same. Most children who make reversals tend to outgrow the behavior after a few months of school. However, if the difficulty persists after several weeks of instruction and the student is making normal progress otherwise, the suggestions listed in this chapter, along with a little patience, should solve the problem.

For many years, reading teachers believed that students who made many reversals or inversions tended to have more severe difficulties than students who made other types of errors. More recent research has tended to refute this belief. We now believe that, if you check carefully, you are likely to find that children who make numerous reversals will also make just as high a percentage of other types of errors.

RECOMMENDATIONS

The suggestions in items A through H can be used effectively with groups of students. The recommendations listed under items I through Q are designed for use with individual students.

A. Use Big Books for beginning readers to point out left-to-right progression (as well as other skills, such as sequencing of words and common sight words). The larger print and the high interest level of most of these books enhance motivation for learning these skills. The *shared book experience* is an instructional technique in which the teacher attempts to duplicate some of the best features of the "lap method" that parents use when reading to their young children. When the teacher glides his hand under the words as they are read (some teachers prefer pointers), he is emphasizing not only left-to-right progression and the return sweep at the end of a line of print, but also the separation of the individual words in the story. When you use this technique with students, be sure to read slowly and with expression. Big Books or language-experience stories that the students have dictated (see the introductory chapter) should be read many times and the children should be encouraged to participate by reading along orally as much as possible.

B. Poetry, songs, and rap music can also be used effectively for shared reading experiences as described in item A. When teachers engage students in reading (or singing) words as they see them, they are using a powerful technique to help students decode words. Remember to insist that the students look at (focus on) the words as you and they pronounce them slowly and clearly.

C. After discussing the problem with the student, give him sentences in which words that he tends to reverse are covered by a small piece of paper. Have him read to the end of the sentence, using the context to determine the word he thinks should be in the sentence. Then have him uncover the word and check the accuracy of his use of context.

D. Provide students with their own copies of the simple sentences, stories, songs, and so on that are being read; have the students underline the words, phrases, or sentences, pronouncing each word as it is underlined or reading the phrases or sentences as they are underlined.

E. Teach students to pace their reading with their hands, practicing a left-to-right movement.

F. Draw arrows pointing from left to right under troublesome words or phrases.

G. Write in pairs the words sometimes reversed (*was/saw, net/ten, war/raw, trap/part*). Use one word in a sentence and ask students to point to or write the word used.

H. Use a colored letter at the beginning of words commonly confused. Discontinue this practice as soon as these words no longer present any difficulty.

I. As mentioned in the "Discussion" section, one of the most effective things you can do to help a student correct the problem of reversals is to call his attention to the context in which the word is used. If the student is made aware of the context, then he will have a tendency to correct the problem on his own. To do this, give the student a number of simple sentences in which the word or words being reversed could only logically be used in one context. It may be helpful to have the student work at the sentence level, rather than at the paragraph or passage level, so he can focus more on the context. Also, try not to put other difficult words in the sentences you prepare. The following is an example:

Bob *was* going with Tom to the store.

Mary *saw* a big dog on the way home.

J. Emphasize left-to-right in all reading activities. The following method may be helpful: Cover words or sentences with your hand or a card and read the word or sentence as you uncover it. Then have the student do the same. The student may find it helpful to make a window marker as shown in Figure 14.1. The student uses it as he would a regular marker but lets the line of print show through the slot.

FIGURE 14.1

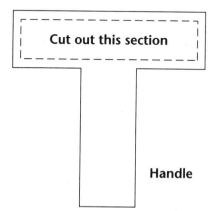

K. Let the child use a typewriter or computer to practice words with which he has difficulty. This will enable him to see the word formed from left to right as he types.

L. Pair the letters that are causing difficulty (such as p and q). Have the student trace the letters with his index and middle fingers, sounding each letter as it is traced. Or, place a thin layer of salt or fine sand in the bottom of a shoebox lid and ask the student to trace letters with his fingers in the sand or salt.

M. If whole words are reversed, you can have the student trace the word and then attempt to write it from memory. It is often helpful to have the student say the word slowly as he writes it, and to repeat this procedure several times. (It is important for the teacher to provide motivation for this type of activity. It is hoped that the student will view this as a game or a fun activity rather than punishment or drudgery.)

N. Use a magnetic board with three-dimensional letters. Have the student manipulate letters to form words commonly reversed. The use of magnetic letters has become very popular in recent years as an outgrowth of their use in practices associated with **Reading Recovery.**

O. Blindfold the student, then form letters or words with which he is having difficulty, using three-dimensional letters. Have the student trace the letter and say it as you trace it on his back, making sure that your finger follows the same part of the letter on the student's back that his finger does in tracing the three-dimensional letter.

P. To help make the student aware of the importance of the sequence of words commonly reversed, place one word commonly reversed above itself. Then have the student draw lines from the first letter of the top word to the first letter of the bottom word, as shown in Figure 14.2. Have the student say each letter as he begins to draw the line from it and each letter as the line reaches it.

FIGURE 14.2

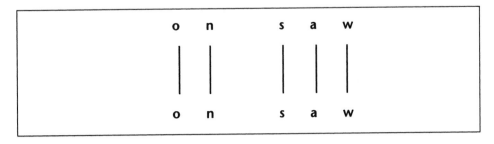

Q. Write two words commonly reversed side by side. Ask the student to number the letters in the first word by placing a number under each letter. Then ask him to assign the same numbers to the letters in the second word:

saw   was   on   no
123   321   12   21

CHAPTER 15

Insertions

RECOGNIZED BY

The student adds words that are not present in the sentence. For example, in the sentence, "The dog chased the little boy," the student may add *big* to make the sentence read, "The *big* dog chased the little boy."

DISCUSSION

Insertions are the third most common type of miscue made by students in oral reading. They are often not as serious as other types of errors. A possible cause of insertions is that the student's oral language development may surpass her reading level or that she may anticipate what is coming next and read that instead of what actually is written. Insertions that make sense within the context of the sentence indicate the student's awareness or comprehension of the material being read. In this case, you may assume the insertions are caused by either poor fluency skills or oral language development beyond the reading level of the student. When insertions do not make sense within the context of the sentence, you may assume that comprehension problems are involved. The suggestions listed under "Recommendations" in items A through I are appropriate when the problem is poor fluency skills or when the oral language development of the student surpasses her reading ability. If students make these types of insertion errors, you should first determine whether they appear often enough, or are serious enough, to cause concern. If they seldom appear, it may be best to ignore them. If the cause of the insertions is a lack of comprehension, then the suggestions in Chapter 22, "Comprehension Inadequate," are recommended.

RECOMMENDATIONS

A. Call the student's attention to the insertion. Sometimes she is not aware of the habit. Allowing the student to continue only provides reinforcement for the mistakes.

B. Encourage the student to read more slowly. Students often believe erroneously that good reading is fast reading. When students try to read more quickly than they are able, insertions may result.

C. Use commercially prepared materials that are designed to promote fluent oral reading.

D. Use one or more of the oral reading techniques described in detail in the introductory chapter. These procedures are highly effective with a variety of oral reading difficulties.

E. Ask questions that require an exact answer. If the student usually follows a certain pattern in making insertions (such as adding adjectives), you may wish to provide questions for the student to review before reading the story. These questions can focus on the objects in the story described by the adjectives that are often inserted. This will cause the student to read more carefully. Use questions such as: "Does it say how big the frog was?" and "Was it a sunny, warm day, a sunny, cold day, or just a sunny day?"

F. Have students read chorally.

G. Play a tape recording in which the student made insertions. Ask the student to follow the written passage, stopping the tape recorder as often as necessary. Have the student write on the written passage the insertions that she made on the oral reading of the material. Use the student-corrected passages as a basis for discussing the problem.

H. Have the student read along with a passage that has been tape-recorded. See Chapter 18 under "Recommendations," item L, for additional activities using the audio tape recorder.

I. If the student makes many insertions, have her point to each word as she reads it. Have the student lift her finger up and bring it down on each word as it is read. Do not allow the student to continue this technique after the habit has disappeared.

CHAPTER 16

Substitutions

RECOGNIZED BY

The student substitutes one word for another when reading orally.

DISCUSSION

Substitutions are the most common type of miscue or oral reading error. The student who substitutes one word for another is either a reader who has not developed adequate decoding skills or one with poor fluency skills. Some readers make substitutions that are nearly correct within the context of the material being read; for example, "The man drove the *automobile*" might be read, "The man drove the *car.*" If these minor mistakes appear rarely, it may be best to ignore the problem. If, however, they occur frequently or consistently, then some steps should be taken. These errors do matter. As students grow older and read increasingly difficult materials, even contextually appropriate substitutions can result in lowered comprehension.

Substitutions that are not in the proper context of the sentence typically are caused by decoding difficulty. When help is given with decoding skills, the problem of substitutions usually disappears. You should determine whether substitutions are caused by inadequate decoding skills or fluency problems and plan help accordingly.

The suggestions listed under "Recommendations" in items A through H should be helpful for students whose substitutions are caused by decoding difficulties. If, however, the substitutions are caused by poor fluency skills, then the suggestions in items I through S should be helpful.

RECOMMENDATIONS

Students whose substitutions are caused by inadequate decoding ability will benefit from the following interventions:

A. Use reading material on a lower level of difficulty.
B. Do not expect students to read material above their meaning-vocabulary level. Generally, use easy materials and encourage students to read widely.
C. If many words are not known, the suggestions listed in Chapters 3 and 4 should be used. When the student's sight vocabulary is increased, the problem of making substitutions will probably decrease.

D. If the student is unable to use phonics or structural analysis sufficiently for decoding, the recommendations in Chapters 5 through 9 will prove helpful.

E. To help students use their existing decoding skills effectively, teach the word-attack strategy shown in Figure 16.1.

FIGURE 16.1

WHEN YOU COME TO A WORD YOU DON'T KNOW:

1. Say the beginning sound.

2. Read the rest of the sentence. THINK.

3. Say the parts that you know. GUESS.

4. Ask someone or skip it and go on.

This strategy and effective ways to teach it are described in Chapter 10, which also presents a number of other recommendations for teaching students to use context clues.

F. Sometimes students feel they must make a continual response while they are reading. When such students do not know a strange word, they are likely to substitute whatever word comes into their minds rather than take the time to use the word-attack strategy. Assure these students that they will be given ample time to attack a word before someone tells them the word.

G. Use the difficult words in multiple-choice sentences, such as in the following examples:

1. John's father gave him a (watch, witch, water) for his birthday.
2. He (though, thought, through) he would be the tallest boy in the class.
3. He asked his father (what, where, when) they would leave.
4. She said, "The books belong to (them, that, this)."

H. Use the words in sentences where the student must complete the word to make the sentence sensible:

1. Can you tell me wh_____ they will be home?
2. Does th_____ book belong to Lori?
3. The stunt driver drove his car thr_____ the wall of fire.
4. Jamie said, "That funny l_____ dog belongs to me."

Students whose substitutions are caused by poor fluency skills will find the following strategies helpful:

I. Call attention to the mistake and correct it when it occurs.

J. In item B, we recommended that you urge students to read in great quantity. This suggestion was aimed at readers whose substitutions result from poor decoding skills. The suggestion is equally valuable for students whose substitutions result from poor fluency skills. Thus, the recommendation bears repeating: Provide abundant opportunities for students to receive practice in the act of reading, both orally and silently.

K. Allow students to preread material silently before asking them to read it orally. You might allow students to ask you for assistance with difficult words during the silent reading phase. If they ask for help on more than 10% of the words, then the material is too difficult and should be replaced with easier material.

L. Use commercially produced materials that are designed to promote fluent oral reading.

M. Use one or more of the oral reading techniques described in detail in the introductory chapter. These procedures are highly effective with a variety of oral reading difficulties.

N. Have the student trace over the first letter or underline the first letter of each word in the sentence, as shown in Figure 16.2.

Do not ask the student to continue this practice for a long period of time. Use it only to break the habit and then stop using it.

FIGURE 16.2

Debbie went with Tom to the movies.

Debbie went with Tom to the movies.

O. Have the students read chorally.

P. Have the students follow a printed copy of what they have read as it is played on a tape recorder. As they listen, have them circle words for which substitutions were made. Use this student-corrected material when discussing the problem.

Q. Have the students read along with a passage that has been tape-recorded. Suggestions for additional tape-recorder activities appear in Chapter 18 under "Recommendations," item L.

R. Ask questions about the subject matter that will reflect the student's mistakes. Have him read to make corrections.

S. Some students, especially when they are under pressure during a test or in a situation somewhat different from their normal environment, will feel pressure to read rather rapidly. If you sense that a student is reading more rapidly than he should or normally does, stop him and explain that it is not necessary to read faster than usual.

CHAPTER 17

Guesses at Words

RECOGNIZED BY

The student guesses at new words instead of analyzing the word to arrive at the correct pronunciation.

DISCUSSION

Guessing at words is similar to, and often difficult to distinguish from, substituting (Chapter 16). Accordingly, the suggestions offered in the previous chapter should also be effective in correcting this problem. Guessing at words may be the result of one or several factors. The student may not possess adequate knowledge of the decoding skills of phonics, structural analysis, or context clues. Before attempting to help the student, you should determine which of the factors are responsible for her guessing at words. An effective way of determining why a student guesses at words is to ask her. You should ask whether she knows the sound of the first letter, the blend, the first syllable, and so forth. Also, you should check to see whether the student knows how to blend sounds together rapidly. Finally, ask questions to determine whether she is aware of the context in which the word is used. If you are unsure about the student's ability to use phonics, structural analysis, or context clues, follow the suggestions listed under "Recommendations" in item A. If she has some knowledge of these decoding skills but does not use them effectively when decoding, the remaining suggestions should prove useful.

RECOMMENDATIONS

A. If the student guesses at phonetically regular one-syllable words, administer the Phonics Assessment (Appendix A-6) and provide help where needed according to the results of the test. If the student guesses at words of more than one syllable, administer the Structural Analysis Assessment (Appendix A-7) and, again, give the student instruction on those aspects of structural analysis in which she is weak. Because an inability to use context clues can cause the student to guess at both one-syllable and multisyllable words, testing for the student's ability to use context clues (Appendix A-10) is also recommended. Recommendations for correcting difficulties in the areas of phonics, structural analysis, and context clues are found in the following chapters:

➡**Phonics—Chapters 5, 6, and 7**
➡**Structural analysis—Chapters 8 and 9**
➡**Context clues—Chapter 10**

B. While the student is reading orally, the teacher should call attention to the words at which she guesses. At the same time, the student should be taught how to systematically attack unknown words. The most effective way to do this is by teaching the student to use the word-attack strategy presented in Chapter 16 and described in more detail in Chapter 10 (see item A).

C. The word-attack strategy teaches students to examine the words that both precede and follow a difficult or unknown word and sound out at least the first one or two sounds of the unknown word. This strategy teaches students to use both the context of the sentence and the letter sounds (or structural parts) of the unknown word. Thus students learn to use more than just the first letter or syllable of the unknown word as the need arises. For example: "The large black dog was ch_____ on the bone." If the student continues past the unknown word and reads *on the bone* after decoding the sound of *ch*, she will in most cases correctly pronounce the unknown word *chewing*.

D. Give the student sentences in which there is one difficult word that she has guessed in her oral reading (or words that you suspect she will be unable to decode in isolation). Have her work independently, using the method described in item C, to correctly decode the difficult words.

E. As the student reads, circle or underline the words that she guesses. Replace these words with blank lines and have the student reread the material. Ask her to fill in the correct words from context.

F. Do not expect the student to read material above her meaning-vocabulary level. Generally, use easy materials and encourage the student to read widely, both orally and silently.

G. Use one or more of the oral reading techniques described in detail in the introductory chapter. These procedures are highly effective with a variety of oral reading difficulties.

H. Allow the student to preread material silently before asking her to read it orally. Encourage the student to ask you for assistance with difficult words during the silent reading phase. If the student asks for help on more than 10% of the words, then the material is too difficult and should be replaced with easier material.

I. Have the student trace over or underline the first and last letters and middle vowel or vowels of words at which she pauses, as shown in Figure 17.1.

FIGURE 17.1

It was a very **hᴜmid** day.

It was a very h̲u̲m̲i̲d̲ day.

J. Teach the student that there are a number of types of context clues. The student does not have to categorize them; however, working with several different kinds of context clues will enable her to become more adept in their use. For example:

1. Definition context clues

   The word *mongrel* sometimes refers to a *dog* of mixed breeds.

2. Synonym context clues

   The team was *gleeful* and the coach was also *jubilant* because they had won the game.

3. Contrasting words

   He was *antisocial* but she was *friendly*.

4. Common sayings or expressions

   It was *dark* as *pitch*.

K. Use commercially prepared materials designed to improve use of context clues.

CHAPTER 18

Word-by-Word Reading

RECOGNIZED BY

The student pauses after each word and does not allow the words to flow as they would in smooth or fluent oral reading.

DISCUSSION

Word-by-word reading may be caused by one or more of the following: (1) failure to apply decoding skills effectively (these include basic sight vocabulary, phonics, structural analysis, and context clues); (2) lack of adequate comprehension; or (3) poor fluency skills. Young students who are beginning to read are often word-by-word readers. However, as their sight vocabulary continues to grow and their word-analysis skills are refined, this habit should disappear.

You should determine which of the previously listed factors is causing the word-by-word reading. Make this determination as follows: Give the student something to read at a much lower reading level than his capablility. If he continues to read poorly, the problem may then be assumed to be poor fluency skills. If he immediately improves, the problem can generally be considered one of either decoding or comprehension. You must then decide between these two difficulties. Ask the student questions about the more difficult material that he was reading word-by-word. If the student can answer approximately 75% or more of the questions correctly, then his problem probably lies in the area of decoding. If he cannot answer approximately 75% of the questions correctly, he may be having trouble with comprehension. You may also take a few of the more difficult words from the reading passage and put them on flash cards to see if the student can recognize these words in isolation.

If the student is unable to decode the words, the recommendations listed under "Recommendations" in items A through G will be helpful. If the difficulty results from poor fluency skills, the recommendations under items H through Q will be more helpful. However, if the student is having difficulty with comprehension, you should follow the suggestions listed in Chapter 22, "Comprehension Inadequate." Remember that students can read fluently only when they are thoroughly familiar with the vocabulary in the material they are required to read. Therefore, if a student is having difficulty with the meaning of the words in the material being read, you should not try the types of suggestions listed in items H through Q. You would be treating the symptoms rather than the actual cause of the difficulty.

RECOMMENDATIONS

Students whose word-by-word reading is caused by inadequate decoding ability will benefit from the following measures:

A. Use reading material on a lower level of difficulty.

B. Do not expect students to read material above their meaning-vocabulary levels. Generally use easy materials and encourage students to read in great quantity.

C. Have the students dictate or write their own stories and read them aloud. Record their readings of these stories and contrast the recordings with their readings of less familiar stories. Discuss the differences and their need for smooth, fluent reading. (This is an adaptation of the language-experience approach.)

D. Use other aspects of the language-experience approach as described in the introductory chapter.

E. If word-by-word reading is caused by an insufficient sight vocabulary, you should follow the suggestions listed in Chapters 3 and 4. Usually a word does not become a sight word until it has been read many times. Some writers and researchers have estimated it takes from 20 to 70 exposures to a word before it actually becomes a sight word. A student who has not built up a sight vocabulary equivalent to his grade level must do an enormous amount of reading to become exposed to as many new words as many times as possible.

F. If the student is unable to use phonics or structural analysis sufficiently for decoding, then the recommendations in Chapters 5 through 9 will prove helpful.

G. To help students use their existing decoding skills effectively, teach the word-attack strategy as described in Chapter 10, item A. That chapter also presents a number of other recommendations for teaching students to use context clues.

Students whose incorrect phrasing is caused by poor fluency skills will benefit from the following instructional strategies:

H. If the student seems unaware of his word-by-word reading, it is often helpful to tape-record the student while he is reading orally. Then play back the recording so he can become aware of the specific problem. If necessary, take time to demonstrate both inappropriate (word-by-word) and fluent reading.

I. In item B, we suggested that you urge students to read in great quantity. This suggestion was aimed at readers whose word-by-word reading results from poor decoding skills. This recommendation is equally valuable for students whose word-by-word reading results from poor fluency skills. The recommendation bears repeating: *Provide abundant opportunities for students to practice the act of reading, both orally and silently.*

J. Use one or more of the oral reading techniques described in detail in the introductory chapter. These procedures are highly effective with a variety of oral reading difficulties.

K. Allow students to preread material silently before asking them to read it orally. You might allow students to ask you for assistance with difficult words during the silent reading phase. If they ask for help on more than 10% of the words, then the material is too difficult for them and should be replaced with easier material.

L. Using an audio tape recorder may also serve as an excellent way for students to practice oral reading. The teacher might set up a "recording studio," providing a tape recorder, microphone, and cassette tapes for the students. The following activities are effective:

1. The student reads orally into the tape recorder, plays back the tape, and
    a. listens to the recording noting errors
    b. reads along silently
    c. reads along orally
2. The teacher or another person reads a selection into the tape recorder and the student plays it back as in item 1. The teacher may make purposeful errors or exhibit poor fluency skills, such as word-by-word reading. The student evaluates the teacher's performance and tries to apply this to his own reading.
3. Two or more students read into a tape recorder together, using some of the techniques in items 1 and 2.

M. Provide experiences in choral reading. This activity may be done with as few as two students (often called *paired reading*) or with the entire class.

N. Give a series of timed silent-reading exercises. The addition of the time factor will often make the student aware of the word-by-word reading.

O. Allow students to choose stories that they feel are exciting and then let them read their selections aloud.

P. Have the children read poetry. They should reread it until it becomes easy for them.

Q. Use commercially produced materials that are designed to develop expressive, fluent oral reading.

CHAPTER 19

Incorrect Phrasing

RECOGNIZED BY

The student fails to read fluently—that is, in natural phrasing or linguistic units. She may fail to take a breath at the proper place and will often ignore punctuation, especially commas.

DISCUSSION

The cause of incorrect phrasing may be inadequate decoding ability, poor fluency skills (including a lack of knowledge about the use of certain punctuation marks), or insufficient comprehension. You should first determine the cause.

Select a passage of 100 words that is at a reading level at which the student is experiencing difficulty. Give the student a disorganized list of the 100 words that appear in that passage. If she recognizes fewer than approximately 95 of the words on the list (word recognition below 95%), you can assume that inadequate decoding ability is contributing to the problem of incorrect phrasing.

If the student does recognize at least 95 of the words on the list, then have her read the story from which the words came and answer at least six questions about that story. If the student phrases incorrectly and fails to answer at least 75% of the questions (but knows 95 or more of the words), then insufficient comprehension is probably a major contributor to the problem. Reading material is probably not too difficult for a student if she can correctly decode 95% or more of the words and can answer at least 75% of the questions about the passage. So, if the material is not too difficult in terms of decoding and comprehension, *and* a student continues to phrase incorrectly, you may assume that she has poor fluency skills.

You should be able to tell if the student fails to recognize how to use punctuation marks by carefully observing the student as she reads orally material that is somewhat difficult. Notice if the student fails to pause at commas or periods or fails to recognize how question marks, quotation marks, and other punctuation cue oral reading. Similar observation should reveal if the student lacks other fluency skills, such as the ability to read smoothly and accurately with the proper speed. Some students *can* decode words successfully and comprehend what they have read, but lack the ability to read in a fluent manner.

If inadequate decoding ability is a contributing factor in incorrect phrasing, the suggestions under "Recommendations" in items A through G should be beneficial. If poor fluency skills—including a failure to understand the meaning of certain punctuation marks—are causing the incorrect phrasing, consult items H through W. If a lack of comprehension is the cause of incorrect phrasing, consult item X and refer to the appropriate chapter. If either a lack of decoding ability or a lack of comprehension is causing the incorrect phrasing, you would be treating only the symptom and not the cause by using the recommendations listed in items H through W.

RECOMMENDATIONS

Students whose incorrect phrasing is caused by inadequate decoding ability will benefit from the following:

A. If the cause of incorrect phrasing is a lack of knowledge of basic sight vocabulary or a limited number of other words in the student's sight vocabulary, then the suggestions recommended in Chapters 3 and 4 will be helpful.

B. Have the student practice reading sight phrase cards such as those described for testing basic sight word phrases in Appendix A-5.

C. Use lists of common prepositional phrases and have the student practice reading these phrases. (See Appendix B-7.) Follow this practice, and that described in item B, with timed tests of the student's ability to read the phrases from flash cards. The teacher, another adult, or other students can administer such tests. Be sure to mix up the phrases or sentences before flashing them. Provide a penalty for missed phrases. After the test, graph and display the student's performance so that she can see her improvement. It is important to emphasize to all students who participate in the timed tests that they are competing only against themselves, not against each other.

D. Have the student read the basic sight word sentences presented in Appendix B-2 with appropriate phrasing.

E. Use one or more of the tape recorder activities described in Chapter 18 under "Recommendations," item L.

F. If the cause of incorrect phrasing is weakness in other decoding skills (phonics, structural analysis, or context clues), then the suggestions recommended in Chapters 5 through 10 will be helpful.

G. Use low-level material that presents no decoding problems, allowing the student to concentrate on phrasing without experiencing difficulty in word attack.

Students whose incorrect phrasing is caused by a failure to understand the meaning of certain punctuation marks will benefit from the strategies that follow:

H. Review the meanings of various punctuation marks and discuss how these help the students to phrase properly. It often helps to draw an analogy between traffic signs and punctuation marks; that is, commas are likened to yield signs and periods are likened to stop signs. Another option is to use guides: three counts for periods, two for commas.

I. Prepare a paragraph with no punctuation marks. Have the student try to read it. Then you and the student together punctuate and read the selection.

J. Use short written paragraphs to demonstrate how punctuation affects the pitch and stress of your voice. Have the student repeat and then reread the paragraphs.

K. Use an overhead projector to display paragraphs without punctuation. Together with the student, fill in appropriate marks and read.

L. Dictate simple paragraphs. Have the student provide the punctuation, in part by listening to your vocal inflections.

M. Use the language-experience approach (see the introductory chapter) and leave out all punctuation marks from the student's dictated story. Then have the student fill them in.

N. Provide cards with words or phrases and cards with punctuation marks. Have the student arrange them properly.

Students whose incorrect phrasing is caused by other poor fluency skills will benefit from the following interventions:

O. Provide direct instruction and guided and independent practice using the strategy outlined below.

   1. Mark the phrases in a passage, using a single vertical slash. Make copies of the passage for each student.
   2. Discuss the purpose of the marks, explaining to students that sentences may be phrased in more than one way.
   3. Read the passage aloud to students, modeling appropriate phrasing. Be sure to have students look at the text as they follow along.
   4. Invite students to participate in a choral reading of the passage. Have them read the selection several times, making sure they attend to the phrasing.
   5. When students demonstrate fluency in phrasing, have them read the passage out loud in pairs. Then have them read to each other in pairs, allowing each person to take a turn.
   6. After students have mastered the selection, provide a copy of the passage without the slash marks and repeat some of the above procedures.
   7. If the lesson is successful, students will likely request that you provide them with another passage. You may wish to have students prepare the next selection.

P. Demonstrate proper phrasing by reading to the class.

Q. Reproduce certain reading passages divided into phrases as in the following sentence.

Fred and Mary   were on their way   to the movies.

In doing this, you may find that there is more carryover if a space is left between the phrases rather than using a dash (—) or a slash (/) to separate the phrases.

R. An alternative to the previous suggestion is to write the sentences using crayons or markers. Make each phrase a different color. After they read sentences in color, have students read them in black-and-white print. In the following example, the different styles of type represent different colors.

Fred and Mary   were on their way   to the movies.

S. Have students read and dramatize conversations.

T. Provide choral reading with several readers who phrase properly.

U. Photocopy songs. Have students read the lyrics without the music.

V. Have students read orally phrases that extend only to the end of the line. After practicing with these phrases, have students read phrases that carry over onto the next line. (However, leave more than the normal amounts of space between each phrase.) Gradually go from this style to normal writing.

W. Use one or more of the oral reading techniques described in detail in the introductory chapter. These procedures are highly effective with a variety of oral reading difficulties.

Students whose incorrect phrasing is caused by insufficient comprehension will benefit from the following:

X. The recommendations in Chapter 21, "Word Meaning/Vocabulary Knowledge Inadequate," or Chapter 22, "Comprehension Inadequate," will be helpful if incorrect phrasing is caused by a lack of comprehension.

GAMES AND EXERCISES

Bouncing for Words

Purpose: To provide practice in basic sight words, other sight words, or sight phrases

Materials: Group-size (6″ × 3″) cards for the basic sight words, sight words in general, or sight phrases to be learned
A chair for each child
A basketball or volleyball

Procedure:

Each student is given one phrase card. She stands behind a chair and places her card face up on the seat of the chair. The leader, one of the students in the group, bounces the ball to the first player. As the student catches the ball, she says the phrase. If the student says it correctly, she then picks up the card. If the student misses the phrase, the card remains on the chair. Play continues until all students have had a turn at their phrases. At the end of the game, players exchange cards and play continues. Any student who could not say the phrase when she caught the ball is told the phrase and keeps the phrase card until all the cards are exchanged at the end of the next game.

Variations:

Use sight word cards or even sight word sentence cards instead of phrase cards, or use two teams. Instead of beginning with students in a circle, have opposite teams face each other with 8 or 10 feet between each team. The leader then rotates the bounces between teams. The team with the least number of cards on its chairs after a certain number of sets or games is the winner.

Search

Purpose: To provide practice in the basic sight words or in phrasing

Materials: Three or more identical packs of sight word cards or three or more identical packs of sight phrase cards

Procedure:

Three or more students sit around a table, each with a pack of phrase or word cards that are identical to those of the rest of the players. One student looks at her pack and calls a phrase. The remaining players then see who can find the same phrase. The player who finds the phrase first places the card face up in the middle of the table and scores a point for herself. Play continues until a certain number of points are scored by an individual.

Pony Express

Purpose: To provide practice in proper phrasing

Materials: Pocket chart
               Sight phrase cards

Procedure:

Fill a pocket chart with sight phrase cards. Each word may represent a letter in the Pony Express saddlebag. Students come one at a time to claim their letters and read them to the rest of the class. After all cards have been removed from the chart, students exchange cards (letters) and begin again by mailing their letters (placing them back in the pocket chart).

A Phrasing Scope

Purpose: To provide practice in proper phrasing

Materials: Pieces of paper about 5" wide
              A piece of cardboard a little larger than the strips of paper
              Two dowel pins about 1/2" in diameter and 7" long

Procedure:

Paste the pieces of paper into a long strip. Type a story, either original or from a book, on the strip. Type only one phrase on a line and double-space the lines. Next, fold the piece of cardboard and seal the sides, leaving the top and bottom open. Cut a window near the top of the cardboard. Slide the strip of paper through the cardboard and attach a 1/2" dowel at each end of the strip of paper. The student rolls the paper from the bottom to the top and reads the story as each phrase passes through the window's opening. (See Figure 19.1.)

FIGURE 19.1

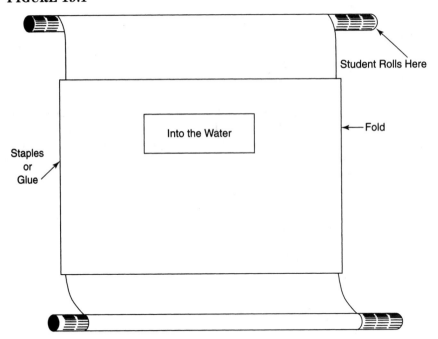

Sets

Purpose: To learn new phrases and to provide practice in reading those already known

Materials: Two decks of identical phrase cards (the number of cards used depends on the number of players; use four phrase cards for each player)

Procedure:

Deal one deck of phrase cards, so each player has four different phrases. Place all duplicate phrases from the second deck face up in several rows on the table. Begin by pointing to a phrase and saying it. The student who has the matching phrase picks it up and says it as she places it in her hand to make a matching "set." Play continues until one player has a complete set of four matches. The student must then read all of the phrases in her hand as they are placed on the desk or table. If the student cannot read them, play continues until another student has a complete matching set and *can* read them without help. The winner is the first student who obtains a complete matching set and is able to read all phrases from the set in his hand.

Drawing for Phrases

Purpose: To provide practice in reading basic sight words and phrases

Materials: Three small boxes
1″ squares of tagboard

Procedure:

In this game, it is beneficial to have a disabled reader work with a good reader. Write a number of different prepositions on 1″ squares of tagboard and place them in box 1. Use words such as *with, in, under,* and *over* that would fit with almost any noun. In box 2, place 1″ tagboard squares with the words *the* and *a.* In box 3, place a few 1″ tagboard squares with nouns on them such as *house* and *chair.* Ask students to draw one square from each box to form a phrase. After all squares have been drawn and the phrases read, the squares may then be rearranged to form more phrases. You may wish to have the students write down the phrases to see who can create the most phrases. The written list is also useful for reviewing the phrases at a later date.

CHAPTER 20

Voicing, Lip Movements, Finger Pointing, and Head Movements

RECOGNIZED BY

When reading silently, the student voices words or reads with visible lip movements; when reading orally or silently, the student points to words with his finger or moves his head while reading.

DISCUSSION

A student who continually voices words or moves his lips while reading silently is not likely to gain any speed until he can be taught that it is not necessary to pronounce each word as it is read. Many people unconsciously pronounce words to themselves even though they do not actually move their lips. Often, voicing and lip movement can be detected by watching for visible signs that are apparent when someone speaks. Other students may voice words and yet show no visible signs of doing so. One way to determine whether students are voicing words is to ask them.

Very slow silent reading is also a sign that a student may be voicing words. That in itself, however, is not enough evidence to support such a diagnosis. Remember that voicing or lip movement is often an indication that a student is reading material that is too difficult for him. By giving him material that is considerably easier and then noting whether the voicing or lip movement continues or stops, you can determine whether they are caused by habit or indicate that the student has been reading at or near his frustration level.

Finger pointing and head movements can also reduce a student's reading speed and interfere with comprehension. All of these behaviors are normal for beginning and severely remedial readers. Usually, they disappear as reading ability improves. When these habits continue in spite of the student's improving reading ability, they can usually be extinguished rather easily. Occasionally, teachers will temporarily encourage a student to finger point to remediate another problem, such as excessive omissions (see Chapter 12 under "Recommendations," item D).

RECOMMENDATIONS

Students with a habit of lip movements and/or voicing of words will benefit from the following interventions:

A. As strange as the technique may seem, a most effective way to alleviate these problems is to ask the student to hum a familiar tune as he reads. While doing this, the student can neither subconsciously nor consciously voice the words he is reading. The student may at first find it distracting and complain about a lack of comprehension. However, if he continues, the student will soon find that his reading speed is not only considerably faster in most cases, but that his comprehension has also improved. The methods that follow are also effective but will usually not work as well as this method.

B. As the student reads, have him hold his mouth shut with the teeth firmly together. Tell the student to hold his tongue against the roof of his mouth.

C. Have the student place a finger against his lips when reading silently.

D. Have the student place a small piece of paper between his lips when reading silently.

E. Discuss with the student the importance of forming mental images when reading silently. Explain that it is not necessary to say each word.

F. Temporarily reduce the amount of oral reading.

G. Have the student pace his reading with his hands. Make sure the rate he uses is faster than his normal speaking rate. This technique may not be effective with children in first, second, or third grade.

Students with a habit of finger pointing will benefit from the following strategies:

H. If you suspect a vision problem, have the student's eyes checked by an appropriate professional.

I. Have the student use a marker *temporarily*.

J. Provide practice in phrase reading.

K. Provide practice in reading from big books, charts, and the chalkboard.

L. Have the student use both hands to hold the book.

M. Use reading material with large, clear print.

Students with a habit of head movements will benefit from the following interventions:

N. Have the student place his elbows on the table and his index fingers against his temples.

O. Demonstrate how to use the eyes to scan a page while the head remains stationary.

PART FIVE

COMPREHENSION SKILLS

CHAPTER 21

Word Meaning/Vocabulary Knowledge Inadequate

RECOGNIZED BY

The student does not understand the meaning of words commonly understood by students of her age level. The student's weakness may be reflected in poor performance on tests of vocabulary knowledge. Inadequate **vocabulary** causes reduced reading comprehension.

DISCUSSION

A strong relationship exists between vocabulary knowledge and comprehension. Authorities have differing notions about what it means to know the meaning of a word. Part of the problem is that one may know the meaning of a word at five different levels or stages. These stages are listed here from lowest to highest level of vocabulary knowledge.

1. A student has no recognition of a word. Indeed, she may never have seen it before.
2. A student has heard of the word (that is, recognizes that it is a word), but has no knowledge of its meaning.
3. A student recognizes the word in context and has a vague understanding of its meaning.
4. A student knows well the meaning of the word in the context in which it appears.
5. A student knows the multiple meanings of the word (if they exist) and can actually use the word in thinking, speaking, or writing.

Knowledge at level 2 is usually required for a student to decode a difficult word, while knowledge at levels 3 or 4 is required for the student to comprehend what she reads. Thus, one of the important reasons that teachers teach vocabulary is to enable students to understand written material. Adequate decoding ability alone will not enable a student to understand material in either a narrative or content-area book.

The most common method of testing students' knowledge of words or overall vocabulary is the use of standardized achievement tests. The most widely used format is the multiple-choice measure in which the student selects, from among several choices, a short definition or a synonym for a target word. Such tests usually measure vocabulary knowledge at level 3, rather than the student's full continuum of word knowledge. If you use such a test, examine the students' raw scores to see if they are above a level that could have been made by chance guessing. A number of standardized reading achievement tests will allow a student who may essentially not read at all to score well into the norms and to have a vocabulary achievement score well above her actual vocabulary ability. Some students do poorly on standardized tests of vocabulary knowledge because they lack sufficient decoding ability. If a student does much better on an individually administered oral vocabulary test, you may then assume that a lack of adequate word-attack skills is contributing to her low score on the standardized test.

Another method of testing students' knowledge of vocabulary is to ask them the meaning of several words that appear in their textbooks (at their grade level). This will give you a general "feel" for their vocabulary knowledge; however, it will not allow you to compare the vocabulary achievement of your students with those in the country as a whole. If you are a teacher in a school with a large group of students from a low socioeconomic level, this method of testing vocabulary knowledge may give you "tunnel vision," because students with only a normal vocabulary may appear very good in comparison to other students in the class.

RECOMMENDATIONS

Because the meanings of many words can be learned through context and repeated exposure, it is not necessary to teach every new word. Only a very small percentage of the total **meaning vocabulary** of adults is achieved through specific vocabulary instruction or through the use of the dictionary. Unfortunately, research has shown that students in **remedial reading programs** usually get little practice in the act of reading. For students with a limited English vocabulary, much practice in oral language is essential. For students who come from an English-speaking background, the single best way of increasing their vocabulary is to encourage them to read widely about a number of subjects. The importance of this cannot be overemphasized.

Direct instruction is also very important. The most effective instructional activities tap into students' prior knowledge and involve students actively in learning new vocabulary. Often it is best for students to practice these strategies while working in small cooperative groups, so that they can learn from each other as well as from the teacher.

A thorough examination of the meaning of only a few words is more worthwhile than having students look up many words in the dictionary, write the definitions of the words, and then use them in sentences. Eldon E. Ekwall and an elementary principal once checked students' knowledge of 20 words that they had just completed writing the meaning of and using in a sentence during a one-hour period. The average number of words known by each student was 2 out of the 20, or 10% of the words. And this was immediately after completing the lesson! This indicates that a little more time spent in discussing several words and making sure that they are well known by each student would be more productive than attempting to introduce many words in a less thorough manner. In addition, the "look it up, write the definition, use it in a sentence" approach tends to be boring for most students.

You will find that the following recommendations are motivating and effective for most students, all the more so when the teacher participates in or directs the activities.

A. Students of all grades can benefit from the use of **semantic feature analysis.** (The word **semantic** means "of or based on the various meanings of words.") To use this technique, pick a theme somewhat familiar to a number of students, such as speech communication. First, discuss various ways in which we communicate through speech and list them—for example, *seminar, congress, forum, debate, dialogue, conversation, symposium, lecture, homily, testimony, caucus, interview, sermon,* and *hearing* (used as a noun). If students are at an age where they are familiar with the use of a thesaurus, they can quickly find synonyms for words first mentioned.

After the list has been completed, discuss characteristics of several of the items on it. Commenting on the list in the preceding paragraph, students may note such characteristics as one-way, two-way, no control over who speaks, one person controls who speaks, anyone can speak, formal, and informal. After a logical set of characteristics has been developed, construct a matrix (on an overhead transparency or on the chalkboard), such as the one shown in Figure 21.1.

When the matrix is complete, ask students to decide whether to place a plus $(+)$ or a minus $(-)$ in each blank space of the matrix, depending on the characteristic of the item in the column. For example, for *seminar,* one would be likely to place a plus in the blanks for "Two-way," "One Person Controls Who Speaks," "Anyone Can Speak," and, perhaps, "Informal." On the other hand, a minus would be likely to appear after "One-way," "No Control Over Who Speaks," and "Formal."

Semantic feature analysis provides students with a much better understanding of terms than definitions from a dictionary. Encourage students to discuss the merits of placing a plus or a minus after various items. Also, allow them to place both a plus and a minus in certain blanks. For example, a seminar might be formal or informal, depending on who is conducting it as well as on its purpose.

After students have completed marking each item with a plus or a minus, have them ask each other questions such as, "Arturo, what is the difference between a debate and a dialogue?" This will, of course, make students more active participants, and they will be much less likely to forget the meanings of various words. The discussion following the completion of the matrix should be considered an essential part of the use of this technique for vocabulary development.

FIGURE 21.1

Semantic Feature Analysis for Speech Communication

	One-Way	Two-Way	No Control Over Who Speaks	One Person Controls Who Speaks	Anyone Can Speak	Formal	Informal
Seminar	-----	-----	-----	-----	-----	-----	-----
Congress	-----	-----	-----	-----	-----	-----	-----
Forum	-----	-----	-----	-----	-----	-----	-----
Debate	-----	-----	-----	-----	-----	-----	-----
Dialogue	-----	-----	-----	-----	-----	-----	-----
Conversation	-----	-----	-----	-----	-----	-----	-----
Symposium	-----	-----	-----	-----	-----	-----	-----
Lecture	-----	-----	-----	-----	-----	-----	-----
Homily	-----	-----	-----	-----	-----	-----	-----
Testimony	-----	-----	-----	-----	-----	-----	-----
Caucus	-----	-----	-----	-----	-----	-----	-----
Interview	-----	-----	-----	-----	-----	-----	-----
Sermon	-----	-----	-----	-----	-----	-----	-----
Hearing	-----	-----	-----	-----	-----	-----	-----

B. **Semantic mapping** also can be fun and challenging to students. Using semantic word maps together with a dictionary and a thesaurus will enable students to learn words that are not in the listening-speaking vocabularies of the students involved in making the map. In using this technique, first pick a word familiar to students, such as *house*. Then ask students simply to list a number of things that come to mind when hearing this word. Examples might include *stone, wood, ice, concrete, electricity, dishwasher, carpenter, mason, skins*, and *concrete*.

After a fairly comprehensive list has been developed, ask students if they see logical categories into which they could fit each of the items. For example, logical categories for this list might be as follows: *equipment* (electricity, dishwasher, garbage disposal), *building materials* (stone, wood, ice, concrete, skins), and *workers* (painter, carpenter, mason).

Show the development of the semantic map as shown in Figure 21.2.

FIGURE 21.2

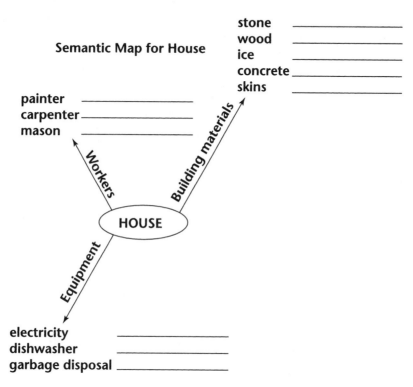

In mapping a word as common as *house*, there would, of course, be more categories than those shown in the example. After the map has been developed, draw lines beside each word in the various categories, as shown. Then have students use a thesaurus to find a word or, preferably, more than one word, that could possibly be a synonym for each listed word. Also, depending on the ages of the students involved, you may wish to use words that are synonyms of the roots of words used in each category. Place these words in the blanks. Examples of words that might be used in Figure 21.2 would be *painter* (tint, dye, pigment, stain); *carpenter* (cabinetmaker, builder, producer); *mason* (bricklayer, plasterer, cement worker); *electricity* (current, juice, power); *dishwasher* (cleaner, cleanse, filter, purify); *garbage disposal* (dirt, filth, muck, slime); *stone* (boulder, gravel, pebble, rock); *wood* (forest, lumber); *ice* (freeze, chill, refrigerate); and *concrete* (cement).

C. The *four-square strategy* (Eeds & Cockrun, 1985) will help students use prior knowledge to increase vocabulary. First, select four important words from an assignment students are about to read and have students fold four papers into quarters. Have students write the first word in square 1, for example, *salubrious.*

Use the word in appropriate context so that the students will have some clues to its meaning; for example, *Joggers lead a salubrious lifestyle by engaging in regular exercise.* Ask, "Is there anything you do that you believe is salubrious?" Label these student examples as salubrious.

Have students write in the second square something they personally find to be salubrious. In the third square, have students write a non-example—something that is not salubrious, for example, smoking. Finally, in the fourth square, have students write a definition of the word in their own words. See the completed example in Figure 21.3.

FIGURE 21.3

salubrious 1	2 **surfing**
4 **any aspect of life that is healthful**	3 **smog**

D. The *context redefinition* strategy (Bean, 1981; Cunningham, Cunningham, & Arthur, 1981) encourages students to predict word meanings, then use oncoming context to confirm their predictions. This strategy is used unconsciously by all good readers and consists of the following five steps:

1. *Select* about four key words from a story or text chapter. (Try to pick at least one that students may know.)
2. *List* these on the chalkboard or overhead projector with a blank space for students' predictions.
3. Have students *predict* what they think each word means, write their predictions verbatim, then vote on the most plausible prediction.

4. Have students read to *verify* their predictions.

5. After reading, have students edit or *redefine* their initial predictions to reflect contextual meaning. (Students can copy these definitions in their own glossaries.)

An example of context redefinition follows.

Write a definition or synonym for the two words that follow:

1. eggrails
2. mushburgers

Now read the following selection (Cunningham, et al, 1981) to see if you need to modify your initial hypotheses.

She preferred a surfboard with *eggrails* for slow, sloppy waves. A board with rounded edges was ideally suited to this afternoon's conditions. The wind was blowing straight onshore, creating bumpy *mushburgers*.

E. Whenever new words come up in lessons, stop and discuss them in sufficient detail so that all students develop a concept of their meaning.

F. When reading stories or books aloud to students, stop occasionally to discuss the meanings of new or unfamiliar words. With practice, teachers can learn to do this without spoiling the flow of the story. For example, when reading books to younger children, vocabulary can be discussed while you are showing the students the illustrations in the book.

G. Appoint a vocabulary committee to preview each new lesson and to identify all words for which they do not know the meaning. Use these words as a guide to the new vocabulary in addition to the vocabulary given in the textbook. You might also have members of this committee find out the meanings of these words and introduce them to the rest of the class. Of course, it is a good idea to rotate membership on this committee.

H. Develop picture files for each unit in the students' textbook. Use the pictures to show the meaning of new words and concepts. These pictures may be placed on a bulletin board or shown and discussed as you introduce each new unit.

I. Place pictures on the bulletin board and have students try to find as many words as possible to describe the pictures. If students are old enough to use a thesaurus, allow them to do so. Place the words under the pictures and discuss them regularly.

J. Brainstorm other words for common words such as *said*. With the assistance of students, prepare charts with lists of synonyms for the overused words. These charts may be hung in the classroom where they can be easily seen by students. Then, when students write creative stories, encourage them to use alternatives to the overused words. Similarly, model the use of these words when speaking to students and encourage students to use them in their conversations.

K. Encourage students to raise their hands whenever someone uses an unfamiliar word. Praise students for asking what a word means and indicate that such students usually have large vocabularies.

L. Develop word awareness by showing students how they often skip words for which they do not know the meaning. Promote awareness of new words by getting students to look for new words for which they or other students may not know the meaning. Write the new word on the chalkboard along with the name of the student who found it.

Vinay's new word—*idealism*
Darcetta's new word—*afterthought*

Discuss these words daily until most students know them. Keep adding new words to the bottom of the list and erase the ones from the top after they have been discussed several times.

M. Encourage students to use vocabulary cards. As students read assignments or any other reading material, have them search for new words. When a new word is found, the student writes it on a vocabulary card. Then she copies the sentence in which it was used and underlines the word. (Encourage the use of context to derive meaning.) After the student completes her reading, she locates the new word in the dictionary and writes its meaning on the card. File the new vocabulary cards in a shoebox and review them periodically.

N. Help students become aware of new words by having contests: Who can find the most words that other students do not understand? Limit the contest to a particular book and one day.

O. Discuss the use of figurative language and have students look for idiomatic expressions such as "Our teacher was a bear today," "She was as quiet as a mouse," or "He lost his cool."

P. Provide a wide background of experiences for students. This can be done, to a certain extent, by taking students on field trips; showing videotapes, films, and filmstrips; and discussing a wide range of topics in the classroom. After returning from field trips, using audiovisual or computer-based materials, or engaging in class discussion, identify and discuss any new words and concepts. Also, encourage students to write down any unfamiliar words as they listen to the narration of a videotape, film, CD-ROM, or computer-based program. After viewing, list students' words on the chalkboard or overhead projector and discuss them. In presenting each word, discuss its meaning with the class and use it in a sentence. Then have several members of the class use the word in sentences they make up. Follow this procedure with all unknown words. Finally, have students write a summary of the field trip, videotape, film, CD-ROM, computer-based program, or class discussion, and use all of the new words that were presented.

Q. Encourage students to use the dictionary to derive a word's meaning. Although only a small percentage of one's total meaning vocabulary comes from the use of the dictionary, all students should learn how to use the dictionary to derive word meaning, as well as to develop the accompanying skills such as understanding a word's first, second, and third meaning.

R. Encourage students to use books marketed for the purpose of building vocabularies. These are constantly being updated, and new ones appear on the market each year. To find them, look under the subject of vocabulary development at a local bookstore. These materials present many words, and most teachers can learn much about the teaching of vocabulary by using them.

S. Teach students to use affixes as clues to word meanings. Although research indicates that the study of prefixes and suffixes is somewhat questionable, a knowledge of affixes is highly useful in understanding words in subject areas such as science, where a student might encounter such prefixes as *bio-*, *sub-*, and the like.

T. Teach students how to use a thesaurus and constantly encourage them to use it in their writing.

U. Use commercial materials, including software programs, that have been designed for vocabulary development.

GAMES AND EXERCISES

Matching Words and Definitions

Purpose: To enrich vocabulary

Materials: Envelopes that contain slips of paper with numbered words printed on them. The envelopes should also contain a larger second set of slips with a definition of each word, numbered on the back to match the first set.

Procedure:

Have students take an envelope and empty it on a desk. They should then place the word slips in a column in numerical order; for example:

1. candid
2. slipshod

Have students try to match the definition slips with the words. Students can check the accuracy of their work when they have finished by checking to see if the numbers match. Number each envelope and give students a number sheet corresponding to each envelope. Have them check off each number as they complete the words in each envelope. Thus, each student will be sure to do each envelope.

Homonym Concentration

Purpose: To enlarge vocabulary

Materials: A set of word cards (about 8–10) with a corresponding set of homonym cards (total of 16–20)

Procedure:

Play the game the same as Concentration. Shuffle the cards and place them face down in rows on a table or on a Concentration board with squares on it. Two students play.

One begins by turning over a card. Then she tries to find its homonym by turning over another card. If the words are not homonyms, she turns both cards face down, and the next student takes her turn. Whenever a student turns over a pair of homonyms, she gets to keep the cards. The student with the most cards at the end of the game is the winner. (This same exercise may be done with antonyms and synonyms.)

Phrase It Another Way

Purpose: To enrich vocabulary

Materials: Phrase cards or phrases written on the chalkboard

Procedure:

On the chalkboard each day, place a new phrase that the students or you commonly use in daily conversation and activities. Opposite the phrase, write another way of saying the commonly used phrase. Each day you and the students concentrate on using the phrase in a new way. You may wish to place the phrases on chart paper and display them as the number grows.

Old phrase	Phrasing it another way
is done	is completed
runs fast	is a rapid runner
couldn't get it	was deprived of it

Variation:

Decide on a new word that can be substituted for one that is commonly used each day (see the example that follows). Place the old and new word in a chart holder. During the day, both you and the students should use the new word instead of the old word. Discuss how this activity will enlarge vocabularies and make students' speech more mature.

Old word	New word
talk	discuss
hate	dislike
do better	improve

Drawing New Words

Purpose: To build vocabulary and improve dictionary skills

Materials: A number of 3" × 5" cards with new vocabulary words written in a sentence (underline the new word)
           Dictionary

Procedure:

The cards are shuffled and placed face down on the table. Students then take turns picking up a card, reading the sentence, and defining the underlined word. Another student looks up the word in the dictionary to see if the definition is correct.

REFERENCES

Bean, T. W. (1981). Comprehension strategies: What makes them tick? In E. K. Dishner, T. W. Bean, & J. E. Readence (Eds.), *Reading in the content areas: Improving classroom instruction* (pp. 188–191). Dubuque, IA: Kendall-Hunt.

Cunningham, J. W., Cunningham, P. M., & Arthur, V. (1981). *Middle and secondary school reading.* New York: Longman.

Eeds, M., & Cockrun, W. A. (1985). Teaching word meanings by expanding schemata vs. dictionary work vs. reading in context. *Journal of Reading, 28,* 492–497.

CHAPTER 22

Comprehension Inadequate

RECOGNIZED BY

The student cannot answer questions about subject matter he has read or cannot retell what he has read.

DISCUSSION

Definitions

The term *reading comprehension* has several different definitions. While most experts agree that reading comprehension is the meaning gained from what is written on the page, they often disagree about the source of the meaning. Currently the three most common models are the **bottom-up, top-down,** and **interactive** models. The bottom-up model emphasizes the material being read and is often described as text driven. Proponents of this model believe that the material being read is more important to the process of reading than the person who reads the material. The top-down model emphasizes the reader and is often described as concept driven. Proponents of this model suggest that the reader is more important to the process of reading than the material being read. This is because readers usually have some prior knowledge (or *schema*) about the topic. Using prior knowledge, the reader makes predictions about the meaning of the material. In other words, the reader's prior knowledge can be a powerful influence on his comprehension of the text.

The interactive model of reading was developed to describe the reading process as both concept and text driven, a process in which the reader relates information stored in his mind with new information in the text. Most experts subscribe to the interactive model, believing that comprehension is a process of constructing meaning by interacting with the text. Many of the suggestions presented in the "Recommendations" section stress interactive strategies as the most effective way to correct and teach comprehension.

Factors That Affect Comprehension

Several factors about the reader affect his comprehension of the reading material. Other factors that affect a student's comprehension are related to the material he reads. Some factors that affect comprehension in terms of the reader are:

1. *The knowledge the reader brings to the subject.* This means that what a student knows about a particular subject is directly related to how much he will

understand about that subject when he reads. This is, of course, a major tenet of the interactive model.

2. *The reader's interest in the subject.* A student will understand more of what he reads if he is particularly interested in the subject. This interest is often a reflection of the student's prior knowledge of the subject.

3. *The reader's purpose for reading.* A student who has a purpose for reading is more likely to understand more of what he reads than a student reading the same material who has no purpose for reading. For example, if a student wishes to learn how to operate a computer to play a particular game, he will be more likely to understand more of what is read than a student of equal ability who has no desire to operate the computer or to play a particular game on that computer.

4. *The reader's ability to decode words rapidly.* If the student must stop to puzzle over new words, he cannot be expected to comprehend well. The whole process of reading, when many of the words are not easily decoded, becomes mind-boggling. The student must give so much attention to the decoding of new words that attending to comprehension to any degree is difficult, if not impossible. Teachers often experience a similar problem when they are reading a book out loud to a group of students. The demands of oral reading, watching the students in the group, showing the pictures, and so on may cause the teacher to have little or no comprehension of the story being read.

Some factors that affect comprehension in terms of the material being read are:

1. *The number of unfamiliar words.* Unfamiliar words are usually considered to be those that are not on a particular word list according to a readability formula. This means that the more words on a higher grade level, the more difficult to comprehend the material is likely to be.

2. *The length of the sentences.* Research has consistently shown that longer and more complex sentences within a passage are more difficult for most readers to comprehend than shorter, simpler sentences.

3. *The syntax.* Syntax is the way words are put together. Some writers use syntax in ways that make material more difficult to comprehend.

Comprehension Subskills

Studies on the nature of comprehension have shown that although teachers of reading often refer to comprehension subskills, they cannot really prove that these subskills exist. Reading researchers definitely know that comprehension involves both a word or vocabulary factor and a group of skills that might be referred to as "other comprehension skills." Even though they cannot prove that these other comprehension skills exist, many teachers find them useful for teaching purposes. These skills include the ability to:

1. Develop mental images
2. Recognize main ideas

3. Recognize important details
4. Follow directions
5. Predict outcomes
6. Recognize the author's organization
7. Read critically

Specific procedures for teaching each of these skills will be presented in the order given beginning on page 165.

Assessing Comprehension Ability

Teachers can often tell if students are having difficulty comprehending by observing their written work, their ability to answer questions, and their participation in discussions about material read. If you suspect that a student has comprehension difficulties that are not related to decoding problems, you might have the student read a passage silently, then retell the contents of the passage to you. Often it is best to have such a student read both narrative and expository selections to see if he is able to comprehend both types of material. You may use a section from a library book, literature, or reading textbook for the narrative material and a section from a science or social studies book for the expository passage. If the student is unable to retell the contents of the selection with adequate comprehension, you may assume that the student will benefit from the recommendations in this chapter.

Several methods are commonly used for more systematic assessment of students' ability to comprehend. One of the most widely used methods is the standardized test. Many standardized tests in the field of reading are divided into two main sections: reading vocabulary and reading comprehension. Perhaps this is a misnomer, as an adequate reading vocabulary is essential for reading comprehension. Thus, reading vocabulary is actually one of the subskills of reading comprehension. Because vocabulary is such an important subskill of comprehension, procedures for dealing with vocabulary were presented in Chapter 21. When using standardized tests to assess reading ability, you should note whether an individual's score is higher than he could have achieved by simply guessing. Some standardized tests have no provision for enabling teachers to measure the performance of students with extremely limited reading ability; that is, by guessing, a student may be able to achieve a score that is one to three levels above that at which he is actually reading. Also remember that standardized reading tests are designed, for the most part, to measure the performance of a large group of students rather than that of an individual.

Another method of assessing reading comprehension ability is to have students read passages from their basal reader or from other material at their grade level. After reading, students should be asked questions that test their ability to remember facts, make inferences, identify main ideas, and understand vocabulary. The major drawback with this approach is that it is difficult for the teacher to construct mean-ingful questions. Some questions that may appear relatively easy are seldom under-stood when they are used with a number of different students. At the same time and for no apparent reason, some questions are almost always answered correctly. When using this method to check comprehension, consider the student to be com-prehending on a level equivalent to that at which the material is written if the stu-dent can answer at least 75% of the questions correctly.

A third approach to measuring comprehension is the use of commercially produced reading inventories. Although some studies have shown that the questions on some of these are sometimes irrelevant or could be answered without reading the pas-sages about which they were constructed, in most cases the teacher can be assured that the questions are appropriate.

Another approach that is sometimes used to determine how well a student com-prehends, as well as how his reading ability matches the level of the material he is reading, is the **cloze procedure.** A detailed description of how to use the cloze pro-cedure is presented in Appendix B-9.

Methods for Teaching Comprehension Skills

Teaching students how to comprehend what they read can be a challenging task. Certain reading methods have contributed to the problem. Comprehension is of-ten tested but seldom taught. In fact, the only instruction some students receive in comprehension skills is in the form of questions over a paragraph or story. While this questioning may help some students to develop a strategy for compre-hending on their own, it does not teach those students who most need to learn how to comprehend.

You are encouraged to have students work in pairs or groups of three to complete many of the recommendations that are presented in this chapter. For example, in the section titled "Ability to Recognize Important Details," the teacher asks stu-dents to write down all the details from a selection, then classify them as (1) im-portant; (2) helpful, but not essential; or (3) unnecessary. If the classification task is done in pairs or groups of three, the resulting discussion may well include some disagreement. However, comprehension flourishes in the presence of interaction! Therefore, such a discussion should be highly beneficial. It is recommended that you limit group size to two or three students because larger groups often result in one or more students not participating actively. The active involvement that occurs when students work with each other is often crucial to the improvement of reading comprehension.

The study of **metacognition** has added much to our understanding of what educa-tors must do to help students learn to comprehend. Cognition is the process of thinking, and metacognition is the process of understanding *how* a person thinks or the process of monitoring one's thinking. Metacognition is sometimes called "thinking about thinking." Practical methods of using metacognition to improve reading comprehension will be emphasized in the first section under "Recommendations."

RECOMMENDATIONS

Metacognitive Strategies

A. Modeling strategies for paragraph meaning[1]—a **think aloud** activity

Definition:

When **modeling strategies for paragraph meaning,** the teacher models, then directs students in the use of, a code for marking reactions to selected paragraphs. This is one of the most effective methods to teach students to monitor their thought processes when reading. The technique can be used with individuals, small groups, or an entire class. It is most effective with intermediate-age or older students, but could be modified and used with primary-grade students. The code system will vary somewhat according to the grade level of the students involved.

This strategy is an example of a think aloud activity. Think alouds are one of the most effective strategies for teaching reading comprehension. This approach usually incorporates four essential instructional steps:

1. Modeling of the strategy by the teacher
2. Students practicing the strategy in pairs while the teacher observes and assists as necessary
3. Students practicing the strategy on their own
4. Students applying the strategy when reading other materials

Steps—Preparation:

You will need to prepare the following materials:

1. Two or more passages of 200 to 400 words, depending on the age and ability of your students. (While experts suggest that you use challenging material, we have found that the technique is successful with passages that are not too difficult.) Choose interesting passages; selections from books on science, social studies, or health make good choices.
2. The first passage should be triple spaced with generous margins and prepared as an overhead transparency (for the teacher to use in modeling the strategy). Other passages should be prepared as hard copies (for students to read on their own) and as overhead transparencies.
3. You may wish to prepare accompanying photographs or illustrations in color on overhead transparencies also.
4. Also prepare an overhead transparency (or enough hard copies for each student) of the symbols you will be using to describe your own comprehension monitoring. Choose 7 or fewer symbols, such as the ones shown in Figure 22.1.

FIGURE 22.1

GVI	=	Got a Visual Image
RA	=	Read Again
🙂	=	No Sweat!
MBI	=	Must Be Important
HW	=	Hard Word
LAP	=	Look at Picture
?	=	I'm Confused!

Steps—Teaching:

The technique may be taught to the whole class as follows:

1. Present the first selection to the students on an overhead transparency or on copied pages (for them to read silently). Prior to reading, you may discuss the title briefly and ask a few questions to access prior knowledge.
2. Have the students read the passage silently.
3. Present and describe your symbols to the students.
4. Place another transparency of the same passage on the overhead projector. This transparency consists of the passage triple spaced with generous margins *and* with your strategy symbols inserted in the passage in appropriate places.
5. Model how you (the teacher) would read the selection by telling students what you did; that is, what you were thinking when you wrote your symbols on the passage. Discuss with students why you made the choices you made and talk about the passage with them, communicating your interest in and enthusiasm about the material being read. Note: There is not one "correct" way to place your symbols. Any logical approach you use will work just fine.
6. Introduce a second selection. You may show a photograph or illustration on the overhead projector to heighten interest and use other techniques to tap into students' prior knowledge about the topic.
7. Pass out the second selection and have students read it, either on their own or in pairs. (It often works well to leave it up to the students to make this choice.) Urge students to monitor their own thinking as they read and explain to them that they may use your symbols or their own symbols to mark this selection as they read it.
8. Circulate around the room while students are working, offering lots of praise and encouragement for their efforts.
9. Go over the second selection and discuss which symbols students used and why. Explain to students that different people may process the same material in different ways, and that is fine. Answer questions about the selection as they arise.

10. Present a follow-up lesson a day or two later. Have students read another selection and repeat steps 6 through 9. Also, find future opportunities to inquire about students' use of comprehension-monitoring strategies when you are working with them individually or in small groups. Similarly, find additional occasions to model your own strategies with other kinds of material.

Variation:

This strategy may also be used with narrative material.

When modeling the strategy with, say, a junior novel, you may want to emphasize imagery (focus on as many of the senses as possible, not just visual), involving oneself in the selection (How would you feel if. . . ? This reminds me of when. . . .), author's purpose (Why do you think the author chose those words? focused on the setting? and so on, and prediction (What do you think will happen next?).

Variation:

To use this procedure with actual books, use a paper cutter to cut a number of strips of paper about 1″ wide and 11″ long from sheets of 8″ × 11″ paper. Have students place the strips along one of the side margins, running top to bottom of the pages next to the material they are to read. Then have students use their codes to mark each paragraph you have assigned.

Summary:

Although the procedure may appear complicated, students catch on quickly and are highly motivated to participate in this activity. It will help all students to think about (monitor) their reading comprehension and to learn successful reading comprehension strategies. It will also enable less skilled readers to learn strategies from their peers who are more able readers.

B. *The Semantic Mapping Technique*[2]—*Definition:* A semantic map is a diagram of relationships and ideas within a reading selection.

Steps:

1. The teacher selects a key word or idea from the upcoming reading selection.
2. During class discussion, students brainstorm to come up with as many ideas as possible that are related to the key word or concept. These ideas are recorded on a chart or the board.
3. As a class, the students categorize these words and ideas.
4. The categories are recorded in a graphic form (map) that shows the relationship of the categories to the main idea (key word) at the core of the map.
5. The class reads the selection.
6. New terms and ideas are added to the map after the reading selection has been read and discussed by the class. Previous categories may be changed or eliminated as the class decides. See Figure 22.2.

Summary:

Semantic mapping has been encouraged for three primary reasons. They are:

1. Development of critical thinking
2. Increased reasoning ability
3. Improvement of memory

FIGURE 22.2

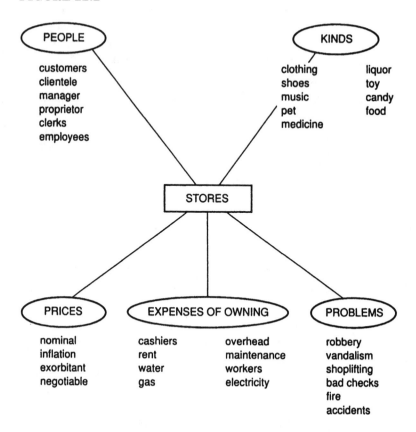

C. The K–W–L Technique

Definition: The **K–W–L technique** is a logical, three-step procedure named for the three basic cognitive steps required: What I *K*now (K), What I *W*ant to Know (W), What I *L*earned (L). This reading comprehension strategy was developed by Donna Ogle (1986).

Steps:

1. The teacher selects a key concept from the upcoming reading selection.
2. The class brainstorms and lists ideas they already know (step K) about this key concept. These ideas are recorded on a chart or board.
3. As a class, the students categorize these ideas.
4. The teacher encourages students to think of questions they wish to know from the reading selection (step W). This may begin as early as step 2. The questions are recorded.
5. The class reads the selection.
6. After reading, the class discusses and records ideas they learned (step L). This may be done in the third column of the K–W–L chart, shown in Figure 22.3.

FIGURE 22.3

K	W	L
What I Know about spiders	What I Want to know about spiders	What I Learned about spiders
1. _____	1. _____	1. _____
2. _____	2. _____	2. _____
3. _____	3. _____	3. _____
4. _____		4. _____
5. _____		5. _____

Variation:

Some teachers add a fourth or even a fifth column to the chart to indicate H: *How* the information was obtained or S: What I *Still* want to know. (See the example in Figure 22.4.)

FIGURE 22.4

K	W	L	S
What I Know about spiders	What I Want to know about spiders	What I Learned about spiders	What I Still want to know about spiders

Summary:

With the K–W–L reading strategy, students are in charge of their learning and actively pursue knowledge. As a result, students learn to use their prior knowledge, locate key concepts in the reading, and recall information.

Other strategies for improving metacognition skills include the following:

D. Research suggests that an important metacognitive skill for students to develop is that of rereading something that does not seem to make sense when read the first time. In the beginning stages, ask students to read one sentence at a time and then ask themselves, "Do I know what the author is saying?" If the answer to this is *yes*, direct students to keep on reading. On the other hand, if the answer is *no*, direct students to reread that sentence. Continue to practice this skill until students have developed the ability to monitor their thought processes while reading.

E. Young students should be counseled on the importance of getting meaning from reading. Young readers, low achievers, and disabled readers all seem to share the belief that fast, fluent, oral reading is their ultimate goal. Do not take it for granted that some students know that comprehension of the material read is the most important purpose for reading. For younger students, it will also be helpful to discuss the vocabulary of reading: what is a *sound*, a *paragraph*, or a *sentence?* Studies have shown that many students, even in first grade, do not know the difference between a letter, a word, and a sentence.

F. Stress the necessity for students to be able to recognize words for which they do not know the meaning while they read. Have students attempt to determine the meaning of unknown words from their context. If students are unable to derive the meaning of the word from context, urge them to ask for help or use the dictionary. Most people become somewhat "expert" at omitting or ignoring words for which they do not know the meaning. Simply being aware of this habit will be most helpful in breaking it. Think back to a time when you looked up a word in the dictionary. You then may have noticed that same word several times in the very near future. Chances are that you had encountered the same word many times in the past, but had simply ignored it. Once you knew the meaning of the word, you became much more aware of how often it appeared in materials that you were reading.

G. Stress the need for students to change their reading speeds depending upon the kind of materials they read. Many students read everything at the same rate. Point out that a story problem in a math book should not be read at the same rate as a newspaper story about a familiar subject. (See Chapter 24 for additional suggestions for helping students adjust their rate of reading.)

H. Teach students to predict what may lie ahead as they read. In teaching this skill, you may wish to have students read up to a certain point in a story or passage, then pause and discuss what they think the author will write next, based on what they have already read.

I. Teach students how to anticipate what questions the author or teacher might ask about a story or passage after it has been read. To do this, have students read a paragraph and then discuss what they think the author or you might ask them about the material. Practice this until students are proficient in this skill. Show students the difference between main ideas or overall comprehension of a passage and the comprehension or learning of only minor facts or details.

J. Use some type of marker for words that you think students will find difficult to understand. For example, you might put an asterisk before words that you believe will be difficult for students or an *X* before words that you believe they will not know. This will help them to be more aware of new words.

K. Demonstrate to students how stories progress from page to page to show a sequence of events; make students aware of the headings in social studies, science, and health text books. Discuss the reason authors use headings and how they may be used to improve the students' understanding of the material they read.

L. Place all of the sentences of a paragraph on the board or on an overhead projector and discuss their importance to an overall understanding of the paragraph. You may wish to have students place the sentences in order according to their importance in the paragraph, for example, putting the most important sentence first, the next most important sentence second, and so on.

M. Teach students to distinguish when text does or does not make sense to them. You may wish to provide practice in this skill by rewriting a passage and adding sentences within the text that contribute nothing to its meaning. Then have students read the material and attempt to locate those sentences that do not contribute to an overall comprehension of the material. This will help students monitor their comprehension in the future.

N. Tell students to think about the material they read, so when they complete a reading assignment, they will be able to explain the material to other students. This, too, will help students monitor their comprehension as they read.

O. Ask students to pretend they are the teacher while they read. Have them attempt to think of as many questions as they can about each paragraph.

P. Many teachers make use of "think-time" in questioning. Teachers allow students 5 seconds to think about a question both before and after they answer it to improve the quality of the answers they give. Teachers often observe that the same few students seem to want to answer any question the teacher asks, often before the asking has been completed. Teachers who are patient and allow think-time will get more responses from students who otherwise might not participate.

Q. Students' ability to monitor their comprehension as they read may be enhanced by using **story frames** such as those suggested by Gerald L. Fowler. Fowler suggests that story frames be introduced shortly after students have read a selection. Five types of story frames are presented in Figure 22.5. Note that not all five types may be appropriate for all types of stories; however, you will find that several can often be used in many stories. It is suggested that you first introduce students to one of the simpler types of story frames, such as the one labeled "1" in Figure 22.5, after students have completed reading a story. Answers to questions posed by the story frames may then be solicited from the entire class. After students become more adept at using each type of story frame, the frames may then be given to students prior to reading a story as an advance organizer to help them monitor their comprehension as they read.

You may have to modify these story frames to be appropriate to particular selections. For example, you may start with "This story begins when" and then add "and then." Following this you may add words that appropriately follow the sequence of events for the story, such as "next," "following that," and "the problem is solved when."

Procedures for Improving Overall Comprehension

A. Teach students to find material that is not too difficult for them by counting out about 100 words of the material they are about to read. Tell them that when they read these 100 words, they should not find more than one or two words they do

FIGURE 22.5

1
Story summary with one character included

Our story is about _____
_____. _____ is an
important character in our story. ____
tried to _____
The story ends when _____
_____.

2
Important idea or plot

In this story the problems starts
when _____. After that,
_____.
Next, _____
_____. Then, _____
_____. The problem is
finally solved when _____
_____. The story ends_____
_____.

3
Setting

This story takes place _____
_____. I know this because the
author uses the words "_____

_____." Other clues that
show when the story takes place are
_____
_____.

4
Character analysis

_____ is an important character
in our story. ____ is important because
_____. Once, he/she
_____. Another time,
_____. I think that
_____ is _____
(character's name)   (character trait)
because _____.

5
Character comparison

_____ and _____ are two
characters in our story. _____
                          (character's name)
is _____ while
              (trait)
_____ is _____
(other character)   (trait)
For instance, _____ tries to _____.
_____ learns a lesson when _____
_____.

From "Developing Comprehension Skills in Primary Students Through the Use of Story Frames" by
G. L. Fowler, 1982, *Reading Teacher, 36,* p. 177. Copyright © 1982 by the International Reading Association.
Reprinted by permission of G. L. Fowler and the International Reading Association.

not know. This refers to material the students would be reading without having
any type of review of the words and content before they begin reading. Research
in this area shows that students cannot be expected to comprehend well unless
they have rapid word recognition of the material; that is, they should be able to
decode at least 98% of the words without assistance.

B. Set a purpose for reading before students begin to read. Have them skim the
material and make predictions about the nature of the material and what they
may expect to get from it. These predictions may be made from captions under pictures, the actual pictures, or from any headings that may appear in the
story or article.

C. Have students combine sentences. This effective writing technique can also
improve students' overall comprehension. Use the basal reader or a literature
selection to find various sentences that can be combined. (Or create your own

sentences for this purpose.) In using this method, call students' attention to connecting words such as *and, but, therefore, however, neither, either, which, that,* and so on. With your students' help, create a permanent list of these words, which can be written on chart paper and placed where all students can readily refer to it.

In arranging this exercise, you might place a number after each sentence and then give students a sheet indicating which sentences should be combined. For example, the sheet may appear as follows:

> Paragraph 1: 1 & 2
> Paragraph 3: 1, 2, & 3

and so on. You may also wish to have them use words from certain sentences to form a new sentence (sometimes called *embedding*). In this case, you may wish to indicate which words are to be embedded using a coding system such as this:

> Paragraph 1: 1, 2 (cute), & 3 (stubborn)
> Paragraph 1: 4, 5, & 6

Example of original paragraph:

Fred had a pet coyote. It was very cute. It was also stubborn. When Fred went to school it sometimes followed him. When the coyote followed Fred, he had to take it back home. Then Fred was late for school.

Example of combined paragraph:

Fred had a pet coyote that was very cute, but also stubborn. Sometimes Fred's coyote would follow him to school and then he would have to take it back home, which made Fred late for school.

D. Constantly make the point to students that reading can be a source of information to help them with hobbies and any other subjects they would like to know more about. Refer them to various source books, encyclopedias, software, and so on.

Ability to Develop Mental Images

A. Some research indicates that the principal differences between students who comprehend well and those who do not are that good comprehenders are able to develop mental images or visualize as they read, and they reread when they do not understand. Thus, teachers should help students develop mental images. You may teach students to be aware of mental images they are forming as they read by doing the following:

1. Select a passage and demonstrate how you visualize. Describe the mental images you are forming as you read the passage out loud to students. Such teacher modeling is highly effective, especially if the teacher demonstrates with enthusiasm.

2. Select another passage. Have students read a sentence or two and then ask if they were able to actually see the scene or the action described in what they read.

3. If students cannot do this, then read the same sentences and tell them what you saw in your "mind's eye" as you read. Ask students to read the same material again and attempt to get approximately the same mental image. In beginning to develop this skill, be sure to use reading passages that contain information with which students are already somewhat familiar. Keep in mind that the mental images students are able to perceive depend on their background or experience.

B. For students to visualize a certain setting or image effectively, they must have actually or vicariously experienced it. Review the setting of a story with students before they begin. You might also supplement their information with a film or videotape or have students bring pictures from books and magazines.

C. As students read a selection, you might stop them from time to time and ask them to describe images gained from the reading. Also, students might be asked questions that combine the images from the passage and their own images. Two examples of such questions are, "What color coat do you think the person is wearing?" and, "How big was the tiger?"

D. Discuss figures of speech such as *big as a bear*, *black as pitch*, or *as cold as a polar bear in the Yukon*. Help students to see that figurative language can either add meaning to a story or, in some cases, be misleading. Ask students to listen for and collect various figures of speech. For younger students, the *Amelia Bedelia* books provide excellent examples of figurative language.

E. Have students draw pictures of certain settings about which they have read. Compare and discuss.

Ability to Recognize Main Ideas

A. Work with students to help them find the main idea and supporting details of a story. You might list the main idea as well as the supporting details, as shown in the following paragraph:

A little bird sang his song day after day. The old man had heard it so many times that he knew the tune by heart. Even the students who played nearby could sing it.

Main idea: A little bird sang his song day after day.
Supporting details: The old man had heard it many times.
                      The old man knew it by heart.
                      Even the students who played nearby could sing it.

B. Another way of bringing out the main idea of a paragraph and showing the supporting details is to draw the paragraph as a diagram, as illustrated in Figure 22.6.

When drawing paragraph diagrams with students, do not expect to find complete agreement on how they should look. Keep in mind that the important thing is to encourage students to think about paragraph structure.

FIGURE 22.6

Some paragraphs have one main idea.

> A little bird sang his song day after day.
>
> > The old man had heard it many times.
> >
> > The old man knew it by heart.
> >
> > Even the students who played nearby could sing it.

Other paragraphs may have two main ideas.

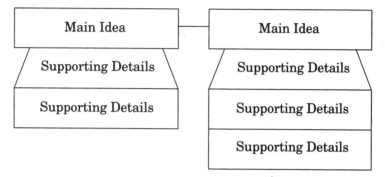

Other types of paragraphs may look like the following.

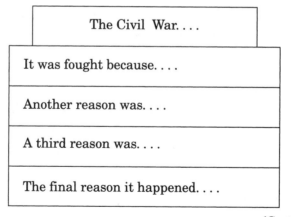

(Continued)

FIGURE 22.6 (Continued)

"X" brand of soap cleans well. . . .

"X" brand leaves no ring in the bathtub. . . .

"X" brand acts as a deodorant. . . .

therefore

You should always buy it.

Many people eat too much. . . .

Many people drink too much. . . .

Many people watch TV too much. . . .

But on the other hand there are people who. . . .

Even some of these do not. . . .

Some do not even. . . .

Sometimes there are those who. . . .

I will run for public office again if. . . .

Senator Brown must. . . .

Governor Turner should. . . .

My health. . . .

If I run I am sure. . . .

(Continued)

FIGURE 22.6 (Continued)

| The first reader introduces. . . . |
| The second reader introduces. . . . |
| The third reader discusses. . . . |

All of the readers in the series are deeply concerned with. . . .

| Once upon a time. . . . |
| Therefore children, you should. . . . |

C. Read the introduction or title to a story or a chapter and then encourage students to predict what the author is going to say.

D. Select appropriate titles for paragraphs, chapters, or short selections. You might also have students select the best title from several listed.

E. After students read a paragraph, have them restate in their own words what the author has said.

F. Many writers use subheadings to help students organize text. Turn these subheadings into questions and then have students read specifically to answer those questions.

G. Have students underline the sentences in paragraphs that best represent the main idea. (Make sure there is a sentence that best represents the main idea, and that the paragraph has a main idea.)

H. Find stories in the newspaper with charts or photos and remove the original captions from each. Give these to students and have them read each story and then write their own captions. Compare students' captions with those of the original stories. Discuss reasons for differences and whether the captions written by students are appropriate.

I. Have each student write a paragraph and place an identifying number at the top of the paper. Then pass the paragraph to another student who reads it and writes the main idea or a caption for it on the back of the paper. Then read the various paragraphs and discuss the appropriateness of each caption or main-idea sentence.

J. Have students write paragraphs, with one sentence being the main idea of the paragraph. Pass these paragraphs around and have other students try to identify the sentence that the writer of the paragraph thought best represented the main idea.

Ability to Recognize Important Details

A. Discuss with students the important details in several paragraphs. Students often focus on minor ideas and details that are not really important. Perhaps the kind of testing often used encourages this type of reading.

B. Help students to find the main idea; then have them find significant details that describe or elaborate on the idea.

C. Have students write down all the details from a selection. Have them classify the details from their list as (1) important; (2) helpful, but not essential; or (3) unnecessary.

D. Have students answer questions or complete sentences that require a knowledge of important details.

E. Have students draw a series of pictures to illustrate details; for example, in the description of a scene.

F. Write three or four paragraphs about a picture; then have students read each of the paragraphs to see which one best describes the picture. The picture may be placed at the top of an 8½" × 11" piece of paper, with each of the paragraphs arranged below it. Encourage students to select a picture and write the paragraphs, which you will duplicate, for other students to complete.

G. Have students read stories in newspapers and magazine articles and then have them attempt to answer the following questions: Who? What? When? Where? Why?

Ability to Follow Directions

A. Make students aware of key words that indicate a series of directions, such as *first, second, then,* and *finally.* Discuss the fact that, in this case, there are actually four steps, although the writer used only the terms *first* and *second.* As students read directions, have them reinforce this knowledge by having them make lists of words that were used to indicate steps.

B. Write directions for paper folding or other activities that students can do at their seats. Have students read and perform these directions step by step.

C. Write directions for recess activities on the chalkboard. Try to get students in the habit of following these directions without oral explanation.

D. Ask students to write directions for playing a game. Have them read their directions and analyze whether they could learn to play the game from a certain student's written directions.

E. Encourage students to read written directions such as those in workbooks and certain arithmetic problems without your help.

F. Write directions for certain designs to be drawn on a certain size of paper. For example, the following directions might be given.

1. Make an X on your paper halfway between the top and bottom edges and 1″ from the left-hand side.
2. Make a Y on the same horizontal plane as the X, but 1″ from the right-hand side of the paper.
3. Make a Z directly below the Y, 1″ from the bottom edge of the paper.
4. Draw a line to connect the X and Y.
5. Draw another line to connect the Y and the Z.

After these are completed, have students examine their pictures in relation to one drawn correctly and shown on the overhead projector or on the chalkboard. Discuss reasons for some common mistakes.

Ability to Predict Outcomes

A. Show a series of pictures from a story and ask students to tell, either in writing or orally, what they think the story will be about.
B. Read to a certain point in a story and then ask students to tell or write their own versions of the ending.
C. Ask students to read the chapter titles of a book and predict what the story will be about. Read the story and compare versions.
D. Encourage students to make logical predictions and be ready to revise their preconceived ideas in light of new information.

Ability to Recognize the Author's Organization

A. Discuss the fact that all authors have some form or organization in mind when writing. Look over chapter titles and discuss other possibilities for organization. Do the same with shorter selections, including paragraphs.
B. Discuss the author's use of pictures, graphs, charts, and diagrams to clarify certain concepts.
C. Discuss the use of introductory material, headings, study questions, and summaries.
D. Explain the value of "signal" words and phrases in showing organizational patterns. Examples of signal words and phrases are: *to begin with, next, not long after, then, finally, several factors were responsible for, these led to, which further complicated it by.*
E. Write down, out of order, a sequence of events from a story students have read and ask them to number the events in the order in which they happened. Explain before they read the story what they will be expected to do.
F. Write each of the sentences from a paragraph on a small, separate piece of paper in mixed-up order. Ask the students to arrange these sentences in a logical sequence to form a paragraph that makes sense.

G. Cut up comic strips or pictures of sequential events and have students assemble them in the correct order.

Ability to Read Critically (a Higher Level Reading Skill)

A. Discuss the use of "loaded" words and have students search through editorials or transcripts of speeches of political candidates for these words. Some examples of these words are: *left-wing, reactionary, rightist, warlord, playboy,* and *extremist.*

B. Examine advertisements for cigarettes or alcohol to see how they are designed to appeal to various age groups. Note statements that are made about such products and examine whether these statements have merit.

C. Examine advertisements for various products in "men's" and "women's" magazines to see how they are designed to appeal to different audiences.

D. Find accounts of a political event as reported by two or more newspapers or magazines. Note ways in which the information differs.

E. Examine political cartoons and discuss whether they are designed to show an individual in a positive or negative way.

F. Examine various advertisements to see how they attempt to get the buyer to infer information about the product, which, in reality, may be quite meaningless. For example, a claim for X brand of aspirin may say, "Nine out of 10 doctors surveyed recommended the ingredients in X brand." What this may mean is that 9 out of 10 doctors recommend that people take aspirin at some time!

G. Analyze editorials to determine whether the writer of the editorial used biased statements or whether the writer wished the reader to make certain inferences. Also discuss why a certain writer may be biased in certain areas.

GAMES AND EXERCISES

Story Division

Purpose: To provide practice in comprehension and oral reading skills for students who lack self-confidence

Materials: A basal reader or other story selection for each student

Procedure:

Divide a story, such as the following, into parts.

1. Toddle was Pam's pet turtle.
   He liked to crawl.
   He got out of his pan of water and crawled all around the house.

2. Toddle bumped into things.
   Bang! Bang! Down they went.
   Mother did not like this.

3. She said, "Please, Pam, put Toddle back into the water, and do make him stay there."

Each student studies one part of the story and reads it orally. After a whole story is read, the students are given a comprehension check. This type of procedure gives the students confidence because they know the part they will be required to read and they can practice reading it silently before reading it orally.

A Matching Board

Purpose: To provide practice in the various components of comprehension

Materials: A piece of 1/2" plywood the same size as a sheet of paper
             Shoestrings

Procedure:

Drill 2 columns of holes 1" apart down the center of the piece of plywood, as shown in Figure 22.7. Make holes the entire length of the board, spacing them the same vertical distance as four linespaces on a typewriter. The holes should be just large enough to let the shoestrings pass through them quite easily. Attach shoestrings through the holes in the left column. Tie a knot on the back side, so they will not be pulled through. Make sure each string in the left column is long enough to thread through any hole in the right column.

Prepare various exercises such as sentence completion, missing words from the context of a sentence, word opposites, sentence opposites, and so on. Space each

FIGURE 22.7

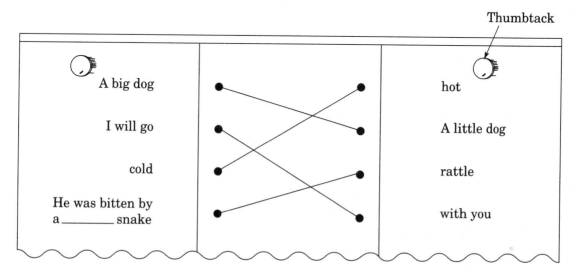

set of opposites four vertical typewriter linespaces apart, so they will correspond with the holes on the board. Use a tack or clear tape at the top and bottom of each column of questions and answers to hold the dittoed material in place. Use these boards with individual students to provide practice in areas in which they need help.

Main Ideas

Purpose: To improve students' ability to concentrate and locate the main idea in a selection

Materials: Basal readers, library books, science or social studies textbooks

Procedure:

Before giving students a reading assignment, show them a list of true-false questions concerning the material in the reading assignment. Construct the questions so that they test for the main ideas. This test will help students determine what they are expected to gather from the assignment, and it will improve their ability to recognize main ideas in future reading. Make sure students understand that the questions test for main ideas and not for details.

Directions: Some of the statements below are true and some are false. Write *T* after the true statements and *F* after those that are not true.

1. Carlos did not really want to race his car.
2. The weather was just right for racing.
3. Someone had been fooling around with Carlos's car.
4. Most of Carlos's friends felt that he could win the race if he wanted to.

Picture Puzzle

Purpose: To help students recognize, evaluate, and describe various situations

Materials: Pictures clipped from magazines or old discarded readers mounted on tagboard
Word cards
Flannel board

Procedure:

Display a picture on the flannel board. Allow students to select from a large number of word cards the ones they believe best describe the given picture. Place these word cards on the flannel board with the picture and discuss their appropriateness to the situation.

Variation:

Substitute sentence strips for the individual word cards or make sentences from the individual cards.

Riddles

Purpose: To provide practice in the comprehension of descriptive details

Materials: Tagboard

Procedure:

Write a series of short stories describing a particular object or animal. Have students read the story and decide what the object or animal is. In the bottom corner, under a flap of paper, place the correct answer. Students may check their answers after they have made their decisions. See Figure 22.8.

FIGURE 22.8

My home is in the country.
I live on a farm.
The farmer's children take care of me.
They give me grain and water.
I give them eggs.
I am a good friend of yours.
What animal am I?

Answer
is here

What Do You See?

Purpose: To develop picture-word description relationships

Materials: Pictures cut from magazines
Tagboard
Flannel board

Procedure:

Place pictures of objects on the flannel board. On tagboard, write some questions about the pictures and some questions that will act as distracters. Have students answer the questions about the pictures posted. See Figure 22.9.

Do you see a frog?
Do you see a hopping rabbit?
Do you see a fat pig?
Do you see a door?
Do you see an open window?
Do you see a red ball?

FIGURE 22.9

The Wizard

Purpose: To provide practice in reading for specific questions

Materials: A basal reader or literature selection for each student

Procedure:

One student is chosen as the Wizard. The student asks a question relating to the reading lesson and calls on a classmate to answer. If that student answers correctly, he is the Wizard, and he makes up the next question. Those students who do not answer a question correctly have another chance to be the Wizard with further play.

Classification Game

Purpose: To develop the ability to classify related words

Materials: Pocket chart
Word cards
Envelopes

Procedure:

Divide the pocket chart into four columns. In the first three columns in each row, place three related word cards. Leave the fourth column blank and have the students select a word card from their envelopes that belongs in the same class as the other three words in that row.

car	boat	airplane	_____
ball	top	doll	_____
Susan	Bill	Lassie	_____
walk	gallop	skip	_____
red	blue	green	_____

Variation:

Instead of filling in the missing word, use a series of four words in which one word does not fit the category represented by the other three words. Have students find and remove the "misfit."

As I See It

Purpose: To provide students with an opportunity to express the visual images they gain from reading or hearing a story

Materials: A story (preferably one with vividly described scenes)
Drawing paper and paints or colors

Procedure:

After students have heard or read a story, have them illustrate various scenes as they perceived them. After drawing the scenes, mix the illustrations up in a box and have one student stand in front of the room and pull out pictures. After he has chosen a picture, he will reconstruct the story on a bulletin board from the many pictures that are in the box. Discuss various differences in drawings and why some students interpreted things differently. At times, you will want to reread parts of the story to see if material was interpreted incorrectly.

Furnish the Empty Room

Purpose: To develop the ability to recognize appropriate visual images

Materials: Flannel board
Pictures of specific objects cut from old magazines or books

Procedure:

At the top of the flannel board, place printed subject headings such as "kitchen" or "playroom." Have the students select object pictures that are appropriate to the given headings. See Figure 22.10.

FIGURE 22.10

My Image

Purpose: To encourage the building of sensory images

Materials: Various materials to create sounds that are very familiar, somewhat familiar, and less familiar to students

Procedure:

Have students close their eyes and listen as you or a classmate makes a noise. Have students open their eyes and write words or phrases that describe the noise. Then have them draw pictures to represent the noise. Encourage them to use a varied vocabulary in their descriptions.

That Makes Sense

Purpose: To develop the ability to associate objects with their sources and to logically complete a given idea

Materials: Pocket chart
Word cards
Envelopes

Procedure:

A series of incomplete statements is placed on the pocket chart. Word cards containing the appropriate missing words or phrases are provided for students. From these, they will select the correct answer and place it in the pocket chart next to the incomplete idea. See Figure 22.11.

FIGURE 22.11

A dress is made from	in the ground
Fish usually	flour
Cocoa is made from	fly
Oil can come from	seeds
Cabbage grows	beans
Parrots can	on the ground
Strawberries have	swim in water
Cakes are made from	whales
Potatoes grow	wool

Ordered Phrases

Purpose: To provide practice in skimming and in determining sequence (comprehension)

Materials: Cards with phrases copied from a story, book, or basal reader

Procedure:

Have students read the passage and place the phrases on the cards in columns in the order that the phrases occurred on the page. You should also write the number order on the back of the cards. Such numbering will enable a student to correct his own work.

Sentence Puzzles

Purpose: To help students see a sequence of ideas

Materials: Envelopes
Paragraphs or short stories that are written in a logical order

Procedure:

Cut up the stories or paragraphs into sentences and paste each sentence on a small rectangular piece of paper. Place one story or paragraph in each envelope. Pass these envelopes out to students and have them assemble the stories in a logical order. Number the envelopes and have students keep a record of the stories or paragraphs (by envelope number) they have assembled. Students continue to exchange these envelopes until all have had a turn at each envelope. In some cases, you might want to have stories or paragraphs graded according to the reading level of a particular group. In such a case, reading group B will do only those envelopes marked 1-B, 2-B, and so forth.

It Does—It Doesn't

Purpose: To help students classify words according to descriptive specifications

Materials: Pocket chart
Envelopes
Word cards

Procedure:

Divide the pocket chart into two columns. Place a statement and its opposite next to each other at the top of the chart. Provide each student with an envelope of word cards containing current vocabulary words. Have students classify the words found in their envelopes according to the given statements. Use a great variety of statements and word cards that will require careful thought. Vocabulary and classification sentences will vary with grade levels. See Figure 22.12.

FIGURE 22.12

It can walk	It cannot walk

Word Cards

boy	top	boat
cup	rabbit	cow
dog	girl	pan
car	bucket	plane
coat	horse	duck

What Did It Say?

Purpose: To develop phrase recognition and the ability to follow directions

Materials: Flash cards

Procedure:

Write specific directions on individual flash cards. As the cards are flashed before the class, call on certain students to respond. Examples of directions are:

Close the door.
Give a pencil to a brown-eyed boy.
Stand up. Turn three circles. Touch the desk behind yours.
Draw a circle inside of a triangle on the chalkboard.

Story Pantomime

Purpose: To provide practice in reading for information and following directions

Materials: Cards on which are printed directions for acting out certain activities

Procedure:

The cards are passed out to all students in the class. One student is selected to act out each set. The other students watch critically for the complete acting of every detail in the directions. Example:

> Pretend you are washing dishes. Stop up the sink, open the doors under the sink, and get the soap. Put the soap in the sink, turn the faucet on, test the water, put the dishes in the water, and then wash and rinse three dishes. Put the dishes in the dish rack to dry.

A story pantomime might also include such things as:

> drawing water from a well
> making the bed
> rocking the baby
> picking flowers for a bouquet
> singing a hymn
> winding the clock
> watering the flowers
> ironing
> picking and eating apples
> playing baseball

Good Words—Bad Words

Purpose: To provide practice in **critical reading**, especially concerning the purpose the author had in mind when the material was written

Materials: Various written or tape-recorded advertisements

Procedure:

Have students locate and circle or make a list of words they can classify as either "good" words or "bad" words. Good words might include words such as *freedom*, *well-being*, *number-one rating*, and *delicious*. Bad words might include words such as *disease*, *cracks*, *peels*, and *odor*. Discuss how the use of these words influences our thinking about a certain product. Carry this exercise into the study of characters in books about whom the author wishes to convey a good or bad impression.

REFERENCES

Ogle, D. M. (1986). K–W–L: A teaching model that develops active reading of expository text. *Reading Teacher, 39*, 564–570.

ENDNOTES

1. This technique is adapted from R. J. Smith and V. L. Dauer, (1984), A comprehension-monitoring strategy for reading content-area materials, *Journal of Reading, 28,* 292–300.
2. Appreciation is extended to Cathy Langmoreland for the description of the semantic mapping and K–W–L techniques.

PART SIX

STUDY SKILLS AND OTHER ABILITIES

CHAPTER 23

Low Rate of Speed

RECOGNIZED BY

The student is unable to read as many words per minute as would be normal for a student of her age on a certain kind of reading material. Low rate of speed usually applies to silent, rather than oral, reading.

DISCUSSION

Harris and Sipay (1990) reported the median reading rates for students as determined by several different standardized reading tests. These rates are summarized in Figure 23.1.

Average reading rates increase through the grades, then level off during high school. It is important to note that these are *average* rates and some students will read considerably faster or slower than these rates at each grade level.

You can determine whether certain students are slow readers by giving a timed reading exercise to an entire class. The various reading speeds listed in words per minute can be graphed or charted to determine which students are considerably below average on a particular kind of material for their class. When giving timed exercises, choose several pages that are typical reading material in story reading. Do not use pages containing questions, lists, and the like. Timed exercises from 2 to 5 minutes should be sufficient.

Speed of reading is an important component of reading fluency. Teachers should provide activities to assist students in developing fluency skills beginning in the elementary grades. One of the most effective ways to accomplish this goal is to apply some of the oral reading activities described in the introductory chapter. You seldom need to worry about achieving a very rapid reading rate in the elementary grades. Therefore, the suggestions listed under "Recommendations" in items A, B, and C may be more appropriate for junior- or senior-high-level students. Activities to increase speed of reading should not be used with students who lack basic decoding skills or who do not comprehend adequately when reading slowly. In all cases, students should be expected to read with accuracy before attempts are made to increase their reading speed.

FIGURE 23.1

Grade Level	Median Reading Rate (Words Per Minute)
2	86
3	116
4	155
5	177
6	206
7	215
8	237
9	252
12	251

RECOMMENDATIONS

A. Focus on speed by using material that can be read quickly. Give timed reading exercises followed by comprehension questions. Let each student keep her own chart on speed and comprehension. See Appendix B-12 for sample charts.

B. Have the students pace their reading with their hands. They should attempt to move across the page slightly faster than their comfortable reading speed normally allows. It should, however, be emphasized that the hand paces the eyes and the reading speed, not the opposite.

C. For students in about fourth grade and above, assign or let them select short paperback novels that are meant to be read rapidly. Use these in conjunction with hand pacing to practice for speed. As students gain more practice reading silently, their speed of reading will gradually increase.

EXERCISE

Timed Stories

Purpose: To encourage rapid reading while still focusing on improving comprehension

Materials: A number of envelopes with short stories in them, along with sets of questions about each story

Procedure:

Before doing this, you should have given speed reading tests to your class and grouped students accordingly; for example, one group that reads 75–100 words per minute, one group that reads 100–125 words per minute, and so on. Cut out a number of short stories from old basal readers or another source. Put one of these stories, along with approximately 10 comprehension questions, in an envelope. Develop norms for each story; for example, a certain story for the 100–125 wpm group may be labeled an 8-minute story. Label the envelopes under headings such as "Dog Stories," "Family Life Stories," and "Science Stories." Allow students to choose the stories they want to read. From the labeling, students will know that they should read the story in a certain number of minutes. This technique is a change from the timed test in which each student is reading the same subject matter. It also avoids having the faster readers wait for the slower readers; when they finish a story, students can get an envelope and begin another selection. Have students keep a record of the stories they have read and their percent of comprehension on each story.

REFERENCES

Harris, A. J., & Sipay, E. R. (1990). *How to increase reading ability* (9th ed.). New York: Longman.

CHAPTER 24

Inability to Adjust Reading Rate

RECOGNIZED BY

The student reads at the same rate regardless of the type of material he is reading. This applies to silent, rather than oral, reading.

DISCUSSION

Many people are in the habit of reading all kinds of material at one speed. They read a newspaper or novel as though it were a science book or a set of directions. This is a habit that can be overcome easily if the student is shown how varying his reading rate can save time and improve comprehension. Students *should* read more slowly when the material is difficult or when seeking high comprehension. Skilled readers generally read such material at rates of 200–300 words per minute (wpm) and expect at least 80–90% comprehension. Medium to fast reading rates are used for reading of novels, newspapers, magazines, or easier textbooks. This rate may range from 250–500 wpm, with an expectation of at least 70% comprehension. When skimming, reading rates may be 800 wpm or faster. At this speed, comprehension may fall to 50%. These reading rates are shown in Figure 24.1.

To determine whether a student is reading all kinds of material at the same speed, give him a speed test on several kinds of material. The first material should be of the type found in novels or in a newspaper. Then give another speed test on material that would require more careful reading, such as the expository writing in a science book. If the student reads all of the material at approximately the same rate, he is having problems adjusting his reading rate to the difficulty of the material.

FIGURE 24.1

Reading Rates of Skilled Readers		
	Difficult Material	Easy Material	Skimming
Speed	200–300 WPM[*]	250–500 WPM	800 WPM+
Comprehension	80 – 90%	70%	50%

[*]WPM = Words Per Minute

To determine reading rate, calculate the total number of words in the passage and the length of time, in seconds, that the student takes to read that passage. Divide the number of words by the number of seconds. Multiply the resulting figure by 60. The result will be words per minute.

RECOMMENDATIONS

A. Differentiate among various types of reading material and show students how reading rates should vary according to the materials read. You may wish to construct a chart like the one shown in Figure 24.2 to facilitate understanding.

FIGURE 24.2

HOW WE READ DIFFERENT KINDS OF MATERIALS

Skim

1. Telephone book
2. Newspaper (when looking for one thing)

Medium

1. Our history assignments
2. A magazine article of high interest

Fast

1. Novels
2. Newspaper (when reading normally)

Slow

1. Procedures for experiments in science
2. Our mathematics book
3. A computer manual

B. Time an entire class on a reading passage from a novel, and then time the class on a reading passage from a mathematics or science book, preferably one that explains a process. Compare the average amount of time taken to read each passage or the number of words read in a certain amount of time. Emphasize that comprehension is necessary in both cases.

C. Check students' comprehension on easy and difficult material when each is read quickly and when each is read slowly. Determine proper reading speeds for adequate comprehension of each type of material.

D. Much of the material in science and social studies is presented with a number of boldfaced headings within the chapters. The student should study this material in the following manner:

1. Turn the first boldfaced heading into a question; for example, the heading may be "The New World." The student might then make a question of this by asking himself, "Where was the New World?"
2. The student then reads to answer that question.

3. When the student has read down to the next boldfaced heading, he should stop and try to answer the question he has just posed. If he cannot answer it, he should read the material again. If he can answer it, he should proceed to the next boldfaced heading and do the same with it.

E. Discuss when it may not be necessary to read every word, such as in a descriptive passage of scenery in a novel or details in newspaper articles. Have students underline only those parts that would be necessary for adequate comprehension. Then have students exchange articles or pages of a novel and read only the parts that other students have underlined. Discuss information derived by various students from reading only the underlined material. Ask the students who underlined the material to comment on the adequacy of the second reader's comprehension.

F. If the reader's rate is much too slow, then discuss when it is desirable to skim. If the reader cannot do this, then see the suggestions in Chapter 26, "Inability to Skim or Scan."

CHAPTER 25

High Rate of Reading at the Expense of Accuracy

RECOGNIZED BY

The student reads quickly, but with poor recall. Often such a student completes reading assignments before the rest of the class, yet lacks comprehension of what she has read.

DISCUSSION

Reading at a high rate of speed is desirable at times. However, certain types of reading material should be read more carefully than others. For example, mathematics, science, and other content reading materials often require slow, careful reading. Many students are not able to adjust their reading rate downward as the reading material becomes difficult. This situation is especially true of the student who regularly reads fiction or the newspaper and then must read material in school that requires considerable concentration.

You occasionally may find a student in the lower elementary grades who reads at a rate that impairs her accuracy. The problem is more prevalent, however, with older students who have become accustomed to reading material that requires little concentration.

RECOMMENDATIONS

A. Demonstrate and then discuss the various reading speeds that are desirable for certain types of material. You may show students how you read different types of material by preparing overhead transparencies of selections that are triple spaced. Use a pointer to indicate the speed at which your eyes move over the material, and stop to explain to students why you are reading at the chosen speed and what you are thinking as you are reading. Take time to thoroughly discuss this and to answer students' questions. Do not be concerned about telling students the *best* way to read different materials. Explain to students that it is acceptable to think about other things while they are reading. What is important is that you model the process of strategic reading. Once students see that their teacher actively thinks while reading, they will begin to do the same thing.

B. Have students react to each paragraph using a code similar to that suggested in ideas for using metacognition, shown in Chapter 22 under "Metacognitive Strategies," item A.

C. Have students use techniques in which they are required to react to each bold-faced heading. (See Chapter 24 under "Recommendations," item D.)

D. Based on material found in a reading passage, ask oral and written questions that require accurate answers. Let students know ahead of time that they will be required to answer questions about the reading passage.

E. Give students worksheets that contain reading passages and related comprehension questions. Have them underline the answers to questions as they read them.

F. Give students study guide questions about material they are to read. Many books contain questions about a unit or chapter at the end of that unit or chapter. Encourage students to read these questions *before* they begin reading the material in the chapter or unit.

CHAPTER 26

Inability to Skim or Scan

RECOGNIZED BY

The student is unable to get a general understanding of reading material through rapid, superficial reading (skimming) or to find specific information or answer specific questions about material that is read quickly (scanning).

DISCUSSION

Skimming and scanning are reading strategies to accomplish specific objectives. *Skimming* requires more comprehension than scanning, but less than normal reading. It can be an effective way for students to preview reading material that they may later read more carefully. One of the causes of the inability to skim is that students have not felt a need for this skill. People who actually need to learn to skim, and who are shown how to do so, soon become adept at this skill. To determine whether a student is able to skim, select material you wish the student to read and skim it yourself. Note how long it takes you to get the gist of the material and add some additional time for the student to do this, depending on the age and reading ability of the student and the difficulty of the material. Next, tell the student that you would like him to look at a reading selection quickly, then tell you what it is about. The best way to judge a student's ability at this task is to compare his performance to that of other students who skim the same material.

To *scan* effectively, the student must know what he is looking for and how to use key words to find specific material or answers to specific questions. Scanning is usually more rapid than skimming and requires less comprehension. To assess students' scanning ability, list 5 to 10 facts, dates, sentences, or the like that appear in a lesson and then ask students to find the material within a reasonable time limit. Watch for those students who have completed only a little when the more skilled scanners have finished.

RECOMMENDATIONS

For Skimming

A. Hold a class discussion on how skimming can be beneficial. Ask students when it might be appropriate to skim. Their list might be similar to the following:
   1. Wanting an idea of what an article or book is about
   2. Previewing a chapter in a textbook prior to studying it more carefully

   3. Looking quickly at a controversial article or editorial to get an idea of the author's opinion
   4. Looking quickly through material to see if it contains the information you are looking for; for example, skimming an article about a medical condition to see if it applies to you

B. Demonstrate to students how to skim by preparing overhead transparencies of selections that are triple spaced. Use your finger or a pointer to indicate the speed at which your eyes move over the material. Stop to explain to students what you are reading or glancing at and what thinking is going on in your mind as you are skimming. Take time to thoroughly discuss this and to answer students' questions. Do not be concerned about telling students the *best* way to skim reading materials. What is important is that you model a process of skimming. Once students see that their teacher does this, they will begin to do the same thing when instructed to do so.

C. Give students copies of newspapers, magazine articles, or other short reading selections and ask them to skim the material, without additional directions, to get a general overall impression of the contents. Use a timer and stop students after the prescribed amount of time has elapsed. Then have students discuss or summarize in writing what they think the material is about.

D. Using a textbook, have students skim the title, headings, introduction, the first sentence of each paragraph, and the summary to get a general overall impression of the contents. Use a timer and stop the students after the prescribed amount of time has elapsed. Then have students discuss or summarize in writing what they think the material is about.

E. List three or four broad questions or issues on the chalkboard. Using a textbook or other reading selection, have students skim to find out if these questions will be answered or if the issues will be discussed in this reading selection.

For Scanning

F. Hold a class discussion on how scanning can be beneficial. Ask students when it might be appropriate to scan. Their list might be similar to the following:
   1. Looking for a name in a telephone book
   2. Looking for a date in a history book
   3. Looking for a certain number of factors to solve a problem
   4. Reading the newspaper and searching for a certain article
   5. Looking for a word in a dictionary

G. Demonstrate to students how to scan using the same procedure described in item B.

H. Show students how to move their hands down a page in a telephone directory to find a certain name. After they have practiced and have become proficient with their hands, they can usually do as well without using their hands.

I. Give students copies of newspapers and have them scan them to locate specific articles, such as one about the president or about a certain baseball pitcher. Another good exercise with a newspaper is to have students find a phrase on a certain page that describes something or discloses a particular fact. After students have found the phrase, ask them to paraphrase the author's meaning.

J. Give study questions on a reading assignment that can be answered by scanning the material. Keep in mind that this is not always the type of reading one wants to encourage.

K. Have students scan to find a certain word in the dictionary.

L. Have students scan to find a certain word (for example, the name of a city) or date in a history book.

M. Tell what a certain paragraph is about and then have students scan to find the topic sentence of that paragraph. (Make sure there is one!)

N. Show students that it is possible to get the meaning of some material when many words are missing. Make paragraphs in which some words unnecessary for comprehension are missing. Make sure students understand that they are not to try to supply the missing words. Another variation of this exercise is to give students paragraphs and have them underline only the words that are really necessary for comprehension. See the following example:

> The <u>superintendent</u> of <u>schools</u> in <u>Huntsville</u> spoke to a large audience. She <u>discussed reasons</u> for the <u>new building program</u>. To some extent, she <u>covered methods</u> by which <u>new revenue</u> might be made available. Everyone thought her <u>speech was excellent</u>.

After students have seen how this process works, have them create similar paragraphs for each other.

GAMES AND EXERCISES

Skim and Sort

Purpose: To provide practice in skimming

Materials: Old textbooks with stories in them that are somewhat varied
            Envelope

Procedure:

Cut three stories from a book and then cut each story into either paragraphs or fairly short passages. Make sure each paragraph or passage contains subject matter that gives a clue as to the story from which it is extracted. Mix all of the paragraphs or passages together, assign each a number, and place them in an envelope. Construct an answer key indicating which passages belong to a particular story. Write the names of the three stories on the outside of the envelope. Give the student this envelope and have him sort through them rapidly, putting each paragraph or passage in one of three piles to match the story title. When a student has finished sorting these, give him the answer key to check his work. (For example, passages 1, 3, 5, 7, 9, 13, 15, and 16 may belong in the first story; passages 2, 6, 8, 14, 17, and 18 may belong in the second story; and passages 4, 10, 11, 12, 19, and 20 may belong in the third story.)

Finish It

Purpose: To provide practice in scanning

Materials: One copy of the same book for each student

Procedure:

Give students the number of a page from which you are going to read. Begin reading somewhere on that page. After reading a few words, stop. Those who have found the place continue to read orally to the end of the sentence.

Scanning Race

Purpose: To provide practice in scanning

Materials: One copy of the same book for each student

Procedure:

Divide students into two teams. You or alternating captains ask a question and tell students in both teams the page where the answer can be found. The first student to find the answer stands by his seat and is called on to read the answer. A correct answer scores one point for the responding team. The object is to see which team can get the most points in a specified amount of time or in a specified number of questions. If a student gives a wrong answer, take away one point from his team.

Rapid Search

Purpose: To provide students with practice in both skimming and scanning

Materials: Multiple copies of an article from a magazine, newspaper, or basal reader.

Procedure:

One student finds a part of the story that represents some action. He then pantomimes this action. The rest of the students skim rapidly to try to find the appropriate part of the story, then scan to find the sentence in the story that describes the actions of the student doing the pantomiming.

CHAPTER 27

Inability to Locate Information

RECOGNIZED BY

The student is unable to locate information on the World Wide Web, in encyclopedias, the card catalog or computer files of the library, almanacs, atlases, and other sources.

The student is unable to use cross-references and parts of books such as the table of contents, index, and appendix.

DISCUSSION

It is almost a necessity for students in the intermediate grades and up to be able to use some of the sources of information listed here. However, students often lack the skills needed to locate information. Even at the high school level, many students are unfamiliar with the use of the index and table of contents in their own textbooks.

Teachers can locate the types of difficulties students are encountering by giving an informal test similar to the following:

1. Name the part of your textbook that tells the beginning page number of the chapter on atoms.
2. Where would you look in your textbook to locate the meaning of the word *negotiate?*
3. Where in your textbook would you find some reference to the subject of atomic reactors?
4. Find the name of the magazine that published the following article: "_____."
5. Explain how you would locate the following book in the library: _____.
6. How would you locate something on the subject of whales in the following set of encyclopedia: _____.
7. What city in the United States has the largest population?
8. What is the purpose of the appendix of a book?

RECOMMENDATIONS

A. Teach students how to locate information that can be accessed on the Internet. Assign reports and other activities that require its use. Have students work with partners to complete some of these assignments.

B. Teach the use of cross-references. Have students locate information about certain subjects that are covered under several headings.

C. Discuss with students the types of information found in encyclopedias. Also assign exercises in which students are required to locate certain volumes and then certain pieces of information using the letter and/or word guides provided.

D. Explain the use of the library card catalog (or computerized catalog).

E. Explain the uses of an almanac. Create exercises that require students to use a variety of almanacs. For example, ask questions such as the following: (1) What city has the largest population in the world? (2) What city covers the most square miles? To increase students' interest in this type of activity, use other general reference materials such as the *Guinness Book of World Records* in addition to an almanac.

F. Explain the use of the table of contents, index, and appendix. Do not take it for granted that older students know how to use these components of a textbook. Ask questions requiring students to use each. For example: (1) What chapter in your geography textbook explains the use of maps? (2) What page of your earth science text contains an explanation of photosynthesis? (3) Where in your math text would you find tables showing the relationships between weights and measures in the English and metric systems?

GAMES AND EXERCISES

Reference Hunt

Purpose: To provide practice in using various reference materials

Materials: Encyclopedia
             Dictionaries
             Thesauruses
             Almanac
             Card catalog
             Other reference materials (including computer-based resources)
             One prepared set of 10 questions for the first reference hunt

Procedure:

The reference hunt should be conducted after you have taught your students how to use the various reference materials. Group students into 10 teams of 3 to 4 students. Identify each team by a different number from 1 to 10. Give each team a copy of the prepared set of 10 questions for the first reference hunt. Direct teams to answer each question and state the source and page number of the answer. See Figure 27.1. The

FIGURE 27.1

REFERENCE HUNT

1. How did John W. Booth earn a living? _____
   Source _____ Page _____

2. What is the meaning of the word *vitiate?* _____
   Source _____ Page _____

3. What is the world record for the mile run? _____
   Source _____ Page _____

4. What is the first sentence of Lincoln's Emancipation
   Proclamation? _____
   Source _____ Page _____

5. Which country leads in the production of cotton? _____
   Source _____ Page _____

6. What is the average summer temperature of Juneau, Alaska? _____
   Source _____ Page _____

7. What are two other words that are synonyms for the word *lumber*
   (when used as a verb)? _____
   Source _____ Page _____

8. For how many years are United States senators elected? _____
   Source _____ Page _____

9. What is the Dewey Decimal classification of the book
   Blue Barns? _____
   Source _____ Page _____

10. What is another name for the gum tree? _____
    Source _____ Page _____

first group to answer all 10 questions correctly, with the proper page indicated from an acceptable source, is the winner. (The answers to some questions may be found in more than one source.) Reward students in the winning group by providing them with special class time so that they may prepare the next reference hunt. When the next reference hunt takes place, these students can serve as judges. (*Caution:* Look over the reference hunt questions to be sure that students' questions are not too difficult for their classmates.)

Student Travel Bureau

Purpose: To provide practice in research and map study skills

Materials: Globes
Road maps
Travel folders and brochures
Various encyclopedias

Procedure:

When students are studying a unit on maps, or at any other time you desire, arrange the room as a travel bureau. Advertise the class's service much the same as a travel bureau would. If students bring in information about future trips their family will be taking, student travel agents can:

1. Present the traveler with a well-marked road map after studying maps from several companies and corresponding with state highway departments.
2. List places they may wish to visit along the way.
3. Provide a history of landmarks along the way.
4. Provide other specific information as it is needed.

Thesaurus Puzzles

Purpose: To help students increase their vocabulary through the use of a thesaurus

Materials: Pocket chart
Word cards
Envelopes

Procedure:

Divide the pocket chart into two columns, as shown in Figure 27.2. In the left-hand column, place a list of words that have synonyms or antonyms. Each student is given an envelope of word cards containing synonyms and antonyms of the word list. Each student then selects a word, which is either the synonym or antonym of

FIGURE 27.2

play	
white	
eager	
rare	
easy	
pleasant	
healthy	
cleanse	
guess	
clear	
dwarf	

one of the given words from her envelope, and places her word card in the appropriate slot on the right-hand side of the chart. A more advanced arrangement of this
game can be made by using a thesaurus. Given a word in column 1, the students can
use the thesaurus to make their own word cards for column 2.

List Completion (for grades 4 and above)

Purpose: To provide practice in the use of the thesaurus

Materials: A thesaurus
              Word lists as shown

Procedure:

Provide lists of words for the student to complete as shown.

Directions:

Complete the lists with words that mean almost the same thing.

1. decide	1. erratic	1. charge
2.	2.	2.
3.	3.	3.
1. deck	1. cage	1. charm
2.	2.	2.
3.	3.	3.

Detective

Purpose: To provide practice in locating information and skimming

Materials: Copies of paragraphs from the basal reader, social studies book, or sci-
              ence book the students are using. (Make multiple copies of a certain
              paragraph, if you desire.)

Procedure:

Copy a certain paragraph from a book that the student has in her desk. Make sure
the paragraph gives enough information to let the reader know from what kind of
book it is taken; for example, a paragraph about clouds would be from a science
book. Use paragraphs that give a clue that can be found in the table of contents or
in the index of the book. Tables and graphs are appropriate if the book has a list of
them. Put one of each of these paragraphs, graphs, or tables in an envelope along
with a blank sheet of paper. Each student is given an envelope and the assignment
to find where the paragraph came from by using the table of contents, index, list of
tables and graphs, or appendix. When the student finds the answer (the same paragraph in her textbook), she writes the information on the blank piece of paper and
hands it back to you. Number the envelopes and have the student keep records of
which envelopes she has completed.

CHAPTER 28

Undeveloped Dictionary Skills

RECOGNIZED BY

The student is unable to locate words in a dictionary, use diacritical markings in determining the correct pronunciation of words, or find the proper meaning for a word as used in a particular context.

DISCUSSION

In addition to remediating the most common errors listed in the preceding section, the student needs to become proficient in a number of other dictionary skills in order to make the dictionary a useful tool. Following is a list of other skills students should learn:

1. The use of guide words
2. The use of accents
3. The use of syllabication
4. Interpreting phonetic respellings
5. Using cross-references
6. Determining plurals
7. Determining parts of speech
8. Determining verb tense

The dictionary can be a useful tool for independent word analysis. Some students become quite adept at using a dictionary in the second grade; however, most students learn in the third grade, and the skill must be learned no later than the fourth grade.

RECOMMENDATIONS

A. Follow the steps listed for teaching students to locate a word in the dictionary according to alphabetical order. Make sure students are adept at each skill before beginning the next one.
   1. Make sure students know the sequence of the letters in the alphabet.
   2. Have students alphabetize a sequence of letters: for example, *a, g, d, b, h,* and *m.*
   3. Have students alphabetize words that have different first letters: for example, *bat, game, calf, dog,* and *man.*

4. Have students alphabetize words that have the same beginning letters, but different second letters: for example, *pie*, *pliers*, *poker*, and *pack*.

5. Have students alphabetize words that have the same beginning and second letters, but different third letters: for example, *pig*, *pie*, *pile*, and *picnic*.

B. Explain the purpose of the guide words at the top of the pages in a dictionary. Have students write the beginning and ending guide words on pages that contain the words for which they are searching.

C. Give students two guide words printed at the top of a piece of paper. List 5–10 words beneath the guide words. Give students a short amount of time (5–7 seconds) to tell whether the words listed would be found on the same page as the two guide words. They should mark a plus (+) after each word that would come on the same page as the guide words and a minus (−) after each word that would not come on the same page. This assignment will enable students to learn to use guide words rapidly.

key	**kick**
keyway	+
kill	−
khan	+
kibe	+
kidney	−

D. Teach the use of diacritical markings. Almost all dictionaries contain a pronunciation key at the bottom of each page that serves as a guide for interpreting diacritical markings.

E. Give students lists of words that they are not likely to be able to pronounce. Have them look up their phonetic respellings and write them beside each word. Have students then take turns pronouncing each word; have other students agree or disagree with each pronunciation.

F. Give students lists of words that have their accent in two places, depending upon the part of speech in which they are used (such as *record* and *research*). Have students look the words up in their dictionaries and inductively decide where like words are usually accented as nouns and where they are usually accented as verbs. Other examples are *combat* and *contract*.

G. Have students use the dictionary to find the proper meanings for the way in which certain words are used in sentences. Use words that are clearly defined by the context of the sentences. Have them write the definitions and then use the words with the same meanings in other sentences.

GAMES AND EXERCISES

Today's Words

Purpose: To provide practice in the use of the dictionary and to increase vocabulary

Materials: A dictionary for each student

Procedure:

Each morning, place three or four new words on the chalkboard. Use words that students have not previously studied. Later in the day, ask students questions using the new words. For example, "Michael, does *pollution* affect our city?"

Synonym Race

Purpose: To provide practice in using the dictionary to find synonyms. This assignment will increase students' vocabulary and improve their comprehension in silent reading.

Materials: A basal reader or other reading material
A dictionary for each student

Procedure:

Select sentences from the current reading lesson that include words you wish students to study. Write these sentences on the board, underlining the words for which the class is to look up synonyms. The students race to see who can supply the most synonyms from their dictionaries.

The starfish does not *please* him.

1. satisfy   3. attract
2. amuse   4. gratify

Water ran in a puddle all over his *clean* house.

1. pure   3. unsoiled
2. spotless   4. immaculate

Written Directions

Purpose: To provide practice in following directions and in the use of the dictionary

Materials: A dictionary for each student
A set of cards or pieces of paper with directions written on them

Procedure:

Give each student a piece of paper on which there is a set of directions. Be sure that the directions are simple, but also include at least one new word that the student will need to find in the dictionary before he can follow the directions. As the students find the meanings of words they have looked up in the dictionary, they can then take turns pantomiming the action described by the directions. The other students try to guess what they are doing and try to guess the word or a synonym for it. If they guess a synonym for a new word, then both the word and the synonym may be written by each student. This practice will help the whole class to remember the meanings of new words. Some examples of directions for the game are:

1. Pretend you are a vagabond.
2. Pretend you are wicked.
3. Pretend you have a halo.

Categories

Purpose: To provide practice on word meaning

Materials: Manila envelopes
             Cards with words on them that the students do not know well 8½″ × 11″
                paper or tagboard

Procedure:

At the top of a number of sheets of tagboard write three categories in which words may fall (see Figure 28.1). Place each sheet of tagboard in a manila envelope along with approximately 30 words that will fit one of the categories listed. Pass the envelopes out to students and have them use their dictionaries to group the words on the small word cards under the proper categories. Number the envelopes and have the students keep a list of the envelopes that they have completed.

FIGURE 28.1

What animals do	*Things that grow*	*Things that are not alive*
fight	trees	rocks
run	cats	books
play	people	paper
jump	weeds	chalk
eat	frogs	chairs
sleep	elephants	pencils
walk	flowers	magnets

Matching Word Meanings

Purpose: To increase vocabulary through the use of the dictionary or thesaurus

Materials: A word sheet similar to the one shown in Figure 28.2
             A dictionary or thesaurus for each student

FIGURE 28.2

goodness	stoop	helpfulness	waning	amiability
kind	philanthropy	senile	cambered	knobby
bias	hooked	charitable	inelegant	arch
vulgar	elder	unsmooth	look	rough
aged	rippling	bowlike	chunky	curved
elderly	choppy	geriatrics	turn	

BENT	COARSE	BENEVOLENCE	OLD

Procedure:

Have students place words from the word list under the capitalized word that would be the best category for them. (You may wish to have students work in pairs. This affords them the opportunity to learn from each other.)

CHAPTER 29

Written Recall Limited by Spelling Skill

RECOGNIZED BY

The student is unable to spell enough words correctly when engaging in purposeful writing.

DISCUSSION

It is important to distinguish spelling from reading. Reading ability is far more important and may be enhanced through the teaching of generalizations that are not necessarily helpful in spelling. Reading proceeds from symbols to sound; the student sees the symbols and must translate them into meaningful sound. Spelling proceeds from sound to symbols; the student knows the sound of the word she wants to spell and must think of and produce the appropriate symbols that represent that word in writing. Unfortunately, many spelling series confuse these language processes and ask students to apply phonics generalizations to spelling. While many of these generalizations are helpful, some are not. The English words most frequently misspelled by nearly all students are those words that are exceptions to the rules of phonics. Therefore, it is usually most helpful to teach students to spell correctly those words that appear most frequently in writing. Although the English language consists of several hundred thousand different words, the following eight words represent 18% of all the words used in writing: *the, of, and, a, to, in, is,* and *you.* The 100 highest frequency words account for 60%, and 1,000 words make up nearly 90% of the words used in daily writing. Yet spelling programs may present students with more than 10,000 words (Sitton, 1990).

Discovering that a student makes a great number of mistakes in spelling is not difficult for the teacher. There is a reasonably high correlation between reading and spelling ability. Most good readers are good spellers and most poor readers are poor spellers. However, it is estimated that about 2% of the population are good readers but poor spellers. It appears that students who are good spellers but poor readers are rare.

A student who is not able to spell correctly as many words as would be normal for her age or grade level should be taught a mastery list of the most commonly used words. If the student must cut down on the total number of words learned, then the words sacrificed should be those of less utility. Be sure that in all subject matter you emphasize spelling. This strategy will help in motivating students to improve their spelling and will reinforce the importance of spelling correctly all the time and not just during the spelling period. Indeed, spelling should not be viewed as a subject, but rather as a skill that will enable students to be more effective writers.

Research on the effectiveness of various techniques for teaching spelling suggests that:

1. It is not helpful to group and teach words based on phonic generalizations or structural analysis.
2. It is not helpful to teach students to spell words that are introduced as new vocabulary words in reading or content area subjects.
3. It is not helpful to teach too many spelling rules.
4. It is not helpful to color-code parts of words.
5. It is not helpful for students to spell words through an oral presentation, such as a spelling bee.
6. It is helpful if the words taught are words that students already know the meaning of and that appear on high-frequency lists.
7. It is better to have students focus on learning the whole word rather than learning to spell the word by focusing on syllables or other parts.
8. It is helpful when students write the word frequently in the context of sentences or stories, rather than writing the word over and over in isolation.
9. It is best to teach only those spelling rules that apply to a great number of words and have few exceptions. It is usually most helpful to teach these rules inductively.
10. It is best to have students use many modalities (such as auditory, visual, and **kinesthetic**) when learning to spell words.

RECOMMENDATIONS

A. Use the following procedure to teach spelling words:
  1. Be sure the student is looking at you.
  2. Pronounce the word clearly, then have the student pronounce it.
  3. Use the word in a sentence and have the student use it in a sentence.
  4. Write the word on the chalkboard in manuscript or printing, not cursive. When working with a single student, write the word on a piece of paper. Have the student write the word on a card.
  5. Have the student spell the word on her card by pointing to each letter with her pencil, marker, or finger while she says it.
  6. The student can use the card for further study. These cards should be kept in a file such as an old shoe box.
B. Increase the spelling vocabulary by adding previously missed words to new lists as well as some words with which students are more familiar. Most students can learn more words than those normally assigned to them in a spelling book.

C. Teaching the following spelling rules will be helpful; however, keep in mind there will be numerous exceptions to rules in the English language. Whenever possible, teach spelling rules inductively. An example of teaching rules inductively would be to list a number of words that exemplify a particular generalization and then let students develop the rule for themselves. This will take time, but students are more likely to remember the rules. Also, it is better to show students certain exceptions to a rule when they learn it than to let them discover exceptions for themselves. At least make clear that there will be exceptions to nearly all of the rules.

    1. Write *ie* when the sound is /ee/, except after *c*, or when sounded as /a/ as in *neighbor* and *weigh.*

    2. When the prefixes *il, im, in, un, dis, mis,* and *over* are added to a word, the spelling of the original word remains the same.

    3. When the suffixes *ness* and *ly* are added to a word, the spelling of the word remains the same. Examples: *mean + ness = meanness, final + ly = finally.*

    4. When a word ends in a consonant + *y*, change the *y* to *i* before adding all suffixes except those beginning with *i*. Do not change the *y* to *i* in suffixes beginning with *i* or those that begin with a vowel + *y*.

    5. Drop the final *e* before a suffix beginning with a vowel. Examples: *care + ing = caring, write + ing = writing.* (Exceptions: *noticeable, courageous, dyeing. Dyeing* is spelled as it is to prevent confusion with *dying.*)

    6. Keep the final *e* in a suffix beginning with a consonant. Examples: *care + ful = careful, care + less = careless.* (An exception is *argue + ment = argument.*)

    7. In one-syllable words that are accented on the last syllable and that end in a single consonant + a single vowel, the final consonant should be doubled when adding a suffix beginning with a vowel. (Examples: *beginning, fanning.*)

Note: Some of the rules noted here are very difficult for even good spellers to comprehend. Keep in mind that not all students learn effectively by the use of rules.

D. Make lists of common prefixes and suffixes, as well as families of sounds. (See Appendices B-4 and B-8.)

E. Teach students how to use the dictionary in locating unfamiliar words. Practice this usage on difficult words that can be found by the sounds of the first few letters. Discuss possible spellings for certain words and sounds. Also teach the use of the diacritical markings in the dictionary.

F. Have students exchange papers and proofread each other's written work. The habit of proofreading will carry over into their own writing.

G. Have students correct their own papers after taking a spelling test. Use steps 1 through 4 under recommendation A above when students correct their spelling tests. Some students are much more adept than others at correcting their own work. You will need to make periodic checks to determine if students are having difficulty finding and correcting their own errors.

REFERENCES

Sitton, R. (1990). A turning point: Three critical connections in the spelling curriculum for the nineties. *California Reader, 23*, 11–14.

APPENDICES FOR LOCATING
READING DIFFICULTIES

Code for Marking in Oral Diagnosis

This section, as explained in the section "How to Use This Book," is designed to teach you a shorthand method of marking oral reading errors. You should find it helpful to read the following information, which should then enable you to use this code effectively.

It is recommended that you tape-record the student's oral reading. In most cases, students do not mind being recorded while reading orally. If you record the reading, you may replay it a number of times, if necessary. This will ensure that your original coding was correct or will give you a chance to make any needed changes from the original reading. Also, if you save the recording, you can compare it to a student's later reading of the same material. This is often an excellent way to document a student's progress. By listening to both the earlier and later reading of the same passages, the student, the student's parents, and you can hear noticeable growth in the student's reading ability over time.

PREPARATION FOR USING THE CODE FOR MARKING IN ORAL DIAGNOSIS

Familiarize yourself with the shorthand method of marking students' oral reading errors before attempting to use it. There are only eight items or eight notations that are to be made to indicate errors or characteristics that readers are likely to make in oral reading. Of these eight items, only the first six are actually used to determine whether the student read a selected passage at the independent, instructional, or frustration level. Each of these notations, of course, denotes a particular kind of error or characteristic of the reader. Once they have been coded and studied, you will find that they will become a blueprint for instruction.

Study each of the eight notations so you understand what is meant by such things as an omission, a reversal, a repetition, and the like. If you were to analyze the coded passage that follows using the code for marking in oral diagnosis, you would find the following types of errors made by the students who read this demonstration passage:

Tom drove his automobile to the county fair. He saw no place to park. He drove up and down between the rows of cars. Finally he decided to go home.

1. Circle all omissions.
2. Insert with a caret (^) all insertions.
3. Draw a line through words for which substitutions or mispronunciations were made and write the substitution or mispronunciation over the word. It really doesn't matter whether the words missed were substitutions, mispronunciations, or reversals. If the student reads too quickly to write in all mispronunciations, draw a line through the word and write a *P* over the word for partial mispronunciation or a *G* over the word for gross mispronunciation.
4. Use parentheses ( ) to enclose the words for which the student needed help; that is, words that you pronounced for the student if he was unable to figure it out on his own after about 5 seconds.
5. Use a wavy line to indicate repetitions.
6. Make a check (✓) over the words that were self-corrected.
7. Use an arched line to connect words for which the student disregarded punctuation. (See line connecting *fair* and *he* in Figure A-1.1.)
8. Draw two vertical lines (| |) to indicate a pause before words.

FIGURE A-1.1

Line 1:   The student inserted *new* between the words *his* and *automobile.*
Line 1:   The student omitted the word *county* between *the* and *fair.*
Line 1:   The student did not stop or pause for the period at the end of the sentence ending with the word *fair* and the next sentence beginning with the word *He.*
Line 1:   The student called the word *saw* as *was.* This could be called a substitution; however, in this case some examiners would refer to it as a reversal or inversion, since *was* is *saw* spelled backwards. For purposes of diagnosis, what you choose to call the error is inconsequential.
Line 1:   The student made no attempt or did not say the word *place* after a period of time (usually 5 seconds) and was, therefore, told or given aid with the word *place.*

Line 1:   The student read the word *park* as *pack* and then corrected it without help from the teacher. Because the student self-corrected the original mistake, this would not be scored as an error in analyzing the student's reading of the passage.

Line 2:   The student repeated the word *He* at the beginning of the sentence. Repetitions *are* counted as errors.

Line 2:   The student paused before the word *drove* for a longer period of time than the scorer believed was normal; however, the period of time was less than 5 seconds, or *drove* would have had parentheses ( ) around it to indicate that the student had been told the word. Pauses of less than 5 seconds, while marked, are not scored as errors.

Line 2:   The student repeated the phrase *up and down*. All three of the repeated words count as only one total error.

Line 2:   The student substituted the word *among* for the word *between*.

Line 2:   The student grossly mispronounced the word *Finally*. In some cases, the teacher might note the improper pronunciation since this might be helpful in analyzing the student's problem with decoding. However, when the student reads too rapidly to write in the improper pronunciation, the teacher usually writes a *G* over the word, indicating that it was grossly mispronounced. This means that the pronunciation was so far off that it did not even sound like the original word. If you have recorded the reading, you can indicate the improper pronunciation when you listen to the tape later.

Line 2:   The student partially mispronounced the word *decided*. If possible, it is best to write the incorrect mispronunciation of the word over the correct word. This will be helpful in analyzing what the student seems to be doing wrong in attacking new words. However, when the student reads too rapidly for the coder to keep up with the coding, then a *P* over the word means that it was only partially, rather than grossly, mispronounced. In this case, the student might have pronounced the word with a hard *c* or *k* sound. This could also have been quickly indicated by crossing out the *c* and putting a *k* over it.

PRACTICE IN USING THE CODE FOR MARKING IN ORAL DIAGNOSIS

In using the code for marking in oral diagnosis, you will need to duplicate something that the student will be reading orally so you have a copy that reads the same as the one read by the student. It will be helpful if the copy on which you will be coding is double- or triple-spaced, so you can more easily write in notations on various oral reading errors made by the student. You should then seat the student so you can easily hear him as he reads the passage. Many examiners find that it is best to seat the student kitty-corner to the opposite side of your handedness. In other words, if you are right-handed, you would seat the student diagonally to your left (see Figure A-1.2).

FIGURE A-1.2

It is a good idea to find a student at a lower grade level who is not a rapid reader when you first begin this procedure, as it may become very frustrating to attempt to mark the errors of a student who reads rapidly, especially if the student makes a considerable number of errors.

INTERPRETING A CODED PASSAGE

Once the student has read the passage or has read several passages that are near his high instructional or frustration level, you can begin to interpret the meaning of the various types of errors or miscues. Chapters 11 through 20 deal directly with these kinds of errors. By studying the error pattern, you will often be able to note whether the student has difficulties with the kinds of problems listed in Chapters 3 through 10.

Preparation and Use of Materials for Testing Phonemic Awareness

PREPARING FOR THE TESTS

For each of the five phonemic awareness tests, you will use the answer sheets on pages 223–231 for your instructions to the student and for marking students' responses to the items tested.

DESCRIPTION OF THE PHONEMIC AWARENESS TESTS

Generally, the Phonemic Awareness tests should be given only to students who are non-readers or who can read only a few words. These tests will help you determine whether the student can successfully complete the following phonemic awareness tasks: Rhyme Production, Initial Sound Recognition, Phoneme Blending, and Phoneme Segmentation. If the student does not succeed at Rhyme Production, an Alternate Test for Rhyme Recognition is provided.

Each of the phonemic awareness tests is easy to administer and score, and all follow a similar format. More than a dozen different phonemic awareness skills have been identified and can be tested. These tests measure only those phonemic awareness abilities that seem to be most closely related to future reading success.

SPECIFIC DIRECTIONS FOR GIVING THE PHONEMIC AWARENESS TESTS

1. Simply follow the instructions as they are provided on the answer sheet.
2. Determine the number of correct responses after each subtest is completed and write this number in the space provided.

Refer to the Phonemic Awareness Scoring Sheet on page 223 as you read the directions that follow. In each subtest, you will model the skill being tested, provide one or two practice items, and eight test items.

The Rhyme Production subtest requires the student to say a word that rhymes with two rhyming stimulus words given by the examiner. Some students will not succeed at this task, even after you have modeled the skill and assisted the student with practice items. When this happens, you should cease testing and move to the Alternate Test, Rhyme Recognition. The rhyme recognition task is a lower level rhyming task. It is easier for a student to recognize two words that rhyme than it is to produce, or say, a new rhyming word after hearing the examiner pronounce two words that rhyme.

The Initial Sound Recognition subtest requires the student to say the beginning sound of words after the examiner pronounces two words with the same beginning sound.

The Phoneme Blending subtest requires the student to pronounce a whole word after the examiner says the word slowly, separating each of the phonemes.

The Phoneme Segmentation subtest is the opposite of the Phoneme Blending subtest. In this case, the examiner pronounces the whole word and the student repeats it by segmenting it into each of its phonemes or sounds.

This test is not set up in a pretest/posttest format. While the tests may be administered at different times to assess progress, criteria for mastery are not provided. This test is designed to assess students' abilities in these areas so teachers may use this information to guide instruction.

IMPORTANT POINTS TO REMEMBER

Emergent literacy tests are generally given to young children who are not test-wise. It is important for the examiner to be especially alert and careful when giving such tests. Children may perform poorly for reasons that may not be obvious. Often children do not fully understand the directions, and their failure may be more a reflection of that rather than their inability to succeed at the task being tested. Sometimes youngsters do not understand the meaning of words such as *beginning, rhyming, sound, letter, word, top, bottom,* and others. Frequently these students will listen for cues in your voice inflection and will try to guess the answer they think will please their teacher, rather than listen carefully to the directions being given or the words in the test items.

PHONEMIC AWARENESS TESTS

Student _____ School _____

Teacher _____ Grade _____ Age _____

Examiner _____ Test Dates _____ _____

1st Test   2nd Test

DIRECTIONS/SCORING	NUMBER CORRECT	
	1st Test	2nd Test
Test 1: Rhyme Production		
Model Item. Say: **"Words that rhyme sound the same at the end. Here are some words that rhyme. Some are not real words. Listen: fit, dit, rit, sit, kit."**		
Practice Item #1. Say: **"Now I will say two words and you say one that rhymes. It doesn't have to be a real word. It can be a silly one. Listen: rake, take...."** (Student says rhyming word. If student gives incorrect response, prompt or assist as needed.)		
Practice Item #2. Say: **"Good. Let's try it again. I will say two words and you say one that rhymes. Listen: fat, rat...."** (If student is successful, go on. If not, go to alternate Test 1a.)		
Test Items. Say: **"Good. Let's do some more."** (Indicate + or − in each space next to the test words. If the student misses 3 consecutive items, stop testing.)		
see - bee _____ **much - touch** _____ **buy - shy** _____ **blue - grew** _____ **big - pig** _____ **hope - soap** _____ **head - bed** _____ **top - mop** _____	/8	/8

DIRECTIONS/SCORING	NUMBER CORRECT	
Test 1a: Rhyme Recognition [ALTERNATE TEST]	**1st Test**	**2nd Test**

Test 1a: Rhyme Recognition [ALTERNATE TEST]

Give this test **only** when the student fails Test 1.

Model Item. Say: **"Words that rhyme sound the same at the end. Here are some words that rhyme. Some are not real words. Listen: <u>cat</u>, <u>sat</u>, <u>gat</u>, <u>fat</u>, <u>rat</u>. Now I will say two words and if they rhyme, I'll put my thumb up. If they don't rhyme, I'll put my thumb down. Listen: <u>big</u> – <u>pig</u>."** (Put your thumb up after you say the words.) **"Now watch and listen while I do another one: "<u>dog</u> – <u>tree</u>."** (Thumb down.)

Practice Item #1. Say: **"Now you try it. Listen: <u>my</u> – <u>fly</u>."** (If the student gives the correct response, give the second practice item. If not, demonstrate again as described in the model item.)

Practice Item #2. Say: **"Good. Now I will say two more words, and if they rhyme, you put your thumb up. If they don't rhyme, put your thumb down. Listen: <u>take</u> – <u>house</u>."** (If the student gives the correct response, go on to the Alternate Test items below. If not, cease testing.)

Items. Say: **"Good. Let's do some more. Remember, put your thumb up if the words rhyme and put your thumb down if the words don't rhyme."** (Indicate + or − in each space next to the test words. If the student misses 3 consecutive items, stop testing.)

top - mop	_____	sat - rat	_____	
try - man	_____	blue - true	_____	
hill - take	_____	an - fog	_____	
red - my	_____	see - be	_____	/8 /8

DIRECTIONS/SCORING	NUMBER CORRECT	
	1st Test	2nd Test

Test 2: Initial Sound Recognition

Model Item. Say: **"Now we're going to listen for sounds at the beginning of words. The first sound in <u>sit</u> is s-s-s-s. The word <u>sit</u> starts with s-s-s-s. You tell me the beginning sound of <u>sit</u>**." (If the student responds correctly, say: **"Very good."** If not, repeat the instructions. Be prepared for the possibility that the student may give you a rhyming word instead of the beginning sound. If this occurs, reemphasize the beginning sound.)

Practice Item. Say: **"Now I will say two words and you tell me the beginning sound of these words. f-ish . . . f-un."** (Emphasize the beginning sound, but do not distort it too much.) If necessary, ask: **"What sound do you hear at the beginning?"** (If the student responds correctly, go on to the test items. If not, try one more example: sock - sun. If the student fails on this item, cease testing.)

Test Items. Say: **"Good. Let's do some more."** (Indicate + or − in each space next to the test words. If the student misses 3 consecutive items, stop testing.)

jump - just _____	land - lake _____
duck - door _____	talk - tell _____
sun - see _____	bat - ball _____
car - can _____	pink - pig _____

/8   /8

DIRECTIONS/SCORING	NUMBER CORRECT	
	1st Test	2nd Test

Test 3: Phoneme Blending

Model Item. Say: **"I have a robot friend. He can say words in a funny way. When he says <u>bad</u>, he says /b/ - /a/ - /d/. When he says <u>fan</u>, he says /f/ - /a/ - /n/."** (Emphasize and distinctly separate each of the letter sounds, but do not distort the sounds. For example, for **<u>bad</u>**, do not say: **/buh/ - /aaa/ - /duh/**.)

Practice Item. Say: **"Now I'm going to say words like a robot and you tell me what the words really are. OK? /c/ - /a/ - /t/, /b/ - /i/ - /g/, /s/ - /ee/ - /m/."** (Student should say <u>cat</u>, <u>big</u>, and <u>seem</u>.)

Test Items. Say: **"Good. Let's do some more."** (Indicate + or − in each space next to the test words. If the student misses 3 consecutive items, stop testing.)

/c/ - /a/ - /t/ _____   /s/ - /u/ - /n/ _____
(cat)   (sun)
/b/ - /oa/ - /t/_____   /m/ - /o/ - /m/ _____
(boat)   (mom)
/st/ - /o/ - /p/_____   /f/ - /ee/ - /l/ _____
(stop)   (feel)
/g/ - /i/ - /v/ _____   /r/ - /ae/ - /z/ _____
(give)   (raze)

| | /8 | /8 |

DIRECTIONS/SCORING	NUMBER CORRECT	
	1st Test	2nd Test
Test 4: Phoneme Segmentation *Model Item.* Say: **"Now *you* get to be the robot. I'm going to say a word and I want you to say all the sounds of the word like my robot friend does. So if I say <u>pat</u>, you would say /p/ - /a/ - /t/."** (Pronounce the whole word slowly and clearly, but do not separate the sounds as you say the word.) *Practice Item.* Say: **"OK, you try it. The word is <u>cat</u>. Say it like my robot friend does."** (Student should say /c/ - /a/ - /t/. If necessary, try one or two more practice items.) *Test Items.* Say: **"Good. Let's do some more."** (Indicate + or − in each space next to the test words. If the student misses 3 consecutive items, stop testing.) sit _____ dog _____ ham _____ wide _____ big _____ rope _____ take _____ just _____		
	/8	/8

Preparation and Use of Materials for Testing Letter Knowledge

PREPARING FOR THE TEST

Before administering the letter recognition inventory, make multiple copies of the answer sheet on page 237, so you will have one for each student to be tested. Also remove the Letter Stimulus Sheet from page 235 and use rubber cement or tape to fasten it to a 5" × 8" card. You may then wish to laminate the card or place it in a plastic sleeve so it will not become soiled from handling.

SPECIFIC DIRECTIONS FOR GIVING THE LETTER RECOGNITION INVENTORY

Before beginning this test, you may first wish to have the student write all of the letters in both uppercase and lowercase. If this is done correctly, then place a plus mark (+) in the blanks by Task 1 on the answer sheet. If they are not all done correctly, you may wish to note exceptions.

A. Give the student the Letter Stimulus Sheet and ask her to read each of the letters in row 1, then row 2, row 3, and so on. Mark them as plus (+) if they are answered correctly, or you may simply wish to place a plus mark (+) in the blanks by Task 2 on the answer sheet to indicate that they were all given correctly. If they are not answered correctly, then write the answer given by the student in each blank. If the student can do this task, stop the test. If she cannot name all of the letters, continue with the following tasks.

B. Show the student the Letter Stimulus Sheet and ask her to point to letters as you name them. Name them in random order from the lowercase letters and then name them in random order from the uppercase letters. Be sure to name all of them, or enough of them so that you are certain the student can identify all letters when they are named. If the student can do this, then place a plus mark (+) in the appropriate blanks by Task 3 on the answer sheet and discontinue the testing. If the student cannot do this task, then note that on Task 3 and continue with the following tasks.

C. Show the student the Letter Stimulus Sheet and ask her to match uppercase letters with lowercase letters; for example, point to the *n* in the lowercase letters and ask the student to point to the *N* from the letters in the upper-case group. You may wish to alternate by first pointing to a letter in the low-ercase group and having the student match it with the corresponding letter from the uppercase group. Be sure to do all of the letters, or do enough of them so that you are certain the student can match all letters. If the student can do this, then place a plus mark (+) in the appropriate blank by Task 4 on the answer sheet and discontinue the testing. If the student cannot do this task, then note that on Task 4 and continue with the following task.

D. Show the student the Letter Stimulus Sheet. Point to a letter from row 11 and ask the student to point to another letter that is exactly the same as that letter. Do this with all of the letters: first *b*, then *m*, and so on, until all pairs have been matched. If the student can do this, then place a plus mark (+) in the appropriate blank by Task 5. If the student cannot do this task, then note that on Task 5.

IMPORTANT POINTS TO REMEMBER

When testing for a student's knowledge of the letters, keep in mind that certain tasks concerning letter knowledge are more difficult than others. For example, note that Task 2 is more difficult than Task 3; that is, naming letters in random order from a stimulus sheet is more difficult than pointing to the letters as they are named by the teacher. Likewise, pointing to the letters as they are named by the teacher (Task 3) is more difficult than being asked to identify a lowercase *g* when shown an upper-case *G* (Task 4). Therefore, in giving this test, begin with Task 1 (if you wish), ask-ing the student to write the letters of the alphabet in both uppercase and lowercase. Then the student will do Task 2. If she can do that task, then there is no need to do Task 3. If the student cannot do Task 3, then she should be asked to do Task 4, and so on.

LETTER STIMULUS SHEET

1.	e	n	i	p	c
2.	v	x	a	j	z
3.	b	o	s	u	q
4.	k	y	f	l	d
5.	g	t	m	r	h	w

6.	C	J	P	H	K
7.	O	G	N	Q	D
8.	L	R	B	Z	Y
9.	A	S	F	M	V
10.	I	W	T	X	U	E

11.   b m g d r p m b g r p d m o

LETTER KNOWLEDGE ANSWER SHEET

STUDENT'S NAME _____ SCHOOL _____
DATE _____
TESTER _____

See directions.

1. e _____	n _____	i _____	p _____	c _____	
2. v _____	x _____	a _____	j _____	z _____	
3. b _____	o _____	s _____	u _____	q _____	
4. k _____	y _____	f _____	l _____	d _____	
5. g _____	t _____	m _____	r _____	h _____	w _____
6. C _____	J _____	P _____	H _____	K _____	
7. O _____	G _____	N _____	Q _____	D _____	
8. L _____	R _____	B _____	Z _____	Y _____	
9. A _____	S _____	F _____	M _____	V _____	
10. I _____	W _____	T _____	X _____	U _____	E _____

TASK 1: _____ Student can write all lowercase letters correctly
_____ Student can write all uppercase letters correctly
Exceptions noted: _____
_____

TASK 2: _____ Student can name all lowercase letters correctly
_____ Student can name all uppercase letters correctly
TASK 3: _____ Student can identify all lowercase letters when named
_____ Student can identify all uppercase letters when named
_____ Student cannot identify all lowercase letters when named
_____ Student cannot identify all uppercase letters when named
Exceptions noted: _____
_____

TASK 4: _____ Student can match all upper- and lowercase letters
_____ Student cannot match all upper- and lowercase letters
Exceptions noted: _____
_____

TASK 5: _____ Student can match a letter with another one that is exactly
the same
_____ Student cannot match letters that are exactly the same
Exceptions noted: _____
_____

APPENDIX A-4

Preparation and Use of Materials for the Quick Check for Basic Sight Words

PREPARING FOR THE TEST

Before administering the Quick Check for Basic Sight Word Knowledge, make multiple copies of page 243, which is the answer sheet to be used in quickly assessing students' knowledge of basic sight words. Also remove the stimulus sheet on page 241. This page can then be placed on a surface such as tagboard and fastened with rubber cement or transparent tape. After it is cemented in place, you may wish to laminate it or place it in a plastic sleeve to keep it from becoming soiled from handling.

SPECIFIC DIRECTIONS FOR TESTING BASIC SIGHT WORDS

Have your answer sheet ready and place the stimulus sheet in front of the student. Ask the student to read the words in the same order as they are numbered. Tell the student to read each word carefully and skip any word that is not known, or instruct the student to say "I don't know" when an unknown word is encountered. Mark the answer sheet as suggested in the directions. If the student pauses more than approximately 1 second before saying a word, count it as wrong.

IMPORTANT POINTS TO REMEMBER

The Quick Check for Basic Sight Word Knowledge is a quick way to test students' knowledge of basic sight words. If there is any doubt in your mind as to whether a student should be given an entire basic sight word test, you may give students this list first. If the student does not miss any words on this test, then he may not need to take the entire basic sight word test. However, if a student misses even one word on this list, he should be given the entire basic word test.

The Quick Check for Basic Sight Word Knowledge was developed by giving Ekwall's basic sight word list to 500 students in grades 2 through 6, using a tachistoscopic presentation. One hundred students were tested at each of these five grade levels. A computer analysis then listed, in ascending order of difficulty, the words students most often missed. From this list, 36 words were chosen. The first few words are the easier ones. However, following the first few easier words are the ones students tended to miss more often. The list also includes words commonly confused by many students. When giving this test, you should make sure that the student is exposed to each word briefly (approximately 1 second). Given more time, the student may use word-attack skills instead of his knowledge of basic sight words. A student who misses even one word in this test should be given the basic sight word tests that appear in Appendix A-5.

Quick Check for Basic Sight Word Knowledge

1. I	13. both	25. every
2. the	14. then	26. ran
3. was	15. shall	27. another
4. down	16. upon	28. leave
5. these	17. while	29. should
6. saw	18. draw	30. there
7. than	19. thing	31. sure
8. start	20. run	32. always
9. this	21. thank	33. carry
10. want	22. once	34. present
11. those	23. wish	35. such
12. went	24. think	36. hurt

Quick Check for Basic Sight Word Knowledge

Answer Sheet

Name _____ Date _____

School_____ Tester _____

Directions: As the student reads the words from the stimulus sheet, mark those words read correctly with a plus (+) and those read incorrectly with a minus (−) or write in the word substituted. If the student says he or she does not know an answer, then mark it with a question mark (?). If a student misses any words on this test, then he or she should be given the full list of basic sight words.

1. I_____		19. thing _____	
2. the_____		20. run_____	
3. was _____		21. thank_____	
4. down_____		22. once _____	
5. these_____		23. wish _____	
6. saw _____		24. think _____	
7. than _____		25. every _____	
8. start _____		26. ran _____	
9. this _____		27. another _____	
10. want _____		28. leave _____	
11. those_____		29. should _____	
12. went _____		30. there _____	
13. both _____		31. sure _____	
14. then _____		32. always _____	
15. shall _____		33. carry _____	
16. upon _____		34. present _____	
17. while_____		35. such _____	
18. draw _____		36. hurt _____	

Preparation and Use of Materials for Testing Basic Sight Words and Phrases

PREPARING FOR THE TEST

Before administering these tests, make multiple copies of pages 249 through 257, the answer sheets to be used in assessing students' knowledge of basic sight words and phrases. You will also need an audio tape recorder and tapes. You will need to prepare flash cards for each of the 220 basic sight words and 143 basic sight word phrases. Your flash cards should be arranged in the same order as the words on the answer sheets.

To do this, purchase $3'' \times 5''$ or $4'' \times 6''$ index cards (either blank or lined) or, if you wish, purchase heavier stock cards in a similar or slightly smaller size. Most school supply stores sell cards ready-made for this purpose in various colors. Also, they often have rounded corners, which makes them last longer. You will need 363 cards, but you should purchase a few more in case you make mistakes preparing the cards.

Once you have selected your cards, look at the lists of words on the answer sheets. Carefully print one word on each flash card, using neat lowercase manuscript printing. An alternative is to use the labelmaking feature of a word-processing program; type all of the words and phrases into the word processor and either print the words and phrases directly onto labels or print the words and phrases onto blank pages and then copy these pages onto labels using a photocopier.

You should also write the list number and the word number on the back of each card. For example, on the back of the first card, *the*, write I-1. (This indicates List I, word 1.) The designation IV-16 would be written on the back of *ride* (List IV, word 16). If your cards ever become mixed up, you will find that it is easy to reassemble them in the correct order if you designate each word on the back as described. You also may wish to use different colored cards for each list.

SPECIFIC DIRECTIONS FOR TESTING BASIC SIGHT WORDS AND PHRASES

Seat the student opposite you and place the microphone near the spot on the table where the cards will be placed after the student has responded to the words on the cards as you flash them. (Make sure the tape recorder is turned on!) Present the cards in the order they appear on the answer sheet. Say to the student: "I am going to show you some words on flash cards and I want you to say them when you see them. I will be flashing the cards quickly, so, if you don't know a word, don't worry about it and go on." Lift off 20 to 30 cards from the ordered stack. At a steady rate of approximately one to two cards per second, flash the cards to the student. Do *not* separate the cards into "right" and "wrong" piles because this may distract you, upset the student being tested, and confuse the order of the flash cards. Continue flashing the cards until the student does not respond to four or five consecutive words or otherwise indicates an inability to successfully complete the test. If the student appears to be pronouncing most of the words correctly, continue the procedure until all cards are flashed.

After you have completed flashing the cards, play back the tape and mark the answer sheet with (+) for correct and (−) for incorrect responses. In scoring, *only the first response counts.* Having mastered a word, the student recognizes it instantly. If the student hesitates, the flashed word is not known *by sight.*

You may test the student's knowledge of basic sight word phrases using the procedures described, this time using the list of basic sight word phrases, also presented in this appendix. Allow up to 2 seconds per phrase when flashing the cards. Each sight word test takes approximately 6 minutes to administer and score.

IMPORTANT POINTS TO REMEMBER

By examining the prepared lists, you can determine specifically which basic sight words and phrases the student has not mastered. These can then be taught without having to misuse instructional time teaching words or phrases that are already known.

A reasonable criterion for mastery of the entire lists is 90% or better. Even students who know all the basic sight words quite well will often miscall a few words because of the speed of the test. You may wish to recheck missed words or phrases a second time to determine whether the errors resulted from the speed of the test or from the student's lack of knowledge.

You must use judgment in evaluating a student's performance on the sight word tests. Young children may have greater difficulty with a speed of one word per second, although ultimately it is essential that the words be recognized at this rate. Similarly, students with speech difficulties may need an adjustment in the rate of flashing.

The modified Dolch list that appears in this appendix includes the 220 Dolch basic sight words, reordered according to frequency of occurrence as found in a study conducted by William K. Durr (1973). The 220 individual words are divided into 11 sublists of 20 words each for ease of scoring and instruction.

The list is presented based on the assumption that not all students will master all the words. It is, therefore, reasonable to begin by teaching the words that appear most often.

The phrase list is compiled so that each word from the isolated words list is presented in a phrase. Only 17 new words are added to complete phrases. These are nouns that are all drawn from the preprimer level of a basal series.

A list of basic sight word *sentences* is provided in Appendix B-2. These sentences are derived from the phrase list presented in this appendix. It is not suggested that you use the sentences for testing; however, they are quite helpful in teaching the student to recognize the individual sight words and sight word phrases in context.

REFERENCES

Durr, W. K. (1973). Computer study of high frequency words in popular trade juveniles. *Reading Teacher, 27*, 37–42.

Name _____ Date _____ Scores: (Pretest) _____ /220

School _____ Tester _____ (Posttest) _____ /220

Directions: Turn on the tape recorder and place the microphone on the table. Tell the student what you are going to do. Flash the cards to the student at a rate of one to two words per second in the order in which they appear on the list. After you have completed the flashing of the cards, play back the tape and mark the answer sheet with a (+) for correct and a (−) for incorrect responses.

Individual Diagnosis of Dolch Words (Listed in Descending Order of Frequency)   pre [/220]   post [/220]

LIST I
	pre	post
1. the		
2. to		
3. and		
4. he		
5. a		
6. I		
7. you		
8. it		
9. of		
10. in		
11. was		
12. said		
13. his		
14. that		
15. she		
16. for		
17. on		
18. they		
19. but		
20. had		
*	/20	/20

LIST II
	pre	post
1. at		
2. him		
3. with		
4. up		
5. all		
6. look		
7. is		
8. her		
9. there		
10. some		
11. out		
12. as		
13. be		
14. have		
15. go		
16. we		
17. am		
18. then		
19. little		
20. down		
*	/20	/20

LIST III
	pre	post
1. do		
2. can		
3. could		
4. when		
5. did		
6. what		
7. so		
8. see		
9. not		
10. were		
11. get		
12. them		
13. like		
14. one		
15. this		
16. my		
17. would		
18. me		
19. will		
20. yes		
*	/20	/20

LIST IV
	pre	post
1. big		
2. went		
3. are		
4. come		
5. if		
6. now		
7. long		
8. no		
9. came		
10. ask		
11. very		
12. an		
13. over		
14. your		
15. its		
16. ride		
17. into		
18. just		
19. blue		
20. red		
*	/20	/20

LIST V
	pre	post
1. from		
2. good		
3. any		
4. about		
5. around		
6. want		
7. don't		
8. how		
9. know		
10. right		
11. put		
12. too		
13. got		
14. take		
15. where		
16. every		
17. pretty		
18. jump		
19. green		
20. four		
*	/20	/20

LIST VI
	pre	post
1. away		
2. old		
3. by		
4. their		
5. here		
6. saw		
7. call		
8. after		
9. well		
10. think		
11. ran		
12. let		
13. help		
14. make		
15. going		
16. sleep		
17. brown		
18. yellow		
19. five		
20. six		
*	/20	/20

* Number of words read correctly

LIST VII

	pre	post
1. walk		
2. two		
3. or		
4. before		
5. eat		
6. again		
7. play		
8. who		
9. been		
10. may		
11. stop		
12. off		
13. never		
14. seven		
15. eight		
16. cold		
17. today		
18. fly		
19. myself		
20. round		
*	/20	/20

LIST VIII

	pre	post
1. tell		
2. much		
3. keep		
4. give		
5. work		
6. first		
7. try		
8. new		
9. must		
10. start		
11. black		
12. white		
13. ten		
14. does		
15. bring		
16. goes		
17. write		
18. always		
19. drink		
20. once		
*	/20	/20

LIST IX

	pre	post
1. soon		
2. made		
3. run		
4. gave		
5. open		
6. has		
7. find		
8. only		
9. us		
10. three		
11. our		
12. better		
13. hold		
14. buy		
15. funny		
16. warm		
17. ate		
18. full		
19. those		
20. done		
*	/20	/20

LIST X

	pre	post
1. use		
2. fast		
3. say		
4. light		
5. pick		
6. hurt		
7. pull		
8. cut		
9. kind		
10. both		
11. sit		
12. which		
13. fall		
14. carry		
15. small		
16. under		
17. read		
18. why		
19. own		
20. found		
*	/20	/20

LIST XI

	pre	post
1. wash		
2. show		
3. hot		
4. because		
5. far		
6. live		
7. draw		
8. clean		
9. grow		
10. best		
11. upon		
12. these		
13. sing		
14. together		
15. please		
16. thank		
17. wish		
18. many		
19. shall		
20. laugh		
*	/20	/20

SCORE

LIST	pre	post
I		
II		
III		
IV		
V		
VI		
VII		
VIII		
IX		
X		
XI		
TOTAL		

* Number of words read correctly

Name _____ Date _____ Scores: (Pretest) _____ <u>/143</u>

School _____ Tester _____ (Posttest) _____ <u>/143</u>

Directions: Turn on the tape recorder and place the microphone on the table. Tell the student what you are going to do. Flash the cards to the student at a rate of one to two words per second in the order in which they appear on the list. After you have completed the flashing of the cards, play back the tape and mark the answer sheet with a (+) for correct and a (−) for incorrect responses.

Individual Diagnosis of Sight Word Phrases   pre [/143] post [/143]

LIST I

	pre	post
1. he had to		
2. she said that		
3. to the		
4. you and I		
5. but they said		
6. on a		
7. for his		
8. of that		
9. that was in		
10. it was		
*	/10	/10

LIST II

	pre	post
1. look at him		
2. as little		
3. at all		
4. I have a		
5. have some		
6. there is		
7. down there		
8. then we have		
9. to go		
10. to be there		
11. look up		
12. look at her		
13. we go out		
14. I am		
*	/14	/14

LIST III

	pre	post
1. look at me		
2. can you		
3. a little one		
4. you will see		
5. what is that		
6. my *cat*		
7. I will get		
8. when did he		
9. like this		
10. get them		
11. so you will see		
12. I could		
13. we were		
14. would not		
15. yes, I do		
*	/15	/15

LIST IV

	pre	post
1. a big ride		
2. went into		
3. if I ask		
4. come over with		
5. they went		
6. I am very		
7. there are blue		
8. a long *book*		
9. an *apple*		
10. your red *book*		
11. its *name*		
12. they came		
13. just now		
*	/13	/13

* Number of phrases read correctly

LIST V

	pre	post
1. I take every		
2. the four green		
3. they don't want		
4. right around		
5. a good jump		
6. a pretty *rabbit*		
7. I know how		
8. where can I		
9. the *duck* got		
10. it is about		
11. don't put any		
12. take from		
13. too little		
*	/13	/13

LIST VI

	pre	post
1. ran away		
2. let me help		
3. going to sleep		
4. five yellow *ducks*		
5. the old *turtle*		
6. by their *mother*		
7. call after *six*		
8. the brown *rabbit*		
9. I am well		
10. will think		
11. will make		
12. you saw		
13. here it is		
*	/13	/13

LIST VII

	pre	post
1. we eat		
2. two may walk		
3. on or off		
4. before seven		
5. today is cold		
6. play by myself		
7. don't stop		
8. it is round		
9. who is eight		
10. have never been		
11. can fly again		
*	/11	/11

LIST VIII

	pre	post
1. black and white		
2. start a new		
3. must try once		
4. don't keep much		
5. it does go		
6. always drink *milk*		
7. will bring ten		
8. *Lad* goes		
9. write and tell		
10. work is first		
11. can give it		
*	/11	/11

LIST IX

	pre	post
1. open and find		
2. *Jill* ate the		
3. those are done		
4. is funny		
5. buy us three		
6. this is only		
7. gave a warm		
8. soon we ate		
9. had a full		
10. run and hold		
11. made a big		
12. it is better		
13. our *duck*		
*	/13	/13

LIST X

	pre	post
1. sit with both		
2. you use it		
3. carry a small		
4. the cut hurt		
5. the fast *car*		
6. then the light		
7. which will fall		
8. pull it in		
9. had found		
10. under here		
11. be kind		
12. pick it up		
13. *Bill* can read		
14. my own *bed*		
15. why is it		
16. I can say		
*	/16	/16

* Number of phrases read correctly

LIST XI

	pre	post
1. wash in hot		
2. because it is		
3. grow best		
4. once upon		
5. sing and laugh		
6. please thank		
7. we draw these		
8. shall we show		
9. the wish is		
10. we clean		
11. they live		
12. too far		
13. all together		
14. many *turtles*		
*	/14	/14

SCORE

LIST	pre	post
I		
II		
III		
IV		
V		
VI		
VII		
VIII		
IX		
X		
XI		
TOTAL		

* Number of phrases read correctly

APPENDIX A-6

Preparation and Use of Materials for the Phonics Assessment

THE FORMAT OF THE PHONICS ASSESSMENT TESTS

The Phonics Assessment consists of nine subtests that evaluate the student's knowledge of all the critical phonics skills. These tests can be administered quickly and easily, and provide considerable information in an easy-to-read format. All of the subtests use a common format on the answer sheets, which contain the following:

☐ Down the left column—a summary of the directions for administering each subtest, including the spoken instructions you will give to the student.

☐ Down the center—places to mark the student's responses to each test item. (Space is provided for both pre- and posttest scores on the answer sheets. You may use different-colored ink to distinguish pretest responses from posttest responses on each subtest.)

☐ Down the right column—spaces to indicate the student's total score on each subtest. (You can determine the student's mastery of each skill on both pre- and posttests by comparing the student's performance to the criterion score for mastery that is provided for each subtest.)

PREPARATION OF THE PHONICS ASSESSMENT TESTS

Before administering the Phonics Assessment tests, make multiple copies of the answer sheets on pages 273 through 279, so you will have one for each student to be tested. Remove pages 265 through 271, the Phonics Assessment test sheets, and rubber-cement or tape them to 5" × 8" cards. You may then wish to laminate the cards or place them in plastic sleeves so they will not become soiled from handling.

DIRECTIONS FOR ADMINISTERING AND SCORING THE SUBTESTS

Subtest 1: Application of Phonics Skills in Context

1. Place the test sheet for Subtest 1 in front of the student and say: "Read this story aloud until I say stop."

2. As the student reads, indicate specific reading errors on the answer sheet. (Refer to Appendix A-1, "Code for Marking in Oral Diagnosis," for instructions on how to mark the student's oral reading errors.)

3. Encourage the student to pronounce as many words as possible. Do *not* provide assistance by pronouncing words for the student, but rather encourage the student to go on and "do the best you can." Cease testing if the student becomes overly frustrated.

4. Only the words underlined on the answer sheet are considered in scoring. The words that are not underlined are basic sight words, which should be pronounced without phonic analysis, or repetitions of previously underlined words.

5. To score this test, compare the oral reading transcription with the response chart just below the paragraph on the answer sheet. The chart lists the 73 phonic elements that are tested, with the underlined words from the paragraph. Circle each phonic element on the response chart that the student failed to pronounce correctly. Some of the phonic elements are tested by more than one underlined word from the paragraph. In such cases, circle the phonic element if even one of the underlined words is mispronounced. Mastery of the phonic element requires that it be pronounced correctly in all cases.

6. Circle the phonic element only if the element itself is mispronounced, regardless of the total pronunciation of the underlined word. For example, to determine the student's symbol-sound association for beginning *b*, the underlined words are *barn* and *bird*. Circle the item if *either* beginning *b* is mispronounced. If, however, the student says "bank" for *barn*, the symbol-sound association for the beginning *b* is correct, so the item is not circled.

7. Determine the number of correct responses, write this number as a fraction, and compare it to the criterion for mastery. To achieve mastery, the student must correctly pronounce 65 of the 73 phonic elements, as indicated on the answer sheet.

Subtest 2: Initial Consonants

1. Place the appropriate test sheet in front of the student and say: "Look at number 1 and point to the letter you hear at the beginning of water."

2. The student must point to the *w* from among the 5 letter choices. If the student makes an incorrect choice, circle the word *water* on the answer sheet. Then pronounce the next word, *dog*, and continue marking the answer sheet in the same way. Continue to pronounce words and circle incorrect responses until the 10 items are completed. (Of course, you may stop sooner if the student's performance reflects a total inability to succeed at this task.)

3. Determine the number of correct responses, write this number as a fraction, and compare it to the criterion for mastery.

Subtests 3–6: Initial Blends and Digraphs, Ending Sounds, Vowels, Phonograms

Subtests 3 through 6 follow the same format as Subtest 2. Subtest 3 assesses initial blends and digraphs, Subtest 4 assesses ending sounds, Subtest 5 assesses short and long vowel sounds, and Subtest 6 assesses common ending phonograms or word elements.

Subtest 7: Blending

1. Place the appropriate test sheet in front of the student, then check to see that the student can recognize and pronounce the two phonograms *at* and *in*. If the student does not know these, they should be taught to the student, which should be easy to do in a short period of time.
2. Complete the sample item for the student, demonstrating how the initial consonant *t* is pronounced /t/, then blended with the phonogram /in/, to arrive at /tin/.
3. Ask the student to do the same with the 10 items provided, while you circle the incorrect responses.
4. On this subtest and on Subtests 8 and 9, you should not only circle the incorrect responses, but also write phonetic transcriptions of the mispronounced words. This will aid in later analysis. Space is provided on the answer sheet for this.
5. Determine the number of correct responses, write this number as a fraction, and compare it to the criterion for mastery.

Subtest 8: Substitution

1. Place the appropriate test sheet in front of the student and say: "Read these words. I will tell you the first one in each column in case you don't know it. Some of these are real words, some are not."
2. The student then reads the 25 words in the 5 columns, while you follow the same scoring procedure as indicated for Subtest 7.

Subtest 9: Vowel Pronunciation

1. Place the appropriate test sheet in front of the student and say: "Read as many of these words as you can."
2. Follow the same scoring procedure as for Subtests 7 and 8.

INTERPRETING THE PHONICS ASSESSMENT TESTS

Subtest 1: Application of Phonics Skills in Context

Subtest 1 evaluates the student's ability to apply phonics skills in a carefully constructed passage. Phonics skills are of most benefit to a student when utilized in conjunction with context clues. For some students, context ability is sufficiently developed for them to decode successfully with only minimal phonics ability.

On Subtest 1, the student is asked to read aloud a short passage. Upon completion, you will be able to evaluate the student's application of 73 phonics elements in context. **If the student performs at mastery level on this subtest, skip the other phonics tests and go on to the Structural Analysis Assessment tests, which are found in Appendix A-7.**

The passage consists of 105 one-syllable words, based on the assumption that only one-syllable words should be utilized in evaluating phonics abilities. (Words of more than one syllable usually require structural analysis, which is a separate decoding skill.) Only 44 of the words in the passage (those that are underlined) are used to evaluate phonics skills. The 61 words that are not underlined include 19 basic sight words that should be recognized instantly without phonic analysis. (Some of these words are also phonetically irregular.) These 19 words appear a total of 52 times in the passage. In addition, 4 of the underlined words are repeated a total of 9 times, and these 9 repetitions are not counted in the analysis. A few of the words that are counted do appear on lists of basic sight words. However, they tend to appear with less frequency than most basic sight words and are phonetically regular.

The 44 underlined words allow for evaluation of 16 beginning single consonant sounds, 13 ending single consonant sounds, 7 beginning consonant blends, 8 ending consonant blends, 4 beginning consonant digraphs, 1 ending consonant digraph, 5 short vowels, 5 long vowels, 5 *r*-controlled vowels, and 9 vowel digraphs, diphthongs, and other vowel combinations for a total of 73 phonic elements.

Depending on the student's reading ability, some or all of the words on this subtest may be in the student's sight vocabulary. However, for those students reading at or below a second-grade level, this subtest provides an opportunity to evaluate the student's ability to use phonic analysis in the act of reading. In addition, if a careful transcription is made, you will be able to observe the student's use of context clues and fluency skills. You should not attempt to evaluate the student's comprehension on this test.

Subtests 2–6: Initial Consonants, Initial Blends and Digraphs, Ending Sounds, Vowels, Phonograms

Subtest 2 evaluates the student's ability to identify the single consonant letter (from a choice of five) that represents the beginning sound in a word pronounced by the examiner. Subtests 3 through 6 provide for similar evaluation of initial blends and digraphs, ending sounds, short and long vowels, and common phonograms, respectively.

Subtests 2 through 6 each consist of 10 items. The mastery level for each subtest is 9 correct out of 10, excepting Subtest 4 (ending sounds), where 8 out of 10 is considered mastery. This is because ending sounds are both more difficult and less important factors in the student's phonics instruction program.

The items and the choices in Subtests 2 through 6 were carefully selected to reflect a sampling of the most critical phonic elements and to require maximum discrimination (minimal guess factor) by the student. Although guessing alone should account for 2 correct answers on the 10 items of each subtest, the mastery level requires sufficient knowledge on the student's part. You will observe that students who have mastered the items tested will work quickly and easily.

It is important to remember that these are *low-level* phonics tests. Failure on these tests does indicate that the student lacks sufficient phonics skills, but mastery does *not* prove that the student possesses adequate phonics ability *in the act of reading.*

Subtest 7: Blending

Subtest 7 evaluates the student's ability to blend a beginning sound with one of two common phonograms. High-level phonics skills are required to pronounce the beginning sound, and blending skills are required to complete the item. Two factors in this subtest may be disconcerting to the student and should be considered when analyzing the results.

First, the appearance of the test items may confuse some students. This is unfortunate, but unavoidable, as it is necessary to separate the word parts. Second, some students may balk at pronouncing nonsense words, especially older students. The use of nonsense words (which also appear in Subtest 8) is necessary to ensure that the student is not relying solely on sight recognition to pronounce the words. The subtest is designed with three nonsense words and a fourth word, *din*, which is not likely to be in the student's meaning vocabulary. Note whether the error pattern consists of only these words.

Because Subtest 7 evaluates two different skills (high-level phonics and blending), note which skill is lacking when errors are made. If the student lacks high-level phonics ability, the beginning sounds will be mispronounced. Blending will go awry if the student lacks blending ability or is confused by the format of the test or the pronunciation of the two phonograms.

The student should be discouraged from reading the words too quickly, as this will also cause errors. Correct pronunciation for each item may occur in either of two ways. For example, for the item /m/ + /at/, the student may pronounce the /m/ and the /at/ separately, then blend them together to pronounce the word /mat/, or the student may simply pronounce the whole word, /mat/. If the student is unable to correctly pronounce the word, the item is failed, even if the separate parts were pronounced correctly. (Some students may say the letter name(s) for the beginning sound, then pronounce the phonogram, and blend the word. This is acceptable, as long as the whole word is pronounced correctly.)

Subtest 8: Substitution

Subtest 8 evaluates the student's ability to substitute a new phonic element and blend it with the rest of the word. The examiner pronounces the first word in each column. The student then reads each word below the first word as a whole word. The first column requires the student to substitute and blend seven beginning single consonants.

Subsequent columns require the student to substitute and blend beginning blends and digraphs, short vowels, long vowels, and ending consonants.

Most students will find that the columns are increasingly difficult. The last column (ending consonants) may be particularly difficult if the student attempts to read the words too quickly.

Subtest 9: Vowel Pronunciation

Subtest 9 evaluates the student's ability to pronounce 15 real words that represent the more difficult vowel patterns: selected digraphs, diphthongs, and r-controlled vowels. Because of the variable pronunciation of these vowel patterns, nonsense words cannot be used. Accordingly, it is possible for students to pronounce these words by relying on sight recognition. However, most of the words are not usually in the meaning vocabularies of remedial readers. This is a difficult subtest for a student who has any difficulty in phonics.

WHEN TO STOP TESTING

If the student masters Subtest 1, stop testing at that point. If the student fails to master Subtest 1, continue administering these subtests until the student consistently fails to attain mastery on the tests or when it is clear that you are no longer obtaining useful diagnostic information. It is important not to overtest. Doing so may lead to unnecessary frustration for the student.

Subtest 1: Application of Phonics Skills in Context

A Job at the Zoo

Ron has a job. He will make the fur of the cat shine. He will use a brush. Ron can fix a cage. He can pat a wet nose. He may hug a cute cub.

Ron may perk up a sad white bird with a nice word. Then Ron will clean dirt from the ground in the owl barn. He can see a fawn rest by a tree. He may bring a toy on a chain to a girl cub. The cub will make a strange noise. Ron will smile. He likes all the things he can do to work and play at the zoo.

Subtest 2: Initial Consonants

1.	l	w	h	t	b	6.	h	b	f	k	t
2.	c	b	k	q	d	7.	t	f	a	j	k
3.	m	l	t	n	b	8.	d	b	p	r	t
4.	c	k	g	b	d	9.	k	c	f	s	r
5.	b	d	p	k	g	10.	t	h	g	i	k

Subtest 3: Initial Blends and Digraphs

1.	cr	gl	gr	tr	dr	6.	sh	cr	bl	ch	sl
2.	bl	tr	br	gl	fr	7.	dr	th	tl	fl	ch
3.	sp	sn	sm	st	sc	8.	dr	bl	cr	pr	br
4.	sh	st	ch	sl	cn	9.	sm	sp	ch	sh	cr
5.	bl	pr	gl	pl	sl	10.	tr	dr	th	ch	tw

Subtest 4: Ending Sounds

1.	q	r	t	k	d	6.	nt	nk	st	ng	rk
2.	k	b	q	d	t	7.	st	ch	ss	ck	sh
3.	b	p	t	k	d	8.	sk	st	sh	ss	ck
4.	r	u	o	l	k	9.	st	nk	ng	nt	rd
5.	d	b	k	t	p	10.	nd	rd	pt	ld	rt

Subtest 5: Vowels

1.	a	e	i	o	u	6.	a	e	i	o	u
2.	e	i	o	u	a	7.	e	i	o	u	a
3.	i	o	u	a	e	8.	i	o	u	a	e
4.	o	u	a	e	i	9.	o	u	a	e	i
5.	u	a	e	i	o	10.	u	o	a	e	i

Subtest 6: Phonograms

1.	ang	and	ime	ing	ame
2.	in	ime	ame	ind	ain
3.	ite	ipe	ike	ice	eek
4.	ick	og	uck	ock	eep
5.	up	eek	ipe	eep	ime
6.	it	ate	ight	ipe	ice
7.	ung	ine	ang	ing	ind
8.	ad	ade	age	and	ape
9.	ean	ime	ad	ang	ame
10.	elp	in	ill	all	ell

Subtest 7: Blending

at   in
t + in

h + at	m + at
ch + in	sh + in
tr + in	str + at
bl + at	f + in
th + at	d + in

Subtest 8: Substitution

fan	track	hat	rade	bib
ran	shack	hit	rode	bif
tan	spack	hot	ride	bid
ban	frack	het	rude	big
jan	chack	hut		bim
lan	plack			
van	stack			
can	whack			

Subtest 9: Vowel Pronunciation

boat	crown	serve
paint	trout	stir
own	hawk	born
soil	haul	word
coy	card	burn

Phonics Assessment Test

Student _____   School _____
Teacher _____   Grade _____ Age _____
Examiner _____   Test Dates _____ _____
                                                                 pretest   *posttest*

Subtest 1: Application of Phonics Skills in Context. Place Subtest 1 in front of the student. Say: "Read this story aloud until I say stop." (Do not assist the student by pronouncing unknown words.)

Write the mispronunciations on the story below and note the weak skill areas.

Ron has a job. He will make the fur of the cat shine. He will use a brush. Ron can fix a cage. He can pat a wet nose. He may hug a cute cub.

Ron may perk up a sad white bird with a nice word. Then Ron will clean dirt from the ground in the owl barn. He can see a fawn rest by a tree. He may bring a toy on a chain to a girl cub. The cub will make a strange noise. Ron will smile. He likes all the things he can do to work and play at the zoo.

Responses—Circle the Letter(s) Representing the Sounds the Student Read Incorrectly

Beginning Single Consonants	*Ending Single Consonants*	*Beginning Consonant Blends*	*Ending Consonant Blends*
b (barn, bird)	*b* (cub, job)	*cl* (clean)	*nd* (ground)
hard *c* (cage, cat, cub, cute)	soft *c* (nice)	*pl* (play)	*ng* (bring)
d (dirt)	*d* (sad)	*br* (bring, brush)	*rd* (bird, word)
f (fawn, fix, fur)	soft *g* (cage, strange)	*gr* (ground)	*rk* (park, work)
hard *g* (girl)	hard *g* (hug)	*tr* (tree)	*rl* (girl)
h (hug)	*k* (make, perk)	*sm* (smile)	*rn* (barn)
j (job)	*l* (owl, smile)	*str* (strange)	*rt* (dirt)
l (likes)	*n* (chain, clean,		*st* (rest)
m (make, may)	fawn, Ron, shine)		
n (nice, noise, nose)	*p* (up)	*Short Vowels*	*Long Vowels*
p (pat, perk)	*r* (fur)	*a* (cat, pat, sad)	*a* (cage, make, strange)
r (rest, Ron)	*s* (likes, noise,	*e* (rest, wet)	*e* (tree)
s (sad)	nose, things, use)	*i* (fix)	*i* (likes, nice, shine,
t (toy)	*t* (cat, cute, pat,	*o* (job, Ron)	smile, white)
w (wet, word, work)	wet, white)	*u* (brush, cub,	*o* (nose)
z (zoo)	*x* (fix)	hug, up)	*u* (cute, use)

Beginning Consonant Digraphs	*Ending Consonant Digraph*	*Vowel Combinations*	
ch (chain)	*sh* (brush)	*ar* (barn)	*aw* (fawn)
sh (shine)		*er* (perk)	*ea* (clean)
th (things)		*ir* (bird, dirt, girl)	*oi* (noise)
wh (white)		*or* (word, work)	*oo* (zoo)
		ur (fur)	*ou* (ground)
		ai (chain)	*ow* (owl)
		ay (may, play)	*oy* (toy)

Sub-Totals	Pretest	Posttest
_____/16 Beginning single consonants		
_____/13 Ending single consonants		
_____/7 Beginning consonant blends		
_____/8 Ending consonant blends		
_____/4 Beginning consonant digraphs		
_____/1 Ending consonant digraph		
_____/5 Short vowels		
_____/5 Long vowels		
_____/14 Vowel combinations		
Total	_____/73	_____/73
	65 = Mastery	

	Pretest	Posttest
Subtest 2: Initial Consonants (Sound-Symbol) Place Subtest 2 in front of the student. Say: "Look at number 1 and point to the letter you hear at the beginning of *water . . ., dog . . .*" Continue for each word listed. 1. water 5. book 9. sit 2. dog 6. kite 10. hide 3. nice 7. fat 4. goat 8. put	/10	/10
	9 = Mastery	
Subtest 3: Initial Blends & Digraphs (Sound-Symbol) Place Subtest 3 in front of the student. Say: "Look at number 1 and point to the letters you hear at the beginning of *great . . ., blue . . .*" Continue for each word listed. 1. great 5. plum 9. spell 2. blue 6. church 10. those 3. small 7. thumb 4. short 8. bring	/10	/10
	9 = Mastery	
Subtest 4: Ending Sounds (Sound-Symbol) Place Subtest 4 in front of the student. Say: "Look at number 1 and point to the letter or letters you hear at the end of *bat . . ., bed . . .*" Continue for each word listed. 1. bat 5. tab 9. pant 2. bed 6. sing 10. card 3. drop 7. bush 4. cool 8. mask	/10	/10
	8 = Mastery	
Subtest 5: Vowels (Sound-Symbol) Place Subtest 5 in front of the student. Say: "Look at number 1 and point to the vowel you hear in *tip . . ., mule . . .*" Continue for each word listed. 1. tip 5. mope 9. cup 2. mule 6. tape 10. keep 3. snap 7. pet 4. dot 8. fine	/10	/10
	9 = Mastery	
Subtest 6: Phonograms (Sound-Symbol) Place Subtest 6 in front of the student. Say: "Look at number 1 and point to the ending part you hear: *ame . . ., ime . . .*" Continue for each part listed. 1. ame 5. eep 9. ang 2. ime 6. ight 10. ill 3. ike 7. ing 4. ock 8. ade	/10	/10
	9 = Mastery	

	Pretest	Posttest
Subtest 7: Blending (Sound-Symbol) Place Subtest 7 in front of the student. 1. h + at 5. th + at 9. f + in Make sure the student can 2. ch + in 6. m + at 10. d + in pronounce the two phonograms 3. tr + in 7. sh + in *at* and *in*. 4. bl + at 8. str + at Say: "You are going to blend letters with *at* and *in*. The first one is *t* plus *in* or *tin*. Now you blend the rest.	/10	/10 9 = Mastery

Subtest Subtest 8: Substitution
(Sound-Symbol)
Place Subtest 8 in front of the student.   fan   track   hat   rade   bib
Say: "Read these words. I will tell   r   sh   i   o   f
you the first one in each column in   t   sp   o   i   d
case you don't know it. some of   b   fr   e   u   g
these are real words, some are not."   j   ch   u   m
                                        l   pl
                                        v   st
                                        c   wh
	/25	/25
		22 = Mastery

Subtest 9: Vowel Pronunciation
(Sound-Symbol)
Place Subtest 9 in front of the student.   boat   crown   serve
Say: "Read as many of these words as   paint   trout   stir
you can."   own   hawk   born
        soil   haul   word
        coy   card   burn
	/15	/15
		13 = Mastery

Preparation and Use of Materials for the Structural Analysis Assessment

THE FORMAT OF THE STRUCTURAL ANALYSIS ASSESSMENT TESTS

The Structural Analysis Assessment consists of eight subtests in a format that is similar to that used in the Phonics Assessment. Subtest 1 assesses the student's ability to apply the structural analysis skills in the context of a passage. Subtest 2 evaluates the student's ability to *hear* the separate parts (syllables) of words, a skill that is a prerequisite for structural analysis. Subtest 3 assesses the student's ability to combine the various inflectional endings with root words and pronounce the resulting new words. Subtests 4 and 5 assess the student's ability to decode prefixes and suffixes, respectively. Subtest 6 assesses the student's ability to recognize the two separate units of compound words for purposes of pronunciation. Subtest 7 assesses the student's ability to pronounce two-syllable words containing one easy affix (prefix or suffix). Subtest 8 assesses the student's ability to pronounce regular three-, four-, and five-syllable words through the use of structural analysis.

PREPARATION OF THE STRUCTURAL ANALYSIS ASSESSMENT TESTS

Before administering the Structural Analysis Assessment tests, make multiple copies of the answer sheets on pages 297 through 309, so you will have one for each student to be tested. Remove pages 287 through 295, the Structural Analysis Assessment test sheets, and rubber-cement or tape them to 5″ × 8″ cards. You may then wish to laminate the cards or place them in plastic sleeves so they will not become soiled from handling.

DIRECTIONS FOR ADMINISTERING AND SCORING THE SUBTESTS

Subtest 1: Application of Structural Analysis Skills in Context

Note: This subtest consists of two passages. The first is easier than the second. The student may read either or both, depending on the student's reading ability. When in doubt, start the student on the first passage and proceed to the second only if the student attains mastery on the first.

1. Place the appropriate test sheet (either Part A or Part B) in front of the student and say: "Read this story aloud until I say stop."

2. As the student reads, follow the procedure for transcribing oral reading errors as described in Appendix A-1, "Code for Marking in Oral Diagnosis." It is essential to determine whether the underlined words are pronounced correctly. All of these words require structural analysis skills for decoding. The words that are not underlined are either basic sight words or words that can be decoded using phonic analysis.

3. Encourage the student to pronounce as many words as possible. Do *not* provide assistance by pronouncing unknown words for the student. Cease testing if the student becomes overly frustrated.

4. To score this test, evaluate the student's oral reading of the underlined words. Each word that is mispronounced should be circled on the response chart on the answer sheet. The words on this chart are categorized according to the structural analysis skill required.

5. Write the number of correct responses as a fraction on the answer sheet to be compared with the criterion for mastery. If the student meets or exceeds the criterion for the first passage (Subtest 1, Part A), then administer the second passage (Subtest 1, Part B), following the same instructions.

Subtest 2: Hearing Word Parts

1. This test requires no test sheet. Hold the answer sheet so that you can read from it and say: "How many syllables do you hear in the word *cowboy?*" Mark the student's response on the answer sheet.

2. Continue the test with the other four items, circling the incorrect responses.

3. Write the number of correct responses as a fraction on the Answer Sheet to be compared with the criterion for mastery.

Subtests 3–5: Inflectional Endings, Prefixes, Suffixes

1. For each subtest, place the appropriate test sheet in front of the student and read the first word (the root word) in each column, then ask the student to pronounce the other words in the columns. (You should not read the first word in column 2 until the student has read all the words in column 1, and so on.)

2. As the student reads the words, circle each incorrect response on the Answer Sheet.

3. Write the number of correct responses as a fraction on the Answer Sheet to be compared with the criterion for mastery.

Subtest 6: Compound Words

1. Place the appropriate test sheet in front of the student and say: "Read as many of these words as you can. Some are not real words."
2. As the student reads the words, circle the errors. On this test, the errors are not determined by imprecise pronunciation, but rather by the student's failure to recognize and attempt to decode the two parts of the compound word. For example, if a student says "baskethorse" for *baskethouse*, this is considered correct; it is clear that the student identified the two pronounceable units. However, if the student attempts to pronounce *baskethouse* by sounding the *th* as a digraph in the middle of the word, this is incorrect. Such an error reflects a lack of recognition of the two obvious word parts.
3. Write the number of correct responses as a fraction on the answer sheet to be compared with the criterion for mastery.

Subtest 7: Affixes

1. Place the appropriate test sheet in front of the student and say: "Read as many of these words as you can. Some are not real words."
2. As the student reads, circle the errors. The determination of errors on this subtest follows the same restrictions as described under the previous subtest.
3. Write the number of correct responses as a fraction on the answer sheet to be compared with the criterion for mastery.

Subtest 8: Syllabication

1. Place the appropriate test sheet in front of the student and say: "Read as many of these words as you can."
2. As the student reads, circle the errors. Although all of the words on this test are real words, most students will not recognize them as sight words. Count as correct pronunciations where the accent is misplaced, as long as each of the syllables is pronounced correctly.
3. Write the number of correct responses as a fraction on the answer sheet to be compared with the criterion for mastery.

INTERPRETING THE STRUCTURAL ANALYSIS ASSESSMENT TESTS

Structural analysis is a decoding skill that is analogous to phonics. It is often referred to as *morphology*, which is concerned with the study of meaning-bearing units such as root words, prefixes, suffixes, possessives, plurals, accent rules, and syllables. To use structural analysis to decode a multisyllable word, the reader first identifies the separate units in the word, then pronounces the units, then blends them together. In using phonics, the reader goes through the same process with phonemes, or individual sounds.

Subtest 1: Application of Structural Analysis Skills in Context

This subtest evaluates the student's ability to apply the various structural analysis skills during contextual reading. The two passages contain a total of 80 words that require the application of structural analysis. Because of the disproportionate number of long words, the readability of these passages is quite high. Part A, according to the Fry readability formula, is written at approximately the low-fifth-grade level. Part B is written at approximately the mid-seventh-grade level. You should not assume, however, that students who successfully read these passages can comfortably read other materials at these levels.

The two passages that compose this subtest are the most difficult of the structural analysis assessment tests. A student who demonstrates mastery on *both* of the passages surely is not lacking in structural analysis skills. In such a case, you should skip the other structural analysis tests. If, however, the student fails to master one or both of these passages, then you should proceed to administer the remaining subtests until you determine that you no longer can obtain useful diagnostic information.

Subtest 2: Hearing Word Parts

This subtest evaluates the student's ability to hear the separate parts (syllables) of words. If the student is unable to do this, instruction should focus on this area prior to other structural analysis skills. You should not be concerned with the student's ability to identify the specific points in words where syllable division takes place. This skill, often called *end-of-line division*, is frequently tested. Unfortunately, it is not useful for decoding purposes.

Subtests 3–5: Inflectional Endings, Prefixes, Suffixes

These subtests evaluate the student's ability to combine various inflectional endings, prefixes, and suffixes with root words, and to pronounce the resulting new words. In every case, you begin by pronouncing the root word for the student, so the task is easier than that which is required in actual reading. The student, however, must pronounce the whole word correctly to receive credit for the item. If the student fails on any of these items, your task is to determine whether the failure results from the student's inability to pronounce the structural part, blend the part with the root, or both.

Subtest 3 presents the six most common inflectional endings. Subtest 4 presents 10 of the most common and easily teachable prefixes. Subtest 5 presents 10 of the most common suffixes.

Subtest 6: Compound Words

This subtest evaluates the student's ability to recognize that many long words are the combination of two shorter, whole words. The five compound words presented consist of one real word and four nonsense words. Since it is more important for the student to recognize the two separate units of the compound words, perfect pronunciation is not required, as long as the student demonstrates recognition of the compound characteristic. Nonsense words must be used to ensure that the student is not recognizing the whole words merely by sight.

Subtest 7: Affixes

This subtest evaluates the student's ability to pronounce two-syllable words containing one common affix. On this test, you do not pronounce the root word, so the task is significantly more difficult for the student than in Subtests 3 through 5. In this case, the student must go through all three steps of decoding through structural analysis: (1) separating the parts, (2) pronouncing the word parts, and (3) blending the separate parts to pronounce the whole word. As with Subtest 6, most of the items on this test are nonsense words.

Subtest 8: Syllabication

This subtest evaluates the student's ability to pronounce 10 multisyllable words. Accurate pronunciation of these words requires the student to use the structural analysis skills previously tested as well as the ability to divide words into parts when obvious affixes are not present. Because they are particularly difficult and not likely to be recognized by sight, these words are all real words.

Subtest 1: Application of Structural Analysis Skills in Context

Part A: Winter in the Countryside

It was a cold winter day. The trees were bare and birds could be seen in the countryside. A grasshopper hopped across the road to hide from the cold and the foxes curled up to keep warm. A brown field mouse and her babies came running out of a hole in the ground. The babies were fighting with each other. Mother mouse looked unhappy as she sat on a big, overgrown stump. It was dangerous for the mice to stay above ground, but the active children wanted their lunches. Mother mouse was also nervous about her children eating the poisonous plants that were in the field. The children were curious and the plants looked so attractive.

Just that morning, Mother mouse had a disagreement with Father mouse. The question was whether or not the children should run in the field in the daytime.

Part B: The Disappearance of Flint

What should have been a great day turned out to be a disappointing one for David King. He found out that he would be the new quarterback for Friday night's game. Unfortunately, he was going to be taking his best friend Ron's place. Ron had gotten a disqualification notice because his grades dropped at the end of the first report. Ron felt that his concentration was poor because of his older brother's recent motorcycle crash. David was sorry about Ron's dismissal from the team, but was shocked by the resentment he saw on Ron's face when he found out who his replacement would be. This was the unfriendliest that Ron had ever treated David.

David thought about the rest of his rather uneventful day as he walked home. He turned on the flashlight he carried with him, for it had grown quite dark. David stopped short when he heard a loud and frightening scream coming from the vacant mansion just up the road.

The place had been empty for three years and was in bad shape. Fixing it up had been estimated to be costlier than most families could afford. David had always felt that the mansion had a mysterious look about it. The man who had built and lived in the mansion was believed to be knowledgeable in the ways of witchcraft. His disappearance three years ago had shocked the people of the town. What made it even scarier was that it happened on a Halloween night when so many children were out on the streets. The imaginative minds of several of the neighbors had come up with many strange stories about what had happened to old Flint.

Subtest 3: Inflectional Endings

bake	pale	slow
baker	paler	slower
baked	paling	slowest
bakes	palest	slowly
		slows

Subtest 4: Prefixes

play	mote	form
replay	remote	conform
display	promote	inform
misplay	demote	deform
take	tend	pack
retake	intend	unpack
intake	contend	prepack
mistake	extend	repack
	distend	
	pretend	

Subtest 5: Suffixes

joy	invent	base	elect
joyous	inventive	basement	election
joyful	inventable	baseness	elective
joyless		baseless	

Subtest 6: Compound Words

overdone   motorplane
laterthought   clockrunner
baskethouse

Subtest 7: Affixes

uncall   treeness
proclaim   sunning
indeem   bookful
demark   raytion
prestrain   darkous

Subtest 8: Syllabication

automotive   premeditate
displacement   imperfection
conformation   unreasonable
remarkable   misplaying
impeachable   complicated

Structural Analysis Assessment Test

Student _____   School _____
Teacher _____   Grade _____ Age _____
Examiner _____   Test Dates _____ _____
                                                                    pretest   posttest

---

Subtest 1: Application of Structural Analysis Skills in Context (Part A). Place Part A in front of the student. Say: "Read as many of these words as you can."
The first story is easier than the second.

Stop if the story becomes too difficult. In both stories the words requiring the structural analysis are underlined.
Write the mispronunciations on the story below and note the weak skill areas.

Part A: Winter in the Countryside

It was a cold winter day. The <u>trees</u> were bare and <u>birds</u> could be seen in the <u>countryside</u>. A <u>grasshopper hopped</u> across the road to hide from the cold and the <u>foxes</u> <u>curled</u> up to keep warm. A brown field mouse and her <u>babies</u> came <u>running</u> out of a hole in the ground. The babies were <u>fighting</u> with each other. Mother mouse looked <u>unhappy</u> as she sat on a big, <u>overgrown</u> stump. It was <u>dangerous</u> for the mice to stay above ground, but the <u>active</u> children <u>wanted</u> their <u>lunches</u>. Mother mouse was also <u>nervous</u> about her children <u>eating</u> the <u>poisonous</u> <u>plants</u> that were in the field. The children were <u>curious</u> and the plants <u>looked</u> so <u>attractive</u>.

Just that <u>morning</u>, Mother mouse had a <u>disagreement</u> with Father mouse. The <u>question</u> was whether or not the children should run in the field in the <u>daytime</u>.

Part A *Responses—Circle Incorrect Responses*					*Number Correct*	
Inflectional	*Endings*	*Compounds*	*Suffixes*	*Syllabication*	*Pretest*	*Posttest*
trees	fighting	countryside	active	dangerous		
birds	wanted	grasshopper	nervous	poisonous		
hopped	lunches	overgrown	question	curious		
foxes	eating	daytime		attractive		
curled	plants			disagreement		
babies	looked	*Prefix*				
running	morning	unhappy			/27	/27
					24 = Mastery	

Part B: The Disappearance of Flint

What should have been a great day <u>turned</u> out to be a <u>disappointing</u> one for David King. He found out that he would be the new <u>quarterback</u> for Friday <u>night's</u> game. <u>Unfortunately</u>, he was <u>going</u> to be <u>taking</u> his best friend Ron's place. Ron had <u>gotten</u> a <u>disqualification</u> <u>notice</u> because his <u>grades</u> <u>dropped</u> at the end of the first <u>report</u>. Ron felt that his <u>concentration</u> was poor because of his <u>older</u> <u>brother's</u> <u>recent</u> <u>motorcycle</u> <u>crash</u>. David was sorry about Ron's <u>dismissal</u> from the team, but was <u>shocked</u> by the <u>resentment</u> he saw on Ron's face when he found out who his <u>replacement</u> would be. This was the <u>unfriendliest</u> that Ron had ever <u>treated</u> David.

David thought about the rest of his rather <u>uneventful</u> day as he <u>walked</u> home. He turned on the <u>flashlight</u> he <u>carried</u> with him, for it had grown quite dark. David <u>stopped</u> short when he heard a loud and <u>frightening</u> scream <u>coming</u> from the vacant <u>mansion</u> just up the road.

The place had been empty for <u>years</u> and was in bad shape. <u>Fixing</u> it up had been <u>estimated</u> to be <u>costlier</u> than most <u>families</u> could afford. David had always felt that the mansion had a <u>mysterious</u> look about it. The man who had built and <u>lived</u> in the mansion was <u>believed</u> to be <u>knowledgeable</u> in the ways of <u>witchcraft</u>. His <u>disappearance</u> three years ago had shocked the people of the town. What made it even <u>scarier</u> was that it <u>happened</u> on a <u>Halloween</u> night when so many children were out on the <u>streets</u>. The <u>imaginative</u> <u>minds</u> of <u>several</u> of the <u>neighbors</u> had come up with many strange <u>stories</u> about what had happened to old Flint.

Part B				Number Correct	
Responses—Circle Incorrect Responses					
Inflectional Endings	*Compounds*	*Syllabication*		*Pretest*	*Posttest*
turned carried	quarterback	disappointing	estimated		
night's stopped	motorcycle	Unfortunately	costlier		
going coming	flashlight	disqualification	mysterious		
taking years	witchcraft	concentration	believed		
Ron's Fixing		dismissal	knowledgeable	/53	/53
gotten families	*Prefixes*	resentment	disappearance	48 = Mastery	
grades lived	report	replacement	Halloween		
dropped scarier	recent	unfriendliest	imaginative	Total Score	
older happened		uneventful	several		
brother's streets	*Suffixes*	frightening	neighbors		
shocked minds	notice				
treated stories	mansion				
walked				/80	/80
				72 = Mastery	

Directions	Responses—Circle Incorrect Responses		Number Correct	
			Pretest	Posttest
Subtest 2: Hearing Word Parts Say: "How many syllables do you hear in the word *cowboy . . . , intention . . . , steam . . . , disagreement . . . , randomly?*"	1. cowboy (2) 4. disagreement (4) 2. intention (3) 5. randomly (3) 3. steam (1)		/5	/5
			4 = Mastery	

	Pretest	Posttest
Subtest 3: Inflectional Endings Place Subtest 3 in front of the student. Say: "Read these words. I will read the first one in each column." bake pale slow er er er ed ing est s est ly s	/10	/10 9 = Mastery

Subtest 4: Prefixes
Place Subtest 4 in front of the student. Say: "Read these words. I will read the first one in each column."
 	
play mote form take tend pack
re   re   con re   in   un
dis pro in   in   con pre
mis de de mis ex re
              dis
              pre
	/20	/20
		18 = Mastery

Subtest 5: Suffixes Place Subtest 5 in front of the student. Say: "Read these words. I will read the first one in each column." joy invent base elect ous ive ment ion ful able ness ive less less	/10	/10 9 = Mastery
Subtest 6: Compound Words Place Subtest 6 in front of the student. Say: "Read as many of these words as you can. Some are not real words." (It is more important for the student to recognize the separate units of the words than to pronounce them perfectly.) overdone motorplane laterthought clockrunner baskethouse	/5	/5 4 = Mastery

		Pretest	Posttest
Subtest 7: Affixes Place Subtest 7 in front of the student. Say: "Read as many of these words as you can. Some are not real words." (It is more important for the student to recognize the separate units of the words than to pronounce them perfectly.)	uncall treeness proclaim sunning indeem bookful demark raytion prestrain darkous	/10 9 = Mastery	/10
Subtest 8: Syllabication Place Subtest 8 in front of the student. Say: "Read as many of these words as you can."	automotive premeditate displacement imperfection conformation unreasonable remarkable misplaying impeachable complicated	/10 9 = Mastery	/10

Preparation and Use of Materials for Testing Knowledge of Contractions

PREPARING FOR THE TEST

Before administering the test, remove page 315 and duplicate it so that you will have multiple copies to use as answer sheets for testing each student. Also remove page 313 and use rubber cement or tape to fasten it to a 5" × 8" card. You may then wish to laminate the card or place it in a plastic sleeve so it will not become soiled from handling.

SPECIFIC DIRECTIONS FOR TESTING FOR KNOWLEDGE OF CONTRACTIONS

Have your answer sheet ready (p. 315) and give the student the stimulus sheet (p. 313). Then read the directions on the answer sheet.

IMPORTANT POINTS TO REMEMBER

A rather high percentage of students have occasional problems with the pronunciation of contractions; however, you are likely to find a greater percentage who do not know what two words each contraction represents. Keep in mind that pronunciation is important for reading purposes, but students will not use a contraction in their writing until they know the two words for which it stands.

Knowledge of Contractions

1. aren't
2. can't
3. don't
4. weren't
5. couldn't
6. didn't
7. wasn't
8. hadn't
9. won't
10. haven't
11. isn't
12. wouldn't
13. anybody'd
14. he'll
15. it's
16. here's
17. I'll
18. let's
19. she'll
20. that's
21. where's
22. they'll
23. I'm
24. who'll
25. there's
26. we'll
27. there'll
28. what's
29. you'll
30. doesn't
31. hasn't
32. you'd
33. he'd
34. you're
35. he's
36. I'd
37. we've
38. I've
39. they've
40. she'd
41. who'd
42. she's
43. they'd
44. we'd
45. they're
46. we're
47. you've

Knowledge of Contractions Answer Sheet

Name _____ Date _____

School _____ Tester _____

Directions: Say, "Here is a list of contractions. I want you to begin with number one and say the contraction and then tell what two words it stands for." Following each contraction are two lines. If the student is able to pronounce the contraction correctly, put a plus (+) in the first blank. If he or she can then tell you what two words it stands for, put a plus (+) in the second blank. Mark wrong answers with a minus (−).

1. aren't	____	____	25. there's	____	____
2. can't	____	____	26. we'll	____	____
3. don't	____	____	27. there'll	____	____
4. weren't	____	____	28. what's	____	____
5. couldn't	____	____	29. you'll	____	____
6. didn't	____	____	30. doesn't	____	____
7. wasn't	____	____	31. hasn't	____	____
8. hadn't	____	____	32. you'd	____	____
9. won't	____	____	33. he'd	____	____
10. haven't	____	____	34. you're	____	____
11. isn't	____	____	35. he's	____	____
12. wouldn't	____	____	36. I'd	____	____
13. anybody'd	____	____	37. we've	____	____
14. he'll	____	____	38. I've	____	____
15. it's	____	____	39. they've	____	____
16. here's	____	____	40. she'd	____	____
17. I'll	____	____	41. who'd	____	____
18. let's	____	____	42. she's	____	____
19. she'll	____	____	43. they'd	____	____
20. that's	____	____	44. we'd	____	____
21. where's	____	____	45. they're	____	____
22. they'll	____	____	46. we're	____	____
23. I'm	____	____	47. you've	____	____
24. who'll	____	____			

APPENDIX A-9

Preparation and Use of Materials for the Quick Survey Word List

PREPARATION OF THE QUICK SURVEY WORD LIST

Remove the Quick Survey Word List on page 319 and rubber-cement or tape it to a 5" × 8" card. You may then wish to laminate the card or place it in a plastic sleeve so it will not become soiled from handling.

DIRECTIONS FOR ADMINISTERING THE QUICK SURVEY WORD LIST

The Quick Survey Word List is designed to enable the tester to determine quickly whether a student has the necessary decoding skills to successfully read material written at an adult level. It may be given to students at approximately the fourth-grade level or above to determine whether it is necessary to administer other decoding tests. Students who fail this test will probably need to be given Test A-6, Phonics Assessment, and/or Test A-7, Structural Analysis Assessment.

The student is simply given the word list and asked to pronounce each word. The student should be told, however, that the words he is about to attempt to pronounce are nonsense words or words that are not real words. The student should also be told that the words are very difficult, but that you would like to know if he is able to pronounce them. If the student can pronounce each of the words correctly, it will not be necessary to administer other decoding tests, as the ultimate purpose of learning phonics and structural analysis is to enable the student to attack new words. On the other hand, if it becomes apparent after one or two words that the student is not able to pronounce the words on the Quick Survey Word List, then it should be discontinued.

The correct pronunciation of the words on the Quick Survey Word List is shown on page 321. This key shows the correct pronunciation as well as the part of each word that should be stressed. It should be remembered, however, that accent rules or generalizations pertaining to the English language are not consistent. Therefore, if the words are pronounced correctly except for the accent or stress shown on certain syllables, they should be considered correct. It is also suggested that the page with the correct pronunciation of the Quick Survey Word List be removed, rubber-cemented, or taped to a 5" × 8" card, laminated, and placed in your diagnostic kit.

IMPORTANT POINTS TO REMEMBER ABOUT THE QUICK SURVEY WORD LIST

The Quick Survey Word List is designed to test a student's knowledge of such word-attack skills as structural analysis and accent generalizations. Because phonics knowledge is prerequisite for successful structural analysis, phonics skills can often be inferred from this test as well. It should be stressed, however, that students who do not do well on the list should be stopped after the first two or three words. Remember, only if the student is able to pronounce all of the words correctly (except for accent) should you continue through the entire list. Having a student attempt to pronounce the words when he is not able to do so without difficulty will only discourage him. If the student does not do well on the first one or two words, then you should simply say, "Let's stop. These words are usually meant for adults, and you are not expected to be able to read them."

Quick Survey Word List

wratbeling

dawsnite

pramminciling

whetsplitter

gincule

cringale

slatrungle

twayfrall

spreanplit

goanbate

streegran

glammertickly

grantellean

aipcid

Pronunciation of Quick Survey Words

răt′-bĕl-ĭng

däs′-nīt

prăm′-mĭn-cĭl-ĭng

hwĕt′-splĭt-tər

jĭn′-kyool

crĭn′-gāl

slăt′-rŭn-gəl

twā′-fräl

sprēn′-plĭt

gōn-bāt

strē′-grăn

glăm′-mər-tĭck-ly

grăn′-tĕl-lēn

āp′-sĭd

Pronunciation Key

l—littl<u>e</u>

ə—<u>a</u>bout

ä—f<u>a</u>ther

ə—tamp<u>e</u>r

hw—<u>wh</u>at

kyoo—<u>cu</u>te

Preparation and Use of Materials for Testing Ability to Use Context Clues

PREPARING FOR THE TEST

Pages 327 through 337 contain materials that you may use to test students' ability to use context clues. Each page contains materials for testing context clues at a level from grade 1 to grade 6. To prepare the materials for testing, remove these pages from this appendix. Cut each page in half along the dotted lines and use rubber cement or magic tape to fasten each half of the page to separate sides of a 5" × 8" card. You may then wish to laminate the card or place it in a plastic sleeve to keep it from becoming soiled with use. In fastening the materials to the 5" × 8" card, make sure that the material on one side of the card is in the same position as the material on the other side, so both you and a student can read the materials at the same time. (An alternative is to place each half page on separate cards, one for the student being tested and the other for you. If you do this, you may wish to use different colored cards to distinguish the student's cards from the examiner's cards. This method has the advantage of allowing the student to hold her card so that it will be easier for her to read.)

When all cards are completed, you should place them in grade-level order, so that the front of the first card contains the material to be read by a student reading at first-grade level, the second card contains the materials to be read by a student reading at second-grade level, and so on. The other side of the cards (to be read by the tester) will then contain the same passages as those to be read by the student, except that the words omitted on the student's passage will be underlined on the side seen by the tester. This side of the card also shows the grade level at which the material is written.

SPECIFIC DIRECTIONS FOR ADMINISTERING THE TEST

Begin the test at a level at which you are sure the student can function at her low instructional or independent reading level. Hold the card so the student can read the material on her side. Read the directions printed at the top of the card and then let the student proceed to read orally the passage printed on the other side. It should not be necessary to record the student's errors; however, as the student reads, if you believe you have chosen too difficult a passage to begin with, or too easy a passage to begin with, then move to the next passage that is either easier or more difficult. If the student uses a word that is a logical substitute for the one that is omitted, count it as correct. No norms have been developed for how well students should do in using context clues. However, in these passages it is suggested that you use the following criteria in determining student performance:

No errors	Excellent
One error	Good
Two errors	Fair
Three or more errors	Poor

IMPORTANT POINTS TO REMEMBER

It is often taken for granted that students will automatically attempt to use context clues even though they have not been taught how to do so. This is simply not true. Many readers require a considerable amount of instruction and a great deal of practice in using this skill.

The pages that follow contain materials for testing students' ability to use context clues. It should be stressed that most students will be unable to use context clues effectively unless they are reading at a level that is rather easy for them (their independent or easy instructional level). Therefore, in using the materials, be sure to use only passages that the student would be able to read fairly easily if no words were omitted. If you wish to develop materials for testing students' ability to use context clues, other than those presented on the following pages, the section that follows will be helpful.

DEVELOPING YOUR OWN MATERIALS FOR TESTING STUDENTS' KNOWLEDGE OF CONTEXT CLUES

In constructing materials for testing skill in using context clues, you should first keep in mind that students must be aware of context in their oral language. Depending upon the age/grade level of the students with whom you are working, the following sequence is suggested:

1. Make a tape recording of a passage in which certain words are omitted. Replace words that are omitted with the sound of a bell or tone of some type. When the bell or tone sounds, ask the student to give orally the word that she feels should have appeared in place of the tone. In making either a tape recording or a written exercise for testing context clues, make sure the words that are omitted are ones that can be gotten from the context of the sentence, as in the following example:

Lupe was going to (beep) a party.

It was going to (beep) on Saturday.

She invited some of (beep) friends to come.

She was (beep) happy.

2. Progress to written materials in which the word omitted is replaced with a _____ for each letter omitted as follows:

Lupe was going to __ __ __ __ a party.

It was going to __ __ on Saturday.

She invited some of __ __ __ friends to come.

She was __ __ __ __ happy.

3. Progress to written materials in which the word omitted is replaced with the first letter of the word omitted, and the rest of the letters are replaced with a blank line as follows:

Lupe was going to h _____ a party.

It was going to b _____ on Saturday.

She invited some of h _____ friends to come.

She was v _____ happy.

4. Finally, progress to written materials in which the word omitted is replaced with a line. At this point, be sure to make all lines equal length.

Lupe was going to _____ a party.

It was going to _____ on Saturday.

She invited some of _____ friends to come.

She was _____ happy.

Teacher reads these directions: Here is a story with some words left out. Each time a word is left out, it has been replaced with a line. When you come to a line, try to figure out what word should be in that blank. Ready—begin.

Jan has a cat.

The cat's name is Tab.

Tab does not like dogs.

One day a dog ran after Tab.

Tab ran up a tree.

The dog could not go up the tree.

Then the dog went away.

Grade one reading level

Jan has a cat.

The cat's _____ is Tab.

Tab does not _____ dogs.

One day _____ dog ran after Tab.

_____ ran up a tree.

The dog could not go _____ the tree.

Then _____ dog went away.

Teacher reads these directions: Here is a story with some words left out. Each time a word is left out, it has been replaced with a line. When you come to a line, try to figure out what word should be in that blank. Ready—begin.

One day Sam was going to school.
He was riding with his father in their car.
He looked out of the window and saw an elephant.
He said, "Look, father, there goes an elephant."
Sam's father did not even look because they were
   in a large city.
That day Sam's father heard that
   an elephant had escaped from a circus.
That evening Sam's father said, "I'm sorry, Sam,
   you did see an elephant this morning."

Grade two reading level

One day Sam was going to school.
He was riding with _____ father in their car.
He looked out of the window and _____ an elephant.
He said, "Look, father, _____ goes an elephant."
Sam's _____ did not even look because they were
   in a large city.
That day _____ father heard that
   an elephant had escaped from a circus.
That evening Sam's father said, "I'm sorry, Sam,
   you did _____ an elephant this morning."

Teacher reads these directions: Here is a story with some words left out. Each time a word is left out, it has been replaced with a line. When you come to a line, try to figure out what word should be in that blank. Ready—begin.

Ann and her brother Mike like to play basketball in a park that is far from their home. When they want to play, they usually take a bus to get to the park. There are other boys and girls who play there, too. Sometimes when they go to the park, their father and mother go with them. Their father and mother like to take some food and have a picnic while they are at the park.

Grade three reading level

Ann and her brother Mike like to play basketball in a park that is far from their home. When they _____ to play, they usually take a bus to get _____ the park. There are other boys and girls _____ play there, too. Sometimes when they _____ to the park, their father and _____ go with them. Their father and mother like to take some food and _____ a picnic while they are at the park.

Teacher reads these directions: Here is a story with some words left out. Each time a word is left out, it has been replaced with a line. When you come to a line, try to figure out what word should be in that blank. Ready—begin.

Most kinds of dogs make excellent pets. They <u>can learn fast, and</u> they also <u>have</u> an excellent memory. An intelligent dog can <u>learn</u> to respond to many commands. Many dogs that have been taught well can learn more <u>than</u> 100 words and phrases.

Grade four reading level

Most kinds of dogs make excellent pets. They _____ learn fast, _____ they also _____ an excellent memory. An intelligent _____ can learn _____ respond to many commands. Many dogs that have been taught well can learn more _____ 100 words and phrases.

Teacher reads these directions: Here is a story with some words left out. Each time a word is left out, it has been replaced with a line. When you come to a line, try to figure out what word should be in that blank. Ready—begin.

Fire is very important to all of us today. Wherever ruins of early man have been found, there has always been evidence of fire in that civilization. It is thought that early man may have first found fire when lightning struck trees and caused them to burn. Some people think that man might have been able to start fires by getting them from active volcanoes.

Grade five reading level

Fire is very important to all of us today. Wherever ruins of early man have _____ found, there has always been evidence _____ fire in that civilization. It is thought _____ early man may _____ first found fire when lightning struck trees and caused _____ to burn. Some people think that man might have been able _____ start fires by getting them from active volcanoes.

Teacher reads these directions: Here is a story with some words left out. Each time a word is left out, it has been replaced with a line. When you come to a line, try to figure out what word should be in that blank. Ready—begin.

One of the most famous eagles in the entire world is not the one we see on stamps or coins. It was an eagle caught by an Indian named Blue Sky who lived in Wisconsin. Blue Sky sold the eagle to a man that sold him to a soldier in the Civil War who named him Old Abe. Before the eagle died, he had been through four years of war and had survived twenty-two battles.

Grade six reading level

One of the most famous eagles in the entire world is not the one we see on stamps or coins. It was _____ eagle caught by an Indian named Blue Sky _____ lived in Wisconsin. Blue Sky sold _____ eagle to a man that sold him to a soldier _____ the Civil War who named him Old Abe. Before the eagle died, _____ had been through four years _____ war and had survived twenty-two battles.

Preparation and Use of Materials for the Reading Interest Surveys

PREPARING FOR THE TEST

Before administering the test, choose the appropriate survey based on the age or interest of the student. The first survey is used with elementary students; the second with high school students. Either survey may be appropriate for junior high or middle school students. Remove the selected test page and duplicate it. If you will be administering this test to many students, duplicate multiple copies to use as test/answer sheets. (With each of these surveys, the one page serves as the total test.)

DESCRIPTION OF THE READING INTEREST SURVEYS

This test is designed to assess quickly the student's attitude toward reading and school, areas of reading interest, reading experiences, and conditions affecting reading in the home.

The test may be given orally to young children or students unable to read the questions. Older students or more able readers may complete the form in writing.

SPECIFIC DIRECTIONS FOR GIVING THE READING INTEREST SURVEYS

1. You might want to give this test orally regardless of the student's reading ability. This will allow you to discuss with the student his responses to some of the questions.
2. Encourage the student to give you candid responses to these items. Reassure the student that there are no right or wrong answers; you want to know how the student honestly feels about these questions.
3. Part I consists of open-ended statements. Write down the student's responses as he finishes the sentences.
4. Part II assesses the student's reading interests. If necessary, explain to the student what some of the categories are on the elementary survey.
5. Part III examines the student's reading experiences and some of the factors that may affect the student's reading behavior at home or outside of school.
6. After you have recorded the student's responses, use this information when you plan the remediation program.

READING INTEREST SURVEY–ELEMENTARY

Student _____   School _____

Teacher _____   Grade _____   Age _____

Examiner _____   Test Dates _____   _____
                                                            Pretest   *Posttest*

I. Open-Ended Questions

I like school if   _____

I wish _____

When I grow up _____

Reading makes me   _____

Books are   _____

I like to read when   _____

Teachers should   _____

II. Reading Interests

I like to read about:

_____ Science	_____ Dogs
_____ Biography	_____ Mysteries
_____ Sports	_____ Science Fiction
_____ People	_____ Riddles
_____ History	_____ Plays
_____ Horses	_____ Monsters
_____ Fantasy	_____ Poetry

I do *not* like to read about   _____

_____

If I had my choice, I would really like to read about   _____

_____

_____

III. Reading Experiences

The last book I read was   _____

My three favorite books are   _____

_____

People in my family read:

_____ Books   _____ Magazines   _____ Newspapers

I watch television, use my computer, or play video games about _____ hours per day.

The hours I watch television or play video games are from _____ to _____.

I visit the public library:

_____ Often   _____ Seldom   _____ Never

READING INTEREST SURVEY–ADULT

Student _____ School _____

Teacher _____ Grade _____ Age _____

Examiner _____ Test Dates _____ _____

                                                                        Pretest   *Posttest*

I. Open-Ended Questions

What are your favorite activities? _____

_____

What are your career or educational goals? _____

_____

How do you feel about school? _____

_____

How do you feel about your classes and your instructors? _____

_____

II. Reading Interests

What do you enjoy reading about? _____

_____

What do you *not* enjoy reading about? _____

_____

What do you usually read: Books? Magazines? Newspapers? Internet? _____

_____

When do you read? When you have to? Or do you also read for pleasure? _____

_____

III. Reading Experiences

What do you remember about your early reading experiences? For instance, did your parents
read to you when you were a child? _____

_____

What was the last book you read? _____

_____

What are your three favorite books? _____

_____

How would you define reading? _____

_____

How do you think reading affects your life? _____

_____

APPENDICES FOR CORRECTING
READING DIFFICULTIES

Books for Emergent Readers

Many book lists include titles that are no longer in print. At the time of publication, all of these titles are available. The lists that follow include both classics and highly rated contemporary books.

Rhyming Books

Bears in Pairs   (Niki Yektai, Bradbury, 1987)

Buzz Said the Bee   (Wendy Lewison, Scholastic, 1992)

Chicken Soup with Rice   (Maurice Sendak, Scholastic, 1962)

Down by the Bay   (Raffi, Crown, 1987)

Each Peach Pear Plum   (Janet and Allan Ahlberg, Viking Press, 1979)

A Giraffe and a Half   (Shel Silverstein, HarperCollins, 1975)

I Can Fly   (Ruth Krauss, Western Publishing, 1992)

Is Your Mama a Llama?   (Deborah Guarino, Scholastic, 1989)

Jake Baked the Cake   (B. G. Hennessey, Viking, 1990)

Jamberry   (Bruce Degen, HarperTrophy, 1985)

Jesse Bear, What Will You Wear?   (Nancy Carlstrom, Simon & Schuster, 1986)

There's a Wocket in My Pocket   (Dr. Seuss, Random House, 1974)

Sheep in a Jeep   (Nancy Shaw, Houghton Mifflin, 1986)

Sheep on a Ship   (Nancy Shaw, Houghton Mifflin, 1989)

Shoes   (Elizabeth Winthrop, Harper Trophy, 1986)

Sing a Song of Popcorn: Every Child's Book of Poems   (Beatrice Schenk de Regniers, Scholastic, 1988)

Sleep Rhymes Around the World   (Jane Yolen, Boyds Mills, 2000)

Street Rhymes Around the World   (Jane Yolen, Wordsong, 1992)

Books With Alliteration

A Mountain Alphabet   (Margaret Ruurs, Tundra Books, 1996)[*]

A, My Name Is Alice   (Jane Bayer, Dial, 1984)[*]

Accidental Zucchini: An Unexpected Alphabet   (Max Grover, Harcourt Brace, 1993)[*]

---

*Books with asterisks are also alphabet books.

Alligators All Around: An Alphabet   (Maurice Sendak, Harper & Row, 1962)[*]

Alphabears: An ABC Book   (Kathleen Hague, Holt, Rinehart & Winston, 1984)[*]

Animalia   (Graeme Base, Abrams, 1987)[*]

Aster Aardvark's Alphabet Adventures   (Steven Kellogg, Morrow, 1987)[*]

Busy Buzzing Bumblebees and Other Tongue Twisters   (Alvin Schwartz, Harper-Collins, 1987)

Dr. Seuss's ABC   (Dr. Seuss, Random House, 1963)[*]

Four Famished Foxes and Fosdyke   (Pamela Duncan Edwards, HarperCollins, 1995)

Six Sick Sheep: 101 Tongue Twisters   (Joanna Cole, Beech Tree, 1993)

Alphabet Books

The ABC Bunny   (Wanda Gag, Coward-McCann, 1933)

Alphabet Art: With A-Z Animal Art & Fingerplays   (Judy Press, Williamson Publishing, 1997)

Alphabet City   (Stephen Johnson, Viking Press, 1996)

Alphabet Soup   (Kate Banks, Knopf, 1994)

The Alphabet Tale   (Jan Garten, Random House, 1964)

Ashanti to Zulu: African Traditions   (Margaret Musgrove, Dial, 1976)

The Butterfly Alphabet   (Kjell Sandved, Scholastic, 1996)

C Is for Curious: An ABC of Feelings   (Woodleigh Hubbard, Chronicle Books, 1990)

Chicka Chicka Boom Boom   (John Archambault, Simon & Schuster, 1989)

City Seen from A to Z   (Rachel Isadora, Morrow, 1983)

The Dinosaur Alphabet Book   (Jerry Palotta, Charlesbridge Publishing, 1990)

Eating the Alphabet: Fruits and Vegetables from A to Z   (Lois Ehlert, Harcourt Brace, 1989)

From Acorn to Zoo and Everything in Between in Alphabetical Order   (Satoshi Kitamura, Farrar, Straus & Giroux, 1992)

Harold's ABC   (Crockett Johnson, HarperCollins, 1981)

I Spy: An Alphabet in Art   (Lucy Micklethwait, Greenwillow, 1992)

K Is for Kiss Good Night: A Bedtime Alphabet   (Jill Sardegna, Doubleday, 1994)

On Market Street   (Anita Lobel, Greenwillow, 1981)

Pigs from A to Z   (Arthur Geisert, Houghton Mifflin, 1986)

26 Letters and 99 Cents   (Tana Hoban, Greenwillow, 1987)

The Z Was Zapped: A Play in Twenty-Six Acts   (Chris Van Allsburg, Houghton Mifflin, 1987)

Basic Sight Word Sentences

HOW TO USE THE BASIC SIGHT WORD SENTENCES

This appendix contains a list of basic sight word sentences that may be used to provide students with practice in learning the basic sight words in context. The basic sight word phrases listed in Appendix A-5 were used to create these sentences.

Students may practice these sentences alone, with other students, or with parents at home. You may also make an audio tape of the sentences as described in Appendix B-7. Because it is important for students to *master* basic sight words, it is appropriate for students to practice these sentences over and over. They may also create their own sentences using the sight word phrases or incorporate them in language-experience activities. The underlined words that appear on the list are nouns drawn from the preprimer level of a basal series.

A common approach that teachers use in teaching the basic sight words, phrases, and sentences follows these steps:

1. The student learns the basic sight words from one sublist at a time. (Each sublist contains 20 words.)
2. The student learns the basic sight word phrases from the same sublist.
3. The student learns the basic sight word sentences from the same sublist.
4. Reinforce the learnings in each previous step by having the student read as much as possible from low-level texts that incorporate many basic sight words and by having the student participate in language-experience activities.
5. After the basic sight words from one sublist are mastered, go on to the next sublist and repeat steps 1 through 4.

BASIC SIGHT WORD SENTENCES

List I

1. She said that it was you.
2. He and I had the <u>duck</u>.
3. They said he had to.
4. But she said it was his.
5. It was on that turtle.
6. He said that it was in it.
7. A <u>duck</u> was for you.
8. They had that for you.
9. She said that of you.
10. <u>They</u> said it was for you.

List II

1. Look at him out there.
2. There is some for her.
3. We have to go out there.
4. Then look up at him.
5. I have to go with her.
6. They had as little as he had.
7. All of it is there.
8. Go down there and look.
9. I am little.
10. Be there with him.

List III

1. I will get them a <u>cat</u>.
2. See what you can do.
3. I like this one a little.
4. Would you look at it for me?
5. My <u>turtle</u> is not little.
6. Could you get some for her?
7. When will you see him?
8. Yes, they were there.
9. He did it for them.
10. Get it so I can see it.

List IV

1. Get the big blue <u>book</u>.
2. When it's over, come to see me.
3. Its ride is very long.
4. No one came to ask her.
5. I would like an apple that is red.
6. He came in just now.
7. If you ask, they will come.
8. They went in to see him.
9. They are your books.
10. He will ride out.

List V

1. I can take it from there.
2. They don't want to do it now.
3. How did you know it was right?
4. She got her four pretty little <u>rabbits</u>.
5. Don't jump around there.
6. Where did he put the good one?
7. It was too little for me.
8. I take every red and green one.
9. It is about this long.
10. Don't put any around there.

List VI

1. They ran away from here.
2. Call after six, then come over.
3. He ran and got his yellow <u>duck</u>.
4. I think I saw the brown <u>turtle</u>.
5. He can help to make her well.
6. I like going to sleep here.
7. Five old <u>turtles</u> are there.
8. Let me ask her to come.
9. He will come by after five.
10. Their cat ran around here.

List VII
1. We can help you eat.
2. The two <u>ducks</u> may walk over there.
3. He will take off the round can.
4. Help him to come before seven.
5. It is very cold today.
6. I do not like to play by myself.
7. I don't know where to stop.
8. When can it fly again?
9. They have never been there.
10. Who had eight yellow ducks?

List VIII
1. Their cat was black and white.
2. May we start to play?
3. You must try once, then try again.
4. Always write your name before you start.
5. Tell her to give it to him.
6. You must drink all of it.
7. Do the work first, then play.
8. You may keep the ten new <u>turtles</u>.
9. How much does he bring?
10. He goes to him for help.

List IX
1. Soon they will find only three of us there.
2. He ate it before it got warm.
3. Our work gave them much help.
4. Will you buy those funny yellow ducks?
5. Hold it open for her.
6. He has made a cold drink.
7. Better start to work right now.
8. It is all done for you.
9. It is cold, so run and jump around.
10. He said he can make it fall.

List X
1. Use the right light when you read.
2. Both of you will sit here.
3. Run too fast and you may fall.
4. They found it under here.
5. Can you pick it up?
6. The cut hurt very much.
7. Say which one you want.
8. I will carry the small one myself.
9. Why pull it up there?
10. My own work is kind of good.

List XI
1. Please thank him for the cold drink.
2. I live far from here.
3. It will grow best over here.
4. I like to laugh and sing, don't you?
5. I wish these were together.
6. How many shall come here?
7. Wash, because you must keep clean.
8. Draw it, then show it to him.
9. She gave him a hot drink.
10. She will start to say, "Once upon. . . ."

A Phonics Primer

SINGLE CONSONANTS

b	bear	*l*	lake	*t*	turtle
d	dog	*m*	money	*v*	vase
f	face	*n*	nose	*w*	wagon
h	hen	*p*	pear	*y*	yellow
j	jug	*q*	queen	*z*	zebra
k	king	*r*	rat		

The following consonants have two or more sounds:

c	cat	*g*	goat	*s*	six	*x*	xylophone
c	city	*g*	germ	*s*	is	*x*	exist
				s	sure	*x*	box

When *g* is followed by *e, i,* or *y,* it often takes the soft sound of *j,* as in *gentle* and *giant.* If it is not followed by these letters, it usually takes the hard sound, as illustrated in such words as *got* and *game.*

When *c* is followed by *e, i,* or *y,* it usually takes the soft sound heard in *cent.* If it is not followed by these letters, it usually takes the hard sound heard in *come.*

Qu usually has the sound of *kw;* however, in some words such as *bouquet,* it has the sound of *k.*

CONSONANT BLENDS

Beginning

bl	blue	*pr*	pretty	*tw*	twin
br	brown	*sc*	score	*wr*	wrench
cl	clown	*sk*	skill	*sch*	school
cr	crown	*sl*	slow	*scr*	screen
dr	dress	*sm*	small	*shr*	shrink
dw	dwell	*sn*	snail	*spl*	splash
fl	flower	*sp*	spin	*spr*	spring
fr	from	*st*	story	*squ*	squash
gl	glue	*sw*	swan	*str*	string
gr	grape	*tr*	tree	*thr*	throw
pl	plate				

Ending

ld	wild
mp	lamp
nd	wind
nt	went
rk	work
sk	risk

CONSONANT DIGRAPHS

ch	chute	*sh*	ship
ch	choral	*th*	three
ch	church	*th*	that
gh	cough	*wh*	which
ph	phonograph	*wh*	who

VOWEL SOUNDS

Short Sounds   # Long Sounds

a	bat	*a*	rake
e	bed	*e*	jeep
i	pig	*i*	kite
o	lock	*o*	rope
u	duck	*u*	mule

W is sometimes used as a vowel, as in the *aw*, *ew*, and *ow* diphthongs (see the following list). *W* is usually used as a vowel on word endings and as a consonant at the beginning of words.

Y is usually a consonant when it appears at the beginning of a word and a vowel in any other position.

Three consonants usually affect or control the sounds of some, or all, of the vowels when they follow these vowels within a syllable. They are *r*, *w*, and *l* (sometimes known as <u>R</u>eally <u>W</u>eird <u>L</u>etters).

r	w	l
car	law	all
her	few	bell
dirt	now	
word		
fur		

VOWEL DIGRAPHS (Most common phonemes only)

<u>ai</u> pain

<u>ay</u> hay

<u>ea</u> each or weather   (Other phonemes are common for *ea*.)

<u>ee</u> meet

ei weight or either   (Other phonemes are common for *ei*.)

ie piece   (Other phonemes are common for *ie*.)

<u>oa</u> oats

oo book or moon

ou tough (digraph) or house (diphthong)

ow low (digraph) or cow (diphthong)

Of the various consonant digraphs, those that are most regular in their pronunciation are underlined here and are represented by this phrase: M*ai*ds m*ay* *ea*t *oa*k tr*ee*s. (Unfortunately, *ea* does have many exceptions!)

DIPHTHONGS (Pronounced: dif´ thongs)

au haul		*oi* soil	
au hawk		*ou* trout	
ew few		*ow* cow	
ey they		*oy* boy	

In a diphthong, both of the vowel letters are heard and they make a gliding sound, which is heard most easily in words like *cow* and *boy*. Some speakers may hear the examples of *au*, *aw*, and *ey* given here as digraphs (one sound) rather than diphthongs.

Phonogram Lists

Research in the field of reading shows that the strategy of looking for "little words" in big or longer words is a poor practice because the shorter word often changes in longer words. For example, in the word *government* we would find the words *go*, *over*, and *men;* yet of these three words, only *men* retains the normal sound of the shorter or smaller word. You may wish to experiment with other words.

However, a similar approach works well for students who need to learn phonics as a tool to pronounce unknown words. In using this approach, one looks for phonograms in words. A *phonogram* is a word part consisting of a series of letters that are often found together, such as *all*, *ell*, *old*, or *ime*. These word parts always begin with a vowel and are frequently referred to as *vowel families* or *word families*. In recent years, the term **rime** has been used as a synonym for *phonogram*. The term **onset** refers to the consonant(s) at the beginning of a syllable. For example, in the word *bat*, the letter *b* is an onset and the letters *at* are a rime or phonogram. Similarly, in the word *street*, the letters *str* are an onset and the letters *eet* are a rime or phonogram.

Whether you use the term *phonogram* or refer to *onsets* and *rimes*, it is important to know that these word parts can be highly useful in teaching phonics skills. In learning phonograms, students also learn many consonant and consonant cluster sounds, as well as the sounds for long and short vowels, vowel pairs, and *r-*, *l-*, and *w*-controlled vowels. Furthermore, a high percentage of phonograms retain the same sounds in longer words that they stand for in the simple phonograms themselves. Therefore, helping students learn many phonograms will, in turn, help them immediately identify these same sounds in longer words.

In the sections that follow, you will find a description of the phonogram lists and an explanation of how to use these lists to teach phonics.

DESCRIPTION OF THE PHONOGRAM LISTS

The phonogram lists were developed initially by identifying and analyzing the phonograms in words that appeared in eight sets of basal readers. In this appendix, a total of 216 different phonograms are presented alphabetically in sets of 10 phonograms per list, except for the final list, which has six phonograms. Each of these phonograms is followed by sample words in which the phonograms appear. The number of sample words per phonogram ranges from a low of two (for the phonogram -*amb*), to a high of 24 words (for the phonogram -*ay*).

When learning to read using a phonogram approach, it is not essential for the student to know the meanings of all the words. Indeed, some phonogram programs include

List 1
Phonograms and Words

1. ab   blab, <u>cab</u>, crab, dab, drab, flab, <u>grab</u>, jab, nab, <u>scab</u>, slab, stab, tab

2. ace   <u>brace</u>, face, grace, <u>lace</u>, mace, pace, <u>place</u>, race, space, trace

3. ack*   back, <u>black</u>, clack, <u>crack</u>, hack, jack, lack, pack, quack, rack, sack, <u>shack</u>, slack, smack, <u>snack</u>, stack, tack, <u>track</u>, whack

4. ad   bad, brad, clad, <u>dad</u>, fad, <u>glad</u>, <u>had</u>, lad, mad, pad, sad

5. ade   blade, fade, grade, jade, made, <u>shade</u>, <u>spade</u>, <u>trade</u>, wade

6. afe   chafe, <u>safe</u>, strafe

7. ag   <u>bag</u>, <u>brag</u>, crag, <u>drag</u>, <u>flag</u>, gag, hag, lag, nag, rag, sag, shag, slag, <u>snag</u>, stag, swag, tag, wag

8. age   <u>cage</u>, page, rage, sage, <u>stage</u>, wage

9. aid   <u>braid</u>, laid, <u>maid</u>, <u>paid</u>, raid

10. ail*   bail, fail, flail, frail, hail, jail, mail, nail, <u>pail</u>, <u>quail</u>, rail, sail, <u>snail</u>, tail, <u>trail</u>, wail

FIGURE B-4.1

nonsense words for students to pronounce. However, we believe it is helpful if students have at least low-level recognition of the words when decoding, as described in the discussion section at the beginning of Chapter 21. Therefore, every real word is not listed for each phonogram because the meanings of some of the words are quite obscure. Even among the words that are listed, you will find some that are not commonly used and will not be known to your students. You may wish to provide students with brief definitions or synonyms to help them understand these words as they appear.

The 37 Most Useful Phonograms*

ack	ap	est	ing	ot
ail	ash	ice	ink	uck
ain	at	ick	ip	ug
ake	ate	ide	it	ump
ale	aw	ight	ock	unk
ame	ay	ill	oke	
an	eat	in	op	
ank	ell	ine	ore	

*Identified by Wylie and Durrell (1970)

FIGURE B-4.2

Each list of 10 phonograms is followed by a set of sentences. The sentences were created so you may provide students with important practice reading the phonograms in context. Each of the phonograms is presented in at least one of the sentences, and most of the sentences include three or more of the phonograms from the accompanying list. The phonograms and words from list 1 illustrate how the phonograms are used in the sentences. (See Figure B-4.1.)

The underlined words are those that were used in the list 1 sentences. As you can see, seven of the ten phonograms on that list were used three or more times in the accompanying sentences, the phonogram *-age* was used twice, and the rare phonogram *-afe* was used once.

Many years ago, Wylie and Durrell (1970) conducted research that identified what they claimed were the 37 most useful phonograms. According to Wylie and Durrell, these 37 phonograms appeared in nearly 500 primary grade words. They are listed on the chart in Figure B-4.2.

Each of these 37 phonograms is designated with an asterisk in the phonogram lists presented in this appendix.

USING THE PHONOGRAM LIST TO TEACH PHONICS

Many students who have problems in learning to read also seem to have problems learning various rules for vowel and consonant sounds. These same students also have difficulty learning sounds in isolation. In using the phonogram approach, the student learns automatically and is not required to learn rules. We have found that many students can greatly expand their knowledge of phonics in a very short time using the phonogram lists. With practice in the act of reading using the sentences and other activities, the transfer to reading behavior can occur rapidly and permanently. Use the following procedure to teach students to decode using the phonogram lists.

Teaching Procedure

1. Prior to teaching the phonograms, check to confirm that the student has mastered the sound-symbol relationships for the beginning consonants, blends, and digraphs. If the student does not know these, they must be taught before proceeding with the following steps.

2. Present the *ab* phonogram. You may write it on chart paper, the chalkboard or white board, or other media.

3. Have the student tell you the names of the two letters and the sounds they make. If necessary, tell the student the individual letter sounds and pronounce the whole phonogram /ab/. Have the student repeat the phonogram sound /ab/ after you.

4. Write an easy single consonant in front of the phonogram, such as *tab*. Ask the student to pronounce the new word. Do the same with other single consonants. If the student is successful, move to the consonant blends and digraphs.

5. Have the student read the phonogram words in order, as shown below:

   ab   blab, cab, crab, dab, drab, flab, grab, jab, nab, scab, slab, stab, tab

6. If the student is successful, point to the words in mixed order and have the student read them as you point.

7. When you believe the student has mastered the first phonogram, introduce the next phonogram. Let the student's success dictate the speed of presentation.

8. Once the student is able to read the phonograms and words on list 1, have her read the list 1 sentences.

9. Provide the student with practice in the act of reading. Have the student read simple sentences or stories that you have created that use the words just taught along with other easy words the student already knows. You may also have the student dictate simple stories to you in which she uses the newly learned words in context. Later, the student can copy her simple stories for additional practice. Finally, have the student read published easy readers that provide repetitive practice on these phonic elements. *This last step is extremely important.*

Alternate Teaching Procedure

If the student is not successful with the approach suggested previously, use the alternate approach that follows:

Say:

"I am going to say a number and then some words. As I say the words, you are to point to each word and say it right after you hear me say it. Be sure to point to the word as you say it.

Number one: ab   blab, cab, crab, dab, drab, flab, grab, jab, nab, scab, slab, stab, tab

Number two: ace   brace, face, grace, lace, mace, pace, place, race, space, trace

In speaking the words, pause slightly after each word so that the student will have time to look at the word and say it before you say the next word. *However, it is very important to keep a rather brisk pace so the student does not become bored. It is also very important that the student be required to point to each word as she says it. The importance of this cannot be overemphasized.*

You may also create a tape recording of the script described above. After you have introduced a few of the phonograms to the student, you may let the student continue on her own by listening to the tape and carefully following the directions.

When teachers first begin to use either of these methods, they often ask, "How many rows should I expect the student to learn at one time?" The answer to this is not a simple one: it depends on how fast the student learns. To make this determination, begin with about 10 rows. Have the student listen to the tape enough times so that she can do the exercise without listening to the tape recording; that is, have her point to the words and say them just as she did when listening to the tape recorder. If you find the student does not know nearly all of the phonograms already studied, or that it takes an inordinate amount of time for her to learn 10 rows, then next time do only five rows. Adjust the number of rows so that the student can learn all the words without a great deal of difficulty. However, this is not to say that the student should not have to listen to the tape and go over the words many times.

Another frequently asked question is, "How many times should the student have to listen to the tape recording and say the words before she learns them?" Again, the answer to this question is not a simple one. The best approach to this is simply to tell the student that you want her to listen to the words enough times to learn all the words on the recording. The student will then be the best judge of just how many times she needs to listen to the tape to learn all of the words.

If the student is learning the phonograms on her own using the tape recorder, you can check on her progress by having her read the sentences that accompany the word lists. If the student is reading the sentences without error, then you will know that she is being successful learning the words on her own.

If you find that approximately 10 rows is best for the student, then continue to give her about 10 rows at a time until she knows all of the phonograms. When she has mastered this task, not only will she know the phonograms found in most words, but she will also have learned nearly all of the beginning sounds (consonants, consonant blends, and consonant digraphs). The student will also have internalized several of the most common vowel rules.

List 1
Phonograms and Words

1. ab blab, cab, crab, dab, drab, flab, grab, jab, nab, scab, slab, stab, tab

2. ace brace, face, grace, lace, mace, pace, place, race, space, trace

3. ack* back, black, clack, crack, hack, jack, lack, pack, quack, rack, sack, shack, slack, smack, snack, stack, tack, track, whack

4. ad bad, brad, clad, dad, fad, glad, had, lad, mad, pad, sad

5. ade blade, fade, grade, jade, made, shade, spade, trade, wade

6. afe chafe, safe, strafe

7. ag bag, brag, drag, flag, gag, hag, lag, nag, rag, sag, shag, slag, snag, stag, swag, tag, wag

8. age cage, page, rage, sage, stage, wage

9. aid braid, laid, maid, paid, raid

10. ail* bail, fail, flail, frail, hail, jail, mail, nail, pail, quail, rail, sail, snail, tail, trail, wail

List 1 Sentences

1. Katie was glad when she ate her snack in the shade.

2. After he fell on the trail, he got a scab and had to wear a brace.

3. Put the snail in the cage and cover it with the flag.

4. Do you want to meet on the stage and trade places?

5. Jill had a braid in her hair and a bag on her arm.

6. His dad paid the cab driver with money from the safe.

7. Her maid tried to grab the quail off of the train track.

8. Don't snag the lace on your black dress on the wall of my shack.

9. Did you brag when you had the spade that won the card game?

10. Drag the pail over the crack in the road.

List 2
Phonograms and Words

11. ain*   brain, chain, drain, gain, grain, lain, main, pain, plain, rain, slain, Spain, sprain, stain, strain, train, twain, vain

12. aint   faint, paint, quaint, saint, taint

13. air   chair, fair, flair, hair, lair, pair, stair

14. ake*   bake, brake, cake, drake, fake, flake, lake, make, quake, rake, sake, shake, slake, snake, stake, take, wake

15. ale*   bale, gale, hale, kale, male, pale, sale, scale, shale, stale, tale, whale

16. alk   balk, chalk, stalk, talk, walk

17. all   ball, call, fall, gall, hall, mall, pall, small, squall, stall, tall, wall

18. am   clam, cram, gram, ham, jam, lam, ram, scam, scram, sham, slam, swam, tram, yam

19. amb   jamb, lamb

20. ame*   blame, came, dame, fame, flame, frame, game, lame, name, same, shame, tame

List 2 Sentences

11. That lamb from Spain has a plain name.

12. The pale man sat in his chair after he saw the snake.

13. There was a squall on the lake, and I thought I would faint.

14. Katie looked pale when we looked at a brain in the lab.

15. In a quake, everything on Main Street will shake.

16. Did you see them paint the train?

17. Walk up the stairs to my room, but don't slam the door.

18. Write your name with the small chalk.

19. Shame on you for being a part of the scam.

20. I will bake a plain small cake and put jam on top.

List 3
Phonograms and Words

21. amp   camp, champ, clamp, cramp, damp, lamp, ramp, scamp, stamp, tamp, vamp

22. an*   ban, bran, can, clan, span, tan, than, van

23. and   band, bland, grand, hand, land, sand, stand, strand

24. ane   bane, cane, crane, lane, mane, pane, plane, sane, cane, wane

25. ang   bang, clang, fang, hang, pang, rang, sang, slang, sprang, twang

26. ange   change, grange, mange, range, strange

27. ank*   bank, blank, clank, crank, dank, drank, flank, frank, plank, prank, rank, sank, shank, shrank, spank, stank, swank, tank, thank, yank

28. ant   pant, plant, slant

29. ap*   cap, chap, clap, flap, gap, lap, map, rap, sap, scrap, slap, snap, strap, tap, trap, wrap, yap, zap

30. ape   cape, drape, nape, scrape, shape, tape

List 3 Sentences

21. The ramp was leaning against the wall at a slant.

22. Strap the grand piano into the van.

23. The damp room really stank.

24. Keep a scrap of the cape in the box.

25. She drank water on the plane.

26. Hang the plant next to the drapes.

27. Shane went to change the music.

28. The purple tie and the tan cap are strange.

29. Did you scrape your arm on the wood plank?

30. I will bang the can with a cane.

List 4
Phonograms and Words

31. ar   bar, car, far, jar, mar, par, scar, spar, star, tar

32. arch   march, parch, starch

33. ard   card, guard, hard, lard, yard

34. arge   barge, charge, large

35. ark   bark, Clark, dark, hark, lark, mark, park, shark, spark, stark

36. arm   charm, farm, harm

37. arn   barn, darn, yarn

38. arp   carp, harp, sharp

39. art   cart, chart, dart, hart, mart, part, smart, start, tart

40. ase   base, case, chase, vase

List 4 Sentences

31. Did you play darts when you were in the barn?

32. The guard was a smart man.

33. Let's march over to the park to play.

34. Would you see a shark if you went to a farm?

35. That is a large scar on your leg.

36. There was a gold star on the top of the harp.

37. Chase the dog across the yard and she will bark.

38. If the bull charges, he will harm you.

39. Use a sharp needle to sew with that yarn.

40. To get past the tar, push the cart hard.

List 5
Phonograms and Words

41. ash*   bash, brash, cash, clash, crash, dash, flash, gash, gnash, hash, lash, mash, rash, sash, slash, smash, stash, splash, thrash, trash

42. ask   bask, cask, flask, mask, task

43. ast   blast, cast, fast, last, mast, past, vast

44. aste   baste, haste, paste, taste, waste

45. at*   bat, brat, cat, chat, fat, flat, gnat, hat, mat, pat, rat, sat, scat, slat, spat, that, vat

46. ate*   bate, crate, date, fate, gate, grate, hate, late, mate, pate, plate, rate, skate, slate, spate, state

47. ath   bath, math, path

48. ause   cause, clause, pause

49. ave   brave, cave, crave, gave, grave, pave, rave, save, shave, slave, stave, wave

50. aw*   caw, claw, draw, flaw, gnaw, jaw, law, raw, saw, slaw, squaw, straw, thaw

List 5 Sentences

41. Do not splash the water when you take a bath.

42. Dave was mad and wanted to smash his dinner plate.

43. We are going to pave the path up to the gate.

44. In a war, people have to be brave when they hear the blast of a gun.

45. Did that skate cause her to crash?

46. At the pool you can bask in the sun and sip your drink through a straw.

47. Can you draw fast or do you have to pause?

48. She called her little brother a brat when he took her toothpaste.

49. We should chat about your math work.

50. Take off your mask so you can taste the food.

List 6
Phonograms and Words

51. awk   hawk, squawk

52. awl   bawl, brawl, crawl, drawl, scrawl, shawl, sprawl

53. awn   brawn, dawn, drawn, fawn, lawn, pawn, prawn, spawn, yawn

54. ay*   bay, bray, day, flay, fray, gray, hay, jay, lay, may, pay, play, pray, ray, say, slay, spay, splay, spray, stay, stray, sway, tray, way

55. ayed   brayed, flayed, frayed, grayed, played, prayed, spayed, sprayed, stayed, swayed

56. ead   bread, dead, dread, head, lead, read, spread, thread, tread

57. each   beach, bleach, breach, leach, peach, preach, reach, teach

58. ead   bead, lead, plead, read, stead

59. eal   deal, heal, meal, peal, real, seal, squeal, steal, teal, veal

60. eam   beam, cream, dream, gleam, ream, scream, seam, steam, stream, team

List 6 Sentences

51. Crawl across the beach and feel the ocean spray.

52. Did she squeal or scream when you sprayed her with water?

53. Can you reach my gray shawl?

54. Did you see the hawk land in the stream?

55. I really like to eat peaches and cream.

56. It is not right to steal.

57. Spread your blanket on the lawn and I will teach you.

58. There are four red beads on the thread.

59. The fawn stayed away from us when we went outside.

60. He will lead us to the team.

List 7
Phonograms and Words

61. ean   bean, clean, glean, Jean, lean, mean, wean

62. eap   cheap, heap, leap, reap

63. ease   please, tease

64. east   beast, feast, least, yeast

65. eat*   beat, bleat, cheat, cleat, feat, heat, meat, neat, peat, pleat, seat, treat, wheat

66. ear   clear, dear, fear, hear, near, rear, sear, smear, shear, spear

67. earn   learn, yearn

68. eck   check, deck, neck, peck, speck, wreck

69. ed   bed, bled, bred, fed, fled, led, shed, sled, sped, red, shred, wed

70. edge   hedge, ledge, wedge

List 7 Sentences

61. Please don't be mean to the puppy.

62. The car sped along the hedge and around the block.

63. I see a speck of dirt in the yeast.

64. The feast was very cheap.

65. If meat is lean, that means it has little fat.

66. A farmer must reap the wheat from his fields.

67. Your sister fled because she knew you would tease her.

68. It was clear we had to wedge the treat in the box to hide it.

69. Did you learn to check your math work?

70. I yearn to be as near to a beach as I can be.

List 8
Phonograms and Words

71. eed   bleed, breed, creed, deed, feed, freed, greed, heed, reed, seed, speed, steed, tweed, weed

72. eek   cheek, creek, Greek, leek, meek, reek, peek, seek, sleek, week

73. eel   feel, heel, keel, kneel, peel, reel, steel, wheel

74. eem   deem, seem, teem

75. een   green, keen, preen, queen, screen, seen, sheen, spleen, teen

76. eep   beep, cheep, creep, deep, jeep, keep, peep, seep, sheep, sleep, steep, sweep, weep

77. eer   cheer, deer, jeer, leer, peer, seer, sheer, sneer, steer, veer

78. eet   beet, feet, fleet, greet, meet, sheet, skeet, sleet, street, sweet, tweet

79. eeze   breeze, freeze, sneeze, squeeze, tweeze, wheeze

80. eft   cleft, deft, left, theft

List 8 Sentences

71. Don't steer the jeep so far to the left on the street.

72. When he was freed, he wanted to cheer.

73. Did you kneel when you went to greet the queen?

74. The creep went to look at himself in his new tweed coat.

75. There is a lot of theft in that mall, but no one has been hurt.

76. Does your grandma squeeze your cheeks when she sees you?

77. The warm breeze came right through the screen.

78. Does it seem as hard as steel?

79. The heel on her shoe was very sleek.

80. You can steer with your left hand on the wheel.

List 9
Phonograms and Words

81. eg   beg, leg, peg

82. eld   held, meld, weld

83. elf   self, shelf

84. ell*   bell, cell, dell, dwell, fell, jell, Nell, quell, sell, shell, smell, spell, swell, tell, well, yell

85. elp   help, kelp, whelp, yelp

86. elt   belt, dwelt, felt, melt, pelt, smelt, welt

87. em   gem, hem, stem, them

88. en   den, hen, men, pen, ten, then, when, wren, yen, zen

89. ence   fence, hence, pence, thence, whence

90. ench   bench, blench, clench, drench, French, quench, stench, trench, wrench

List 9 Sentences

81. The Frenchman lived in the city, and on hot days he thought he would melt.

82. The food has started to rot, hence the bad smell.

83. Did you clench your teeth when you felt the pain in your leg?

84. The men said the new fence looks swell.

85. He stood on the bench and held the shelf for me. I used a peg to hang it on the wall.

86. He yelled for help when he fell down.

87. If you go to the sea, you will find kelp and shells.

88. Don't hurt yourself when you cut the rose stem.

89. Did you see the water drench them?

90. I heard a yelp when he hurt himself with the wrench.

List 10
Phonograms and Words

91. end   bend, blend, fend, lend, mend, rend, send, spend, tend, trend

92. ent   bent, cent, dent, lent, pent, rent, scent, sent, spent, tent, vent, went

93. ept   crept, kept, slept, swept, wept

94. er   her, per

95. ere   here, mere

96. esh   flesh, fresh, mesh, thresh

97. ess   bless, chess, cress, dress, guess, less, mess, press, stress

98. est*   best, blest, chest, crest, guest, jest, nest, pest, quest, rest, test, vest, west, zest

99. et   bet, fret, get, jet, let, met, net, set, wet, whet, yet

100. ew   blew, brew, chew, crew, dew, drew, few, flew, grew, hew, Jew, knew, mew, pew, screw, shrew, skew, slew, spew, stew, threw, yew

List 10 Sentences

91. He wept when he saw the dent in his car.

92. Who left such a wet mess in here?

93. Can you guess how much stress she felt when she saw the big test?

94. Spend your money on a new tent and ice chest for our trip.

95. The pest crept out the door, and we couldn't find him.

96. Can you smell the fresh scent of flowers?

97. Blend the meat into the stew before you eat it.

98. In the net they found a shrew, which is an animal that looks like a mouse.

99. Because of the new trend, she grew her hair long.

100. He slept here a few hours, then flew to his home out west.

List 11
Phonograms and Words

101. ext   next, text

102. ice*   dice, lice, mice, nice, price, rice, slice, spice, splice, thrice, twice, vice

103. ick*   brick, chick, click, crick, flick, kick, lick, nick, pick, quick, sick, slick, stick, thick, tick, trick, wick

104. id   bid, did, grid, hid, kid, lid, rid, skid, slid, squid

105. ide*   bide, bride, chide, glide, hide, pride, ride, side, slide, snide, stride, tide, wide

106. ife   fife, knife, life, rife, strife, wife

107. ift   drift, gift, lift, rift, sift, shift, thrift

108. ig   big, brig, dig, gig, jig, pig, rig, sprig, twig, wig

109. ight*   bright, fight, flight, fright, light, might, plight, right, sight, tight

110. ike   bike, dike, hike, like, pike, spike, strike

List 11 Sentences

101. Use ice on the side of your right hand after the next fight.

102. You need to strike a match to light the wick on the candle.

103. Use that knife to cut a thick slice of bread.

104. You pay a smaller price at the thrift store.

105. The big squid will drift past us in the water.

106. Don't kick the spike in the ground or you'll hurt your toe.

107. That twig is not a big enough stick to use for this job.

108. Slide your textbook over to me.

109. He might drift or skid if he rides past the red light.

110. You should feel pride about what you do in your life.

List 12
Phonograms and Words

111. ile   bile, file, mile, Nile, pile, rile, smile, stile, tile, vile, while, wile

112. ilk   bilk, milk, silk

113. ill*   bill, chill, dill, drill, fill, gill, grill, hill, kill, mill, pill, sill, shrill, skill, spill, still, thrill, till, will

114. im   brim, dim, grim, him, prim, rim, shim, skim, slim, swim, trim, vim, whim

115. ime   chime, crime, dime, grime, lime, mime, prime, slime, time

116. in*   bin, chin, din, fin, gin, grin, kin, pin, shin, sin, skin, spin, thin, tin, twin, win

117. ince   mince, prince, quince, since, wince

118. inch   cinch, clinch, finch, pinch, winch

119. ine*   brine, dine, fine, line, mine, nine, pine, shine, shrine, spine, tine, twine, vine, whine, wine

120. ing*   bring, cling, ding, fling, king, ping, ring, sing, sling, spring, sting, string, swing, thing, wing, wring, zing

List 12 Sentences

111. The prince will smile if you bring him a gift.

112. Do you want string or twine to tie up the box?

113. We will use a thin white tile to trim the garden.

114. She will give a shrill scream if you pinch her skin.

115. Fill my glass to the brim with milk and I will grin.

116. Don't get any grime on my new silk dress.

117. Since it is time to eat, let us go light the grill.

118. You can hear the bells chime in the spring.

119. Don't hurt your spine when you fly off the rope swing.

120. The king will sing and fill the hall.

List 13
Phonograms and Words

121. ink*   blink, brink, clink, drink, kink, link, mink, pink, rink, shrink, sink, slink, stink, think, wink

122. int   flint, glint, hint, lint, mint, print, splint, sprint, squint, stint, tint

123. ip*   blip, chip, clip, dip, drip, flip, grip, hip, lip, pip, quip, rip, ship, sip, skip, slip, snip, strip, tip, trip, whip, zip

124. ipe   gripe, pipe, ripe, snipe, stripe, swipe, tripe, wipe

125. ird   bird, gird, third

126. ire   dire, fire, hire, mire, spire, squire, sire, tire, wire

127. irl   girl, swirl, twirl, whirl

128. irt   dirt, flirt, shirt, skirt, squirt

129. ish   dish, fish, swish, wish

130. iss   bliss, hiss, kiss, miss, Swiss

List 13 Sentences

121. I think you'll have to squint in the bright light.

122. Don't drink the water that squirts out of this pipe.

123. Her pink skirt went over the gate with a swish.

124. The shirt will shrink in the wash.

125. The squire went to kiss the princess, but she ran off.

126. Sprint down the path and start on your trip right away.

127. The fish would flip and twirl to get away from the bear.

128. There was a fire on the ship, and I heard the engine hiss.

129. The girl in the third desk had a stripe on her paper.

130. The bird came up to us and ate the ripe berry.

List 14
Phonograms and Words

131. ist   fist, grist, list, mist, twist, wrist

132. it*   bit, fit, flit, grit, hit, kit, knit, lit, pit, quit, sit, skit, slit, spit, split, wit

133. ite   bite, cite, kite, mite, rite, quite, site, smite, spite, sprite, trite, white, write

134. ive   chive, dive, drive, five, hive, live, strive, thrive

135. ix   fix, mix, nix, six

136. ize   prize, size

137. oach   broach, coach, poach, roach

138. oad   goad, load, road, toad

139. oak   cloak, croak, soak

140. oal   coal, foal, goal, shoal

List 14 Sentences

131. The foal will thrive at the new farm.

132. Soak the white shirt in warm water with soap.

133. The road will split at the end of the drive.

134. Twist the cap to open the bottle of Sprite.

135. The coach told his team not to quit when the star player broke his wrist.

136. She tried to hit the roach, but it ran over her wrist.

137. Strive to make a goal and your team may win the prize.

138. I can hear the six toads as they croak in the pond.

139. You will have to knit my top in a large size.

140. The five birds will dive near the hive, then sit by the road.

List 15
Phonograms and Words

141. oar   boar, roar, soar

142. oast   boast, coast, roast, toast

143. oat   bloat, boat, coat, float, gloat, goat, moat, throat

144. ob   blob, bob, cob, fob, glob, gob, job, lob, knob, mob, rob, slob, snob, sob, throb

145. ock*   block, chock, clock, dock, flock, frock, hock, knock, lock, mock, pock, rock, shock, smock, sock, stock

146. od   clod, cod, God, mod, nod, plod, pod, prod, rod, scrod, shod, sod, trod

147. ode   bode, code, lode, mode, node, rode, strode

148. oft   loft, soft

149. og   bog, clog, cog, dog, flog, fog, frog, grog, hog, jog, log, smog, tog

150. oice   choice, voice

List 15 Sentences

141. We will float through the fog until we see the dock.

142. A sob came out of her throat, and she couldn't find her voice.

143. There was a soft knock on the door, and the man strode across the room to open it.

144. He hit his head on the top of the loft, and it started to throb.

145. You will be able to hear the roar of the waves when we get to the coast.

146. She made her choice and rode in the other car.

147. If you just plod along, we'll never make it out of this smog.

148. They put a rod through the beef to roast it over the fire.

149. Did you look at the clock when you saw the man rob the store?

150. He saw the flock of birds soar over the boat, then fly to the coast.

List 16
Phonograms and Words

151. oil   boil, broil, coil, foil, soil, spoil, toil

152. oin   coin, join, loin

153. oke*   broke, choke, coke, joke, poke, spoke, stoke, stroke, woke, yoke

154. old   bold, cold, fold, gold, hold, mold, scold, sold, told

155. ole   bole, dole, hole, mole, pole, role, sole, stole, whole

156. olt   bolt, colt, dolt, jolt, molt, volt

157. ond   blond, bond, fond, frond, pond

158. ong   gong, long, prong, song, strong, thong, throng, tong

159. ood   good, hood, stood, wood

160. ood   brood, food, mood

List 16 Sentences

151. A strong yoke can hold two oxen together.

152. I will scold her if she broke the whole stack of glasses.

153. He was in a good mood when the new colt was born.

154. I stood in a hole to fix the pipe.

155. There was a long line to get your food.

156. I told them that these bolts will hold the bookcase to the wall.

157. Her hair was so blond it looked like she had gold in her hair.

158. Join me at the pond later and we'll fish.

159. The cold food will spoil if left in the sun.

160. Did you find my lost coin in the pot of soil?

List 17
Phonograms and Words

161. ook   book, brook, cook, crook, hook, look, nook, rook, shook, took

162. oof   goof, poof, proof, spoof

163. ool   cool, drool, fool, pool, school, spool, stool, tool

164. oom   bloom, boom, broom, doom, gloom, groom, loom, room, zoom

165. oon   boon, coon, moon, noon, soon, spoon, swoon

166. oop   coop, droop, goop, hoop, loop, scoop, sloop, snoop, stoop, swoop, troop, whoop

167. oose   goose, loose, moose, noose

168. oot   boot, coot, hoot, loot, moot, root, scoot, shoot, toot

169. op[*]   cop, chop, crop, drop, flop, fop, hop, lop, mop, plop, pop, prop, shop, slop, sop, stop, top

170. ope   cope, dope, grope, hope, lope, mope, pope, rope, scope, slope

List 17 Sentences

161. The cook had to stand on a stool to scoop our soup with a spoon.

162. I will have to groom the moose for the silly show.

163. Snoop around for the proof you need to catch the crook.

164. Soon we hope to sell in our shop the things you need for school.

165. Please don't shoot the goose that got loose. I will swoop him up with my rope.

166. After it blooms, I will chop down this cherry tree and dig it out by the roots.

167. At high noon, it is hard to cope in the hot sun.

168. Put on your boots, get the broom and mop, and let's do our job and not goof around anymore.

169. He shook the tree, and a lemon fell in the pool.

170. She took a look at the shop room in the school.

List 18
Phonograms and Words

171. ore*   bore, chore, core, fore, gore, lore, more, pore, score, shore, snore, sore, spore, store, swore, tore, wore, yore

172. ork   cork, fork, pork, stork

173. orn   born, corn, horn, morn, scorn, shorn, thorn, torn, worn

174. ort   fort, port, short, snort, sort, sport, tort

175. ose   chose, close, hose, nose, pose, prose, rose, those

176. oss   boss, cross, floss, gloss, loss, moss, toss

177. ost   host, most, post

178. ot*   blot, clot, cot, dot, got, hot, jot, knot, lot, not, pot, plot, rot, shot, slot, spot, tot, trot

179. ote   dote, mote, note, quote, rote, smote, tote, vote, wrote

180. oud   cloud, loud, proud, shroud

List 18 Sentences

171. The thorn on the rose bush tore my skin.

172. I like the sport where they toss a ball around and score when it goes through the basket.

173. When their pet died, they picked out a plot at the graveyard and put a cross on the grave.

174. I am going to post my note on the door.

175. When you were born, your mom and dad were so proud that they chose a great name for you.

176. That cloud sort of looks like a nose and two eyes.

177. It is a chore to get the knot out of your shoelace.

178. The cork made a loud noise when it shot off the top of the bottle.

179. She wrote most of the prose while she was on her deck, looking at the shore.

180. Give her a fork so she can try this pork.

List 19
Phonograms and Words

181. ought   bought, brought, fought, sought, thought, wrought

182. ould   could, should, would

183. ound   bound, found, ground, hound, mound, pound, round, sound, wound

184. ount   count, mount

185. our   dour, flour, hour, scour, sour

186. ouse   blouse, douse, grouse, house, louse, mouse, spouse

187. out   bout, clout, flout, gout, grout, lout, pout, rout, scout, shout, snout, spout, stout, trout

188. ove   clove, cove, drove, grove, stove

189. ow   brow, chow, cow, how, now, plow, sow, vow, wow

190. ow   blow, crow, flow, glow, grow, low, mow, row, show, slow, snow, sow, throw, tow

List 19 Sentences

181. The lemons we bought are round and sour.

182. She drove through the snow to come to our house.

183. The ground was hard and would take a lot of time to plow.

184. Could you throw me the ball when I shout for it?

185. We thought the hour was too late for us to call.

186. Count how many Boy Scouts are in the room.

187. He found it was not easy to mount the new horse.

188. Her blouse got too close to the stove and caught on fire.

189. We fought over who should mow the lawn.

190. They want to show you the mouse they brought home.

List 20
Phonograms and Words

191. ox   box, fox, lox, pox, sox

192. oy   boy, coy, joy, ploy, soy, toy

193. ube   cube, lube, rube, tube (*Note:* Cube is not an exact rhyme.)

194. uch   much, such

195. uck*   buck, chuck, cluck, duck, luck, muck, pluck, puck, shuck, struck, stuck, truck, tuck

196. udge   budge, drudge, fudge, grudge, judge, nudge, sludge, smudge, trudge

197. uff   bluff, cuff, fluff, huff, gruff, muff, puff, ruff, scuff, scruff, snuff, stuff

198. ug*   bug, chug, drug, dug, hug, jug, lug, mug, plug, pug, rug, shrug, slug, smug, snug, thug, tug

199. um   bum, chum, drum, glum, gum, hum, plum, rum, scum, slum, strum, sum, swum

200. umb   crumb, dumb, numb, plumb, thumb

List 20 Sentences

191. The truck would not budge out of the mud where it was stuck.

192. Roy hurt his thumb when he grabbed for my stuff.

193. That is such a dumb toy; it isn't worth a buck.

194. Did you feel smug when the judge ruled that you were right?

195. There isn't much glue in that tube.

196. When I gave her a crumb, she got mad and left in a huff.

197. A fox ran after a duck and made such a fuss.

198. I saw him shrug when asked about the smudge on the wall.

199. Have you ever seen a drum in the shape of a cube?

200. The drug made my hands go numb!

List 21
Phonograms and Words

201. ump*   bump, chump, clump, dump, frump, grump, hump, jump, lump, plump, pump, rump, slump, stump, thump, trump

202. un   bun, fun, gun, nun, pun, spun, stun, sun

203. unch   brunch, bunch, crunch, hunch, lunch, munch, punch, scrunch

204. une   dune, June, prune, tune

205. ung   clung, flung, hung, lung, rung, slung, sprung, strung, stung, sung, swung

206. unk*   bunk, chunk, drunk, dunk, flunk, hunk, junk, punk, shrunk, skunk, sunk, trunk

207. up   cup, pup, up

208. ur   blur, cur, fur, slur, spur

209. ure   cure, lure, pure, sure

210. urn   burn, churn, spurn, turn

List 21 Sentences

201. Sit down on the stump and we'll eat our lunch.

202. After Ma spun some wool, it was time to churn the butter.

203. Do you always scrunch up your face like that when you eat a prune?

204. That hunk of junk you call a car won't turn up this street.

205. As she swung high in the seat, all she could see became a blur.

206. When the pup saw the cat, he sprung from my lap and his fur stood on end.

207. I'm sure I heard a tune coming out of that trunk.

208. There is pure water in your cup.

209. Can you cure this lump in my throat?

210. Pick the clump of grapes that is growing in the sun.

List 22
Phonograms and Words

211. us   bus, plus, thus

212. usk   dusk, husk, musk, tusk

213. uss   fuss, muss, truss

214. ust   bust, crust, dust, gust, just, must, rust, thrust, trust

215. ut   but, cut, glut, gut, hut, jut, nut, rut, shut

216. uzz   buzz, fuzz

List 22 Sentences

211. Shut the door so the dust doesn't blow in.

212. Don't make a fuss about the cut on your hand.

213. We must get back to the house at dusk, before the sun is gone.

214. Did you trust that the bus would get here on time?

215. I hear the buzz of a bee around my head.

216. Let's buy the shirt because it's on sale, plus there is no tax.

REFERENCE

Wylie, R. E., & Durrell, D. D. (1970). Teaching vowels through phonograms. *Elementary English, 47,* 787–791.

Words for Teaching Short and Long Vowels

USING THE WORD LISTS TO TEACH THE MOST COMMON VOWEL RULES

You may use the word lists that appear in this appendix for teaching the most common vowel rules. The two vowel rules that beginning readers should learn are as follows:

1. *When a single vowel appears in a closed syllable, it usually stands for the short sound of the vowel.* This is often referred to as the CVC (consonant-vowel-consonant) rule. A closed syllable is one that has a consonant at the end; for example, the words *in*, *did*, *on*, and *Fred* are all closed syllables. On the other hand, the words *go*, *he*, and *me* are open syllables. Remember that a closed syllable is one that has a consonant at the end and an open syllable is one that has a vowel at the end.

2. *When a word has a vowel, consonant, and final* e, *the first vowel will be more likely to be long and the final* e *will be silent.* This is often referred to as the VCE (vowel-consonant-final *e* rule). More accurately, the student should be taught that when he encounters a word with a VCE ending, he should try the long sound first. This is because this rule has many exceptions.

To use the word list to teach these two vowel rules, use the following strategy:

A. Write the following words and ask the student to say each word (or help him, if necessary):

> can   pan   gap   tap

After doing this, explain to the student that the *a* sound heard in these words stands for the short *a* sound. Pronounce for the student a few rhyming words such as *fan*, *ran*, *lap*, and *nap*, and point out that these words also have the short *a* sound.

B. Write the following words and then ask the student to say each word (again, help him if necessary):

> cane   pane   gape   tape

Following this, explain to the student that the *a* sound heard in these words stands for the long *a* sound. Pronounce for the student a few rhyming words such as *mane*, *sane*, *grape*, and *nape*, and point out that these words also have the short *a* sound.

C. Write the word *cane*. Then cross off the *e* at the end. Ask the student what word you now have. Do the same with the words *pane*, *gape*, and *tape*. Following this, ask the student what happens to the vowel sounds in the words when you remove the *e* from the end. He should, of course, tell you that removing the *e* changes the vowel sound of the first vowel from long to short.

D. Following this, present words the other way around. That is, write words such as *mad*, *fat*, and *man* and have the student pronounce them. (Help him again, if necessary.) Then put an *e* at the end of each word and ask him to pronounce the words as they now appear. Ask him what happens when you add an *e* to the end of words such as these. The student should, of course, tell you that the first vowel sound changes from short to long when an *e* is added.

In doing this it is not necessary to use real words all of the time; therefore, you may wish to use the phonogram lists (See Appendix B-4) to supplement the word lists. Students enjoy doing the same exercises with nonsense words; for example, changing *slam* to *slame*, or *bam* to *bame*.

E. After teaching the two vowel rules, dictate various words and nonsense words to students and have them write them from your dictation. *This is a very important part of learning these rules.*

F. Provide the student with practice in the act of reading. Have the student read simple sentences or stories that you have created that use the words just taught along with other easy words the student already knows. You may also have the student dictate simple stories to you in which he uses the newly learned words in context. Later, the student can copy over his simple stories for additional practice. Finally, have the student read published easy readers that provide repetitive practice on these phonic elements.

For students who have difficulty pronouncing the words or remembering the short- and long-vowel pattern, teach the skill using discrete steps, easier to more difficult, as follows:

1. Begin by teaching two examples of *one* phonogram for the letter *a*, such as *can* and *man* for the short vowels and *cane* and *mane* for the long vowels.

2. Next, present four examples of *two* phonograms for the letter *a*, as shown in the sample lesson presented previously.

3. Next, present *three* or *four* different examples of phonograms for the letter *a*.

Once the student has mastered the short- and long-vowel pattern for *a*, move to *e*, then *i*, and so on. After the student demonstrates mastery of the individual vowels, check his ability to pronounce phonograms that represent all the different vowels, such as *bat / bate, ten / teen, kit / kite, slop / slope*, and *tub / tube*.

A Vowels

can	cane
cap	cape
fad	fade
gap	gape
hat	hate
mad	made
nap	nape
pal	pale
pan	pane
plan	plane
Sam	same
tam	tame
tap	tape
scrap	scrape
sham	shame

E Vowels

bet	beet
fed	feed
Ken	keen
pet	Pete
red	reed
ten	teen

I Vowels

bit	bite
dim	dime
fin	fine
grim	grime
grip	gripe
hid	hide
kit	kite

I Vowels (continued)

pin	pine
prim	prime
quit	quite
rid	ride
rip	ripe
shin	shine
sit	site
slid	slide
slim	slime
snip	snipe
spin	spine
strip	stripe
Tim	time
twin	twine
win	wine

O Vowels

cod	code
glob	globe
hop	hope
mop	mope
not	note
rob	robe
rod	rode
slop	slope
tot	tote

U Vowels

cub	cube
cut	cute
plum	plume
tub	tube

Words, Sentences, and Stories for Teaching Structural Analysis

The materials in this section were developed by Cheryl Milner, Senior Program Associate, Western Assessment Collaborative at WestEd. The word lists, sentence lists, and stories contained herein have been used to teach thousands of students how to decode "big words" in both one-to-one settings and small groups in classrooms.

Unfortunately, most developmental reading programs (basal readers) provide teachers with few materials or lessons to achieve this important goal. Students who get off to a good start in reading and continue to read widely as they progress through the grades usually have little difficulty in figuring out on their own how to attack (pronounce) multisyllable words. Many students, however, have no strategy other than guessing to assist them in this aspect of decoding.

These materials provide you with two important tools to teach students to decode using structural analysis. First, a sample direct instruction lesson is provided. This lesson consists of six critical steps. The first three teach students how to strategically identify, separate, and blend parts of multisyllable words. Students then get guided assistance in pronouncing whole words (step 4), reading the words in sentence context (step 5), and finally reading the words in story context (step 6).

The scope and sequence of the program is as follows:

Lesson 1:   Inflectional endings *-s, -ed, -ing*
Lesson 2:   Inflectional endings *-er, -est*
Lesson 3:   Inflectional endings *-es, -ies, -ied, -ier, -iest*
Lesson 4:   Inflectional endings *double consonants*
Lesson 5:   Inflectional endings *-ly, -en, final -e*
                  Inflectional endings: Review Story
Lesson 6:   Compound Words
Lesson 7:   Contractions
Lesson 8:   Prefixes *re-, un-*
Lesson 9:   Prefixes *pre-, pro-*
Lesson 10: Prefixes *com-, im-*
Lesson 11: Prefixes *con-, dis-, ex-*

Lesson 12:	Prefixes *de-, in-*
	Prefixes: Review Story
Lesson 13:	Suffixes *-ion, -ive*
Lesson 14:	Suffixes *-able, -ment*
Lesson 15:	Suffixes *-ful, -less, -ness*
Lesson 16:	Suffixes *-al, -ous*
	Suffixes: Review Story
Lesson 17:	Syllabication

For each lesson, a word list, a sentence list, and a story are provided.

The sample lesson was created for teaching the very first lesson in the program: Inflectional Endings *-s, -ed, -ing.* However, the same six steps in the sample lesson may be used along with the word lists, sentence lists, and stories to teach the full range of structural analysis skills. Students begin this program learning how to read words with simple inflectional endings, such as *sees* and *asking.* By the end of the program, you will see that you can teach these same students to decode long, difficult words, such as *paleontologist* and *uncontaminated.*

The sample lesson is presented on the following page. Following that are the word lists, sentence lists, and stories.

Sample Lesson

Step 1. Identify Word Parts

Materials: Chalkboard or chart paper, word list

1. Review roots: clean, born, cover, dress
2. Write on the chalkboard or chart paper:

   List 1

look	looked
looks	looking

   List 2

asks	worked
works	calling
called	asked
asking	working
calls	

3. Direct students' attention to List 1.

   Say: "How are these words alike?" (They all have the root look.)
4. Circle the root *look:*

look	s
look	ed
look	ing

   Say: "How are these words different?" (They have different endings.)
5. Write these headings across the chalkboard:

   s   ed   ing

6. Direct students' attention to List 2.

   Say: "These words have some of the same endings you saw on the word look. Which column would you place the word asks under? (Under the s because it has an -s ending.)
7. Repeat step 6 with the words: called, asking, calls, worked, calling, asked, and working.
8. Ask students to read the -s words, the -ed words, and the -ing words.

Step 2. Separate Word Parts (Optional)

Materials: Each student should have a magnetic board with magnetic letters, a small chalkboard, a magic slate, a white board with a marker, or a pencil and paper

1. Review roots: turn, help

2. Using the medium you have chosen, have students form or write the word turns. Say: "Show me how you take away the s from turns." Assist the student to separate the magnetic letters (between the n and the s), or draw a line between the appropriate letters on the chalkboard, magic slate, white board, or paper.

3. Repeat Step 2 for helping, turning, helps, and helped.

Step 3. Blend Word Parts (Optional)

Materials: Same as Step 2

1. Say: "Make or write the word turn. Now add the ending -ed. Put the parts together. What is the word?" (turned)

   "If you take away the -ed, what is left?" (turn)
   "If you take away the turn, what is left?" (-ed)
   "What is the whole word?" (turned)

2. Repeat Step 1 for: helped
                          turns
                          helps
                          helping
                          turning

3. Ask each student to read all the words aloud.

Step 4. Pronounce Whole Words

Materials: Word List 1

1. Select a number of words from the word list with -s, -ed, and -ing endings.

2. Have the students read these words out loud, chorally, to themselves, and with a partner.

3. Have the students read these words as often as necessary until they can be read quickly and easily.

Step 5. Read in Sentence Context

Materials: Sentence List 1

1. Read the first sentence slowly to students. Have students look at the words, not at you, and have the students point to each word in the sentence as you read it.

2. Repeat your reading of the sentence (slowly). This time, have students read out loud (chorally) with you while they also point to each word in the sentence as it is read.

3. Have students read the first sentence to a partner, then switch and listen while the partner reads the sentence.

4. Repeat steps 1, 2, and 3 with the remaining sentences. (If the students catch on quickly and you find that you can skip some of the steps, then do so. But remember: accurate decoding is the goal, not speed of reading.)

5. Provide opportunities for students to read the sentences over and over, to the teacher, to an aide, to another student, or into a tape recorder.

6. Encourage students to read the sentences to parents or siblings at home.

7. If a student is able to do steps 1 through 4 successfully but has difficulty reading the words in sentences (step 5), try color-coding the variants. To draw the student's attention to the root plus the inflectional ending, underline or write the roots with one color and the inflectional endings with a different color.

Step 6. Read in Story Context

Materials: Story 1—A Long Camping Trip

1. The story *should* be:
   a. Copied and distributed to each student in the group
   b. Introduced to the group
      Say: "This is a story about a boy with a problem. Some strange things happen to him that do not make sense. We are going to read to find out what they are."
   c. Read silently
   d. Read chorally (all students reading out loud together) after silent reading
   e. Discussed by the group
   f. Practiced as seatwork or a free-time activity
   g. Read orally by each student to an aide, into a tape recorder, with a partner (either together or taking turns), and/or to the teacher
   h. Taken home to be read to parents or siblings *after* mastery at school

2. The story *may* be:
   a. Placed on a transparency for introduction to the group
   b. Read to the principal or another group of children for extra oral practice
   c. Placed along with other stories into a booklet

3. If a student has successfully completed steps 1 through 5, but has difficulty reading variants in context:
   a. Color-code the variants on one copy of the story. Underline the roots with one color and the endings with another color.
   b. Ask the student to read the color-coded story orally. Direct her attention to the color-coded ending and root when she has difficulty with the longer word.
   c. *Encourage the student to read the whole sentence and think of a word that makes sense as well as focusing on the word parts.*
   d. After she has mastered the color-coded story, have the student read the same story without color-coding.
   e. Remember that repeated readings of the same story are helpful to students who are learning to decode longer words, and students are usually highly motivated by such repeated readings. This is especially true when students discover that practice leads to success in the form of fluent reading of the story.

Words, Sentences, and Stories for Teaching Structural Analysis

Contents

Word List 1:
Inflectional Endings -s, -ed, -ing

-s

acts	eyes	mothers	slams
answers	fades	naps	sleeps
apples	finds	Nells	slows
asks	flowers	news	smells
backs	friends	nuts	smiles
bangs	frowns	odds	stairs
bats	gaps	opens	starts
birds	gets	paints	steps
blows	girls	pants	stops
boys	glares	pats	streets
bumps	grows	pets	tags
burns	gusts	picks	takes
cakes	hands	plants	tells
calls	hates	plays	thinks
camps	helps	pleases	ticks
cans	hems	pops	times
casts	hints	puffs	tips
chugs	hopes	punts	tracks
clears	hops	puts	trees
clicks	hugs	reds	trips
climbs	jabs	rings	trunks
comes	jams	rolls	tugs
costs	jumps	rows	turns
cuts	kicks	runs	uses
days	kills	sands	waits
dims	kinds	says	walks
dogs	knows	schools	warms
doors	lights	scores	waters
dots	likes	scrubs	waves
dreams	loads	sees	weds
drills	longs	shakes	works
drips	looks	shines	years
dusts	logs	shorts	
eats	makes	skates	
ends	melts	skips	

Word List 1 (continued)

-ed

acted	crashed	lighted	shocked
answered	crossed	loaded	shorted
asked	dreamed	looked	slowed
backed	dressed	melted	smelled
banged	drilled	mothered	started
boxed	dusted	opened	ticked
bumped	filled	painted	tossed
burned	fixed	panted	tracked
called	flowered	picked	turned
calmed	frowned	planted	waited
camped	gusted	played	walked
casted	handed	puffed	warmed
clashed	helped	punted	watered
cleaned	hinted	reached	wished
cleared	jumped	sanded	worked
clicked	kicked	schooled	
climbed	killed	seemed	

-ing

acting	dreaming	knowing	singing
answering	dressing	lighting	sleeping
asking	drilling	loading	slowing
backing	drying	longing	smelling
banging	dusting	looking	starting
blowing	eating	melting	teaching
boxing	eyeing	morning	telling
bumping	feeling	mothering	thinking
burning	finding	opening	ticking
calling	fixing	painting	tossing
calming	flowering	panting	tracking
camping	flying	picking	treeing
casting	freeing	planting	trying
clashing	frowning	playing	turning
cleaning	frying	puffing	waiting
clearing	going	punting	walking
clicking	growing	reaching	warming
climbing	gusting	ringing	watering
cooking	handing	sanding	wishing
costing	helping	saying	working
crashing	hinting	schooling	yelling
crossing	jumping	seeing	
crying	kicking	shorting	
doing	killing	shying	

Sentence List 1:
Inflectional Endings -s, -ed, -ing

She turns and helps the girls.

She turned and helped the girl.

She is turning and helping the girl.

Mother knows when the family eats, plays, and sleeps.

The family likes being mothered.

The family will be eating, playing, and sleeping here.

He opens the doors for his friends.

He opened the door and called his friend.

He is opening the door and calling his friend.

Bob stops and looks up and down the streets.

Bob looked before he crossed the street.

Sis likes trees, walks, and dogs.

Sis watered and walked the dog.

Sis will be watering and walking my dog.

Sam waits and thinks about how many days it takes.

Sam played while he waited.

Sam is waiting and thinking about the day.

Story 1:
Inflectional Endings -s, -ed, -ing

A Long Camping Trip

It all started when I came home from camp. I was walking home from the bus stop. As I turned down my street, I saw some friends a block away. I called hello, but they acted like they did not hear me.

I was feeling a little sad as I opened the doors to our house. I needed a snack, so I went to find Mom and get some nuts and apples. When I saw her, I laughed and said, "Here I am!" Mom seemed not to hear or see me. I started yelling. I jumped up and down. It was no use. She just went on cooking. "She does not look the same as before," I thought.

I walked out the back door. First my friends, and now my mother! What had I done? Was no one glad to see me? The trees were blowing and the birds were singing, but I felt like crying as I climbed a tall tree near the gate.

I started thinking. My dog Rags would be happy to see me! I jumped from the tree and ran to find Rags. He would be in my room sleeping. I ran up the steps. When I walked into my room, I was shocked to find it filled with trunks, junk, and all kinds of odds and ends.

Just then my little sister Kate ran up the stairs. To my surprise, she walked right by me, too. She looked to be about five years too old to be little Kate! As I walked down stairs, I saw the date in the hall—July 16, 2013. But this is only 2003!

Word List 2:
Inflectional Endings *-er, -est*

-er

asker	faster	painter	starter
backer	finder	passer	stronger
boxer	fixer	picker	swifter
brighter	frowner	planter	taller
bumper	grower	player	teacher
burner	helper	puffer	teller
caller	higher	punter	ticker
calmer	hinter	quicker	thicker
camper	jumper	quieter	thinker
clearer	kicker	reacher	tosser
clicker	killer	ringer	tracker
climber	kinder	sander	turner
colder	leader	sayer	waiter
crasher	lighter	shorter	walker
crosser	loader	sleeper	warmer
damper	longer	slower	wisher
dreamer	looker	smaller	worker
dresser	melter	smarter	younger
driller	newer	smeller	
duster	older	softer	
eater	opener	sooner	

-est

brightest	highest	shortest	swiftest
calmest	kindest	slowest	tallest
clearest	longest	smallest	thickest
coldest	newest	smartest	warmest
crossest	oldest	softest	youngest
dampest	quickest	soonest	
fastest	quietest	strongest	

Sentence List 2:
Inflectional Endings *-er, -est*

The ball player used to be a boxer.

He is slower than Roger, but he is not the slowest.

This is the longest I have seen you work.

You have been a faster worker than I have.

I am a quieter eater than you are.

Tom is the longest passer on our team.

When the baby is older she can sit in a walker.

The sky is clearest after a rain.

That moon is the brightest I have ever seen.

He is the quickest fox in the woods.

This has been the warmest day all week.

I have the oldest bike, but the newest paint job.

Story 2:
Inflectional Endings *-er, -est*

The Slowest Kid on the Block

Jack was the smartest, the strongest, the tallest, and the oldest kid on our block. The younger kids always came to him for help. He was also kinder than most older boys I knew. Bob was like a teacher or leader to us, a big brother.

I went to him for help once a few years ago.

"I am slower than all my friends," I told him. "I am also the smallest and the shortest. I would not mind being slower at SOME things. I would not mind being slower than SOME of my friends. But ALL of my friends are faster at ALL things. My friend Bob is a faster climber, a faster eater, a faster walker, and a faster worker. Bob is the fastest at all things."

I went on talking to Jack. "I thought that if I grew taller, I would get faster. So at each meal I ate longer than any of my friends. I did not get taller. I am still the shortest, thickest kid on the block. What can I do?" I asked. "I need your quickest answer."

Jack told me to wait one week and I would find an answer quicker than I thought. I thought it would be the longest week of my life.

Three days after our talk, I went to Fun Park U.S.A. with some friends. We were having fun at the Killer Whale Show when I looked down and saw Bob's sister, Sue, looking over the wall of the pool. The killer whales began their fastest swim across the pool to make their highest jump to grab the smallest ring from the pole over Sue's head. When the whales came down, they would hit Sue!

I made the swiftest move of my life and reached Sue sooner than Bob. I pulled her away just as the two whales shot out of the water.

Bob said, "You were by far the quickest thinker and the fastest on your feet this time, Mike. Sue may be quicker than me, but not quicker than my best friend, Mike." He took Sue's hand. "And you, little one, are the dampest girl at the park. We should go home before you get any colder."

I guess Jack knew I couldn't always be the slowest at all things.

Word List 3:
Inflectional Endings
-es, -ies, -ied, -ier, -iest

-es

boxes	clashes	fixes	teaches
branches	crashes	foxes	tosses
bushes	crosses	goes	watches
buzzes	dishes	reaches	wishes
churches	dresses	searches	

-ies

babies	cries	funnies	scurries
berries	dries	hurries	tries
carries	flies	muddies	
copies	fries		

-ied

babied	copied	fried	muddied
busied	cried	hurried	tried
carried	dried	married	scurried

-ier

busier	flier	merrier	slier
carrier	frier	muddier	sneakier
copier	funnier	prettier	speedier
crazier	furrier	rustier	tinier
crier	happier	scarier	uglier
drier	heavier	sillier	

-iest

busiest	happiest	rustiest	tiniest
craziest	heaviest	scariest	ugliest
driest	merriest	silliest	
funniest	muddiest	sneakiest	
furriest	prettiest	speediest	

Sentence List 3:
Inflectional Endings
-es, -ies, -ied, -ier, -iest

After the rain, the ground was muddier than before.

He jumped in the mud and tried to be the muddiest of all his friends.

His mother cries when she tries to wash the mud out of his clothes.

These boxes are the heaviest I have ever carried.

My brother lives alone and has never married.

Tom cried when he saw that the rain had made his bike rustier.

The foxes hurried across the field.

The mother fox watches her babies.

He was the tiniest baby I had ever seen.

That tinier bee buzzes as it flies.

If I had three wishes, I would wish to be the funniest, craziest clown, so that I could make people happier.

The funnies in the paper are funnier than before.

Story 3:
Inflectional Endings
-es, -ies, -ied, -ier, -iest

The Ugliest Ogre

In the very deepest part of the woods lived the ugliest ogre that had ever lived. Every ogre said that he was scarier and uglier than any other ogre. I had tried many woods before I came here to live. I came here because of the many bushes and tall trees. It was the prettiest place I had ever been. It was prettier than any picture I had ever seen. I was happier here than I had ever been. One day, all of the ogres in the woods came to visit me.

They all cried at once, "We must go away from our beautiful woods, away from the trees with their beautiful branches, away from the sliest foxes, away from the sweetest berries, away from each little mouse who scurries around under our feet, and away from all of our friends. We will miss the woods."

"If you like it so much, then why must you leave?" I asked. "That is the silliest thing I have ever heard."

"Over near those bushes lives the ugliest, meanest ogre of the woods. He searches for the tiniest ogres he can find, and he fries them for his dinner!"

With that, the tiny ogres hurried and scurried away to look for a new home.

"How do you know this?" I called after them. They did not hear me.

I did not think that the ugliest ogre fried tiny ogres like me.

I went to visit him. I thought he looked funnier than any ogre I had seen before, but not scarier. I tried to say hello, but the ugly ogre just cried.

"I was much happier before I came here," he said. "My life was merrier. I am going away."

"That's the craziest thing I ever heard of," I said. "You must talk to the others and let them know that you are *not* the ugliest, scariest, sneakiest ogre, but that you are the merriest and the friendliest. They will like you if they get to know you. Why, I like you already, and I just met you."

I took his hand and we both felt happier.

Word List 4:
Inflectional Endings
Double Consonants

Roots

bat	gap	pet	step
beg	get	plan	stop
bet	hem	pop	swim
big	hit	put	tag
bob	hop	rob	tip
can	hot	run	trap
chug	hug	scrub	trot
dig	jab	shop	wed
dim	jam	sit	wet
dot	log	skip	zip
drip	nap	slam	
flap	pat	spot	

Sentence List 4:
Inflectional Endings
Double Consonants

The digger used a shovel to do the digging of the hole.

Some days I can hear the water dripping, dripping while I am napping.

This must be the hottest day of the year.

She petted and patted the dog.

The corn is popping in the corn popper.

The bride planned a big wedding.

The boy zipped up the zipper of his coat and skipped out to play.

When she tugged on the strap, the horse trotted down the path.

The rabbit stopped hopping.

We stepped across the brook on the stepping stones.

Story 4:
Inflectional Endings
Double Consonants

Monster from Outer Space

It was the hottest day of the year when that strange shape popped out of the sky and zipped back and forth before my eyes. I was sitting by the pool thinking about going in swimming when there it was! It stopped over the pool, and a strange dotted monster hopped out.

I jumped up to run just as the monster was hitting the water. He bobbed in and out of the pool three times, tipped his head to one side, and was still dripping as he stepped back into the ship. The door slammed, and the ship zipped off.

I never saw the strange dotted monster again. What a strange swimmer to have dropping in my pool!

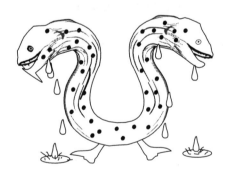

Word List 5:
Inflectional Endings -*ly*, -*en*

-*ly*

brightly	dimly	openly	strongly
calmly	dryly	quickly	swiftly
churchly	freely	sadly	thickly
clearly	friendly	shortly	timely
costly	greatly	shyly	warmly
crossly	lightly	slowly	
daily	motherly	softly	

-*n*, -*en*

brighten	hidden	quicken	soften
broken	known	redden	sunken
dampen	lengthen	sadden	taken
eaten	lighten	shaken	thicken
grown	olden	shorten	widen

Sentence List 5:
Inflectional Endings *-ly, -en*

The friendly boy has broken the glass.

I saw his face redden when I said, "My, how quickly you have grown."

"We must go home shortly," Mother said calmly.

It will sadden me greatly to give away my bike.

The fox will be running very swiftly.

She timed Bob running, while I was timing Jack.

The sunken ship was found under the water.

Mother will shorten my dress after baking a cake.

The book was hidden under some papers.

We were hoping to find a seat in the front.

Story 5:
Inflectional Endings -*ly*, -*en*

The Hidden Mummies

One day as I was walking home from school, I saw a sunken door in the broken brick wall near the old Miller place. I pushed on the door. As the opening began to widen, I felt my heartbeat quicken. I wanted to run swiftly away.

"Lighten up!" I thought calmly as I peered into the dimly lit room.

That is when I saw them! Four hidden mummies! The white tapes of one mummy slowly waved in the wind. They were clearly not friendly mummies.

There I was, a hater of mummies, glaring at four of them. Or were they glaring at me? One wrong move could be very costly.

I quickly turned and closed the sunken door. I must say, I was pretty shaken. How was I to have known there were mummies at the old Miller place?

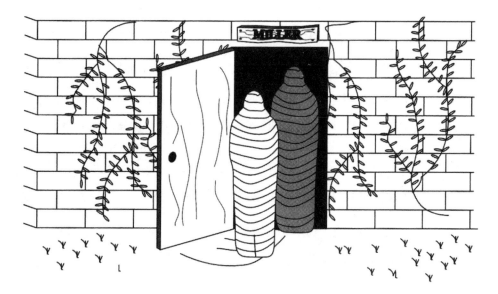

Inflectional Endings: Review Story

The Land of Giants and Elves

Who could have known that there really was a land of thrilling giants and friendly elves? Joe had found this olden land one evening while trimming the hedges for his Aunt Sue. As he clipped the back of the largest hedge, he spotted a good-sized hole hidden there, covered with ivy.

He started trimming the ivy when he spied a flowered path leading to a funny-shaped building. Cutting through the ivy to get a better look, he saw newly made tracks. The only thing Joe could do was follow the tracks.

No sooner had Joe started walking than he saw a motherly looking elf brightly dressed in the prettiest clothes Joe had ever seen. She was watering the plants. The elf clearly did not see Joe at all.

Joe crossed a bubbling stream and then sat down while his dripping boots dried. All of a sudden he heard a crashing, bumping noise. He looked up just in time to see a frowning giant swiftly rushing down the hill to the building at the end of the winding path. All around the building with its tall towers were lots of the littlest people Joe had ever seen. As the giant rushed nearer, the little elves scattered and ran away. The giant went into the building, and things were much quieter than they had been earlier. The elves did not come back.

Slowly Joe walked back to the hole in the hedge. He could hardly wait to go home and find Tom!

Word List 6:
Compound Words

aircraft	butterfly	hardwood	pineapple
airfield	classmate	headline	playground
airliner	cowboy	herself	policeman
airplane	cupcake	highlight	popcorn
airport	doghouse	himself	racecar
anywhere	downhill	homesick	railroad
babysit	draftsman	horseshoe	rainbow
backboard	dragonfly	however	raincoat
backbone	dressmaker	icebox	rattlesnake
background	drugstore	indeed	raygun
bagpipe	earache	inside	roadblock
barnyard	everyone	into	roadside
baseball	fairway	kingfish	rooftop
basketball	firebell	landslide	rowboat
bathtub	firehat	lifeboat	sailboat
because	fireman	lipstick	schoolhouse
bedside	fisherman	mailbox	seafood
bedspread	flagman	mailman	seaman
bedtime	flapjack	mainland	seaport
behind	flashlight	milkman	seesaw
beside	flatworm	motorbike	shipmate
birthday	football	myself	shipwreck
birthmark	foremost	nearby	shotgun
birthplace	forgot	newspaper	skyline
birthright	freeway	oatmeal	skyscraper
birthstone	fruitcake	onto	slipknot
blackberry	glassblower	outdoors	smallpox
blackboard	glassware	outfit	snowball
blacklist	godfather	outlaw	snowflake
blackmail	grandfather	outline	snowman
blackout	grandmother	outrage	snowmobile
blindfold	grapevine	outside	snowshoe
blowhole	groundwork	overdone	someone
bluebell	grown-up	overdose	something
bluebird	gunpowder	overnight	sometime
brainstorm	hailstorm	pancake	somewhere
brakeman	hairbrush	peanut	sourdough
briefcase	haircut	peppercorn	southeast
buckskin	halfback	peppermint	southwest
buckwheat	hallway	pigtail	spaceman

Word List 6 (continued)

spaceship	storyteller	toadstool	waistline
spotlight	strawberry	today	waterproof
staircase	streamline	toenail	watershed
stairway	sunburn	trademark	weekend
steamboat	sunshine	turnpike	wheelchair
steelhead	supermarket	underground	windmill
stepladder	tadpoles	upstairs	without
stereotype	tailbone	waistband	

Sentence List 6:
Compound Words

The airplane landed on the airfield at the airport.

The butterfly flew around the barnyard in the sunshine.

The little boy took a bath in the bathtub with his toy sailboat.

Mother sits at my bedside to read a story at bedtime.

The boys and girls ran downhill and onto the playground.

The boys are playing football nearby.

My grandmother and grandfather gave me a horseshoe game for my birthday.

The mailman left the mail in my mailbox.

The spaceman jumped into his spaceship and flew away.

The flagman stood on the freeway to flag the cars by.

Story 6:
Compound Words

Little Brother, Anyone?

My little brother Bobby just had his fifth birthday. He can be very hard to live with. He likes to make everyone think he is something he is not. Like cute! Cute indeed! If they knew him like I do, they would not think he was so cute. I sometimes think I would like to live by myself.

Today Bobby thinks he is a fireman. He even ate lunch with his raincoat and firehat on. Mom would have a fit if I came to the table with a hat on! Bobby said that he needed to be ready when the firebell rang.

Last weekend I took Bobby to the playground beside the schoolhouse. Mom will not let him go by himself, so I always have to take him. She does not seem to know that I have better things to do than babysit my little brother. First he wanted to play spaceman. He cried because his swing did not look like a spaceship. He cheered up when I let him shoot me with his raygun, however. Next, he climbed the staircase to the rooftop. He said he was an airplane and could land on the grass like a butterfly. I had to say that I would buy him a cupcake and give him my old flashlight before he would come down. Then Bobby wanted to make a snowman. There was not a snowflake to be found anywhere. We made snowballs without snow. Bobby made a snowman in a snowmobile. After it was done we had a snowball fight. Bobby used rocks for snowballs. It was like being hit by a landslide. I hid behind a nearby mailbox. It was a good thing none of my classmates saw me hiding from my little brother.

On the way home we passed the drugstore and the supermarket. Bobby wanted his cupcake.

Every day with Bobby is like that. The last time he went to stay overnight with Grandmother and Grandfather, he called home at bedtime. He wanted to come home because he had forgotten his cowboy outfit. He said that cowboys never sleep without their guns. Dad had to take the freeway and bring Bobby home. I think he was homesick. Sometimes I do not know why they put up with him.

I like to hunt tadpoles, look at motorbikes, make model racecars, and play football and baseball. Bobby wants to do all of these things, too. He never lets me be alone. Mom says it is because I am such a great brother that Bobby wants to be grown-up like me.

I guess Bobby is not such a bad brother. He just may be as good a brother as I am someday.

Word List 7:
Contractions

aren't	he'll	o'clock
can't	he's	one's
couldn't	I'd	that's
didn't	I'll	they'll
doesn't	I'm	wasn't
don't	isn't	you're
haven't	it's	you've
he'd	I've	

Sentence List 7:
Contractions

He doesn't know that it's six o'clock.

We can't find the keys, so we aren't ready to go.

Tom couldn't play handball because he didn't have anyone
to play with.

I don't think he'll be home because I've been calling all day.

I'm sure we haven't met before.

Dad said he'd be home soon, but he's not here yet.

I'd like to know what time you're having dinner.

I'll make sure the meat isn't too well done.

This one's not as big as that one is.

That's not a nice thing to say.

They'll be here before you've cleaned up.

She wasn't at school today.

Story 7:
Contractions

Jumping Seeds

Mexican jumping beans aren't beans, but they'll sure jump. The bean isn't really a bean but a seed. It's a seed with a caterpillar inside.

A moth lays an egg on the plant. After the egg hatches he'll chew his way into a seed. The seed doesn't jump, but it does fall to the ground. The larva in the seed can't do much but wiggle around. This makes the bean or seed move. Some people think he's jumping because of the heat from the ground.

Now, the larva couldn't live in the seed forever. He'd run out of food. I'll tell you how he gets out. He chews a hole in the seed. Next he turns into a pupa and then into a moth. The moth climbs out the hole. He didn't go in as a moth, but that's how he comes out.

If you've ever kept a jumping bean for a long time, you may have seen a moth come out. If you have some jumping beans, and you haven't seen one move for a long time, it may mean that that one's a pupa. If you wait, you're sure to have a moth.

I'd better warn you! If your jumping bean stops moving, don't keep the seeds in your house, unless you don't mind sharing your home with a moth or two.

Word List 8:
Prefixes *re-*, *un-*

re-

react	refill	remorse	respond
readjust	refine	remote	response
rebate	reflect	remove	restore
rebel	reflex	renew	restrain
rebirth	reform	reorder	restrict
rebloom	refrain	repack	result
reborn	refresh	repair	retail
rebuild	refuse	repay	retain
rebury	refute	repeat	retard
rebut	regain	replace	retest
recall	regard	replay	retire
recap	regress	reply	retold
recede	regret	report	retouch
receive	rehearse	repress	retrace
recess	reject	reproach	retreat
recharge	rejoice	repulse	return
recite	relate	request	reveal
reclaim	relax	require	revenge
reclean	relay	rerun	reverse
record	release	research	revert
recount	relent	resemble	review
recover	relief	resent	revise
redeem	relieve	reserve	revolt
redo	rely	resist	revolve
redone	remain	resort	revue
redress	remind	resource	reward
reduce	remiss	respect	rewrite

un-

unable	uncertain	uncover	uneven
unafraid	unchain	uncross	unfair
unaware	unclaim	uncut	unfasten
unbalance	unclean	undo	unfit
unbecoming	unclear	undone	unfold
unbolt	unclench	undress	unfurl
unborn	unclose	undue	unglue
unbroken	uncoil	undying	unhappy
unbuckle	uncommon	unearth	unhealthy
unbutton	unconcern	uneasy	unheard
uncap	uncork	unequal	unhook

Word List 8 (continued)

un-(continued)

unjust	unmask	unsaddle	untidy
unkind	unpack	unsafe	untie
unknown	unpaid	unscramble	until
unlace	unpin	unscrew	untouch
unlatch	unpleasant	unseal	untrue
unlearn	unplug	unseat	untwist
unleash	unravel	unseen	unused
unless	unread	unsnap	unveil
unlike	unready	unsnarl	unwell
unload	unreal	unsteady	unwind
unlock	unrest	unstrung	unwise
unlucky	unripe	unsung	unwrap
unmarried	unroll	unsure	unzip

Sentence List 8:
Prefixes *re-*, *un-*

The weatherman will repeat the report on our unpleasant weather at six o'clock.

My dog will refuse to unclench his teeth and release the stick after I throw it.

Unlace and remove your shoes, unzip your coat, and relax until dinner is ready.

Unless we repair the old chair it will be unsafe, and we will be unable to sit in it.

Please remind me to unload the washer after we return from the store.

Bob was feeling a little uncertain and very uneasy about trying out for the class play.

They had to unwind the ropes and release the sails as a wind came up in order to return the boat to the dock.

It would be unwise to unfasten the ribbon and unwrap the present before the party.

You must review the story and rewrite this paper before I retest.

As he began to unsaddle his horse and unpack the saddlebags, the sheriff said, "I regret having to lock you up, Sam, but I can't let you get revenge for your brother's death."

Story 8:
Prefixes *re-*, *un-*

The Mystery of Sea Creatures

Long ago, unlucky sailors would relate unpleasant stories about unknown sea creatures when they returned from the sea. These creatures had long arms and might attack the ship. They might refuse to release it until the ship sank or many men were eaten or drowned.

Today, scientists who review those stories think that some of them were untrue. The creatures may have been real, but the size may have gotten larger each time the story was retold.

A sailor who looked into the water as he tried to unfasten the ropes or unfurl the sails might become very uneasy if he saw a large animal with long arms. Today we know these were not uncommon monsters, but an octopus or a giant squid.

Other sea creatures that may have made fishermen and sailors a bit unsteady on their feet are eels, lizards, and whales. How would you feel if, as you bent to recover your fishing net, you found a seven-foot eel? The result could be another untrue story about sea monsters.

Some iguanas, or lizards, remove food from the sea bottom by prying it loose with their teeth. They can remain underwater for fifteen minutes. These uncommon creatures are found around the islands off the coast of South America.

After much research, or study, scientists think that many of the creatures thought to be monsters were whales. Grey whales have bumpy backbones, grow to be fifty feet long, and have been reported to attack boats. These attacks may have been the result of a mother whale trying to keep her baby safe.

In a storm or thick fog, anything might be reported to look like a monster. Even a remote island in an unclear fog could resemble a sea monster. Maybe unknown creatures do live in the sea, but so far scientists have been unable to uncover real sea monsters, only real animals.

Word List 9:
Prefixes *pre-*, *pro-*

pre-

prearrange	prejudice	pretend
precede	prepack	pretense
precise	prepare	pretest
preclude	prescribe	prevail
precook	present	prevent
predict	preserve	preview
prefect	preside	prewash
prefix	presume	

pro-

proceed	program	proscribe
proclaim	project	protest
procure	prolong	proton
produce	promote	protrude
profane	pronoun	provide
profess	pronounce	provoke
profile	propane	
profound	propose	

Sentence List 9:
Prefixes *pre-*, *pro-*

We must promote the program before the preview show on March 10th by putting up posters.

I presume, or take for granted, that my pretest score will be lower than my posttest score.

At a yellow blinking light, proceed with care to prevent an accident.

Sometimes I pretend to know how to pronounce very long words when I don't.

If you provoke me again by calling me names, I will project my voice throughout this whole room in an angry protest.

If you precook the meat and prewash the produce, it is easier to prepare meals when camping.

Story 9:
Prefixes *pre-*, *pro-*

Gerbils

I don't profess to like gerbils, but I can't pretend that they don't make perfect pets because they do. Most people love the furry animals. They are clean and easy to feed. These animals have a mouselike profile with tiny feet, whiskers, and long tails.

In the wild, gerbils dig tunnels in the desert sand and live underground, but you can prepare a good home for a pet gerbil almost anywhere. If you proceed as follows, I predict you will have lots of fun with your pet.

First, procure a healthy gerbil from a pet store. Provide the gerbil with a tank or wire cage, wood chips for bedding, a water bottle, and gerbil food. Prearrange the supplies so that you will be able to find them as you need them. If your gerbil acts slow or sleepy, I prevail upon you to take it to a pet doctor. Protect your pet from dogs, cats, and small children. Try not to provoke or upset your pet. Preserve or keep a quiet place for your gerbil. Finally, I presume you will also give your gerbil lots of love.

Word List 10:
Prefixes *com-*, *im-*

com-

combat	common	complex
combine	commune	comply
comfort	commute	compose
command	compact	compound
commence	compare	compress
commend	compass	comprise
comment	compel	compute
commerce	compile	comrade
commit	complain	
commode	complete	

im-

image	impact	imply
imbed	impair	import
imbue	impale	impose
immature	impart	impound
immense	impasse	impress
immerse	impeach	imprint
immobile	impede	improper
immodest	impel	improve
immoral	impend	impulse
immortal	implant	impure
immune	implore	

Sentence List 10:
Prefixes *com-*, *im-*

It is common for mothers to complain that their children's rooms are messy.

It would impress me if you would improve your math grades.

Mr. J. P. Marsh bought the four smaller farms to combine them into one immense 15,000-acre ranch.

Everyone tries to compare me with my brother, but we are nothing alike.

If you like to sleep in comfort, try a waterbed.

You can make an imprint in the wet sand with a shell.

It is improper to clean your teeth at the dinner table.

The map was too complex for me to follow.

Story 10:
Prefixes *com-*, *im-*

Dinosaurs

The word *dinosaur* means "terrible lizard." Try to compare the dinosaurs that lived more than 65 million years ago to the animals of today, and you may think of lizards or snakes. Some scientists believe that common birds of today and the dinosaurs may both be related to early reptiles that crawled on the land over 200 million years ago. The history of the dinosaur is very complex and not at all complete.

Scientists learn more every day. Not all dinosaurs were immense in size. Some were as small as a chicken. Scientists have found fossils, or imprints of bones and footprints that became imbedded in the earth.

In 1964, Dr. John Ostrom found some unusual fossils in Montana. He found the remains of a four-to-five-foot dinosaur that must have run fast on its hind legs to catch its prey. Research seems to imply that this animal may have been a warm-blooded ancestor of today's birds.

Some dinosaurs were very terrible and would have been unpleasant to meet. One such dinosaur was the Sauropod (*SOAR*-oh-pod), which weighed about 30 tons. It might impel you to run if it were not for the fact that its size would impede your path.

Of course, humans did not live during the age of the dinosaurs. Everything we know is just what scientists think from studying the remains they have found. We should commend scientists like Dr. Ostrom for their hard work and study.

Word List 11: *con-, dis-, ex-*

con-

concave	conform	consume
conceal	confound	contain
conceit	confront	contempt
conceive	confuse	contend
concept	congest	contest
concern	congress	context
concert	connect	continue
concise	connote	contort
conclude	conquer	contour
concord	conquest	contract
concrete	consent	contractor
concur	conserve	contrast
condemn	consider	control
condense	consist	convene
condone	console	converge
conduct	conspire	convert
confess	constant	convex
confide	constrain	convey
confine	constrict	convict
confirm	construct	convince
conflict	consult	

dis-

disaffect	discomfort	disloyal
disagree	disconnect	dismiss
disallow	discontinue	dismount
disappear	discord	disobey
disappoint	discount	disorder
disapprove	discourage	disown
disarm	discover	dispatch
disarray	discrete	dispel
disaster	discuss	dispense
disband	disfigure	disperse
disbar	disgrace	displace
disbelief	disguise	displease
disbelieve	disgust	dispose
discard	dishonest	disprove
discern	dishonor	disserve
discharge	disinfect	distend
disclaim	disjoin	distort
disclose	dislike	disturb
discolor	dislodge	

Word List 11 (continued)

ex-

exact	exhaust	explode
exam	exile	exploit
excel	exit	explore
except	expand	export
excess	expanse	expose
exchange	expect	express
excite	expel	extend
exclaim	expend	extent
exclude	expense	extinct
excrete	expert	extract
excuse	expire	extreme
exhale	explain	

Sentence List 11:
Prefixes *con-*, *dis-*, *ex-*

I must confess that I did not win the contest fairly.

Tom had to convince his father to consent to drive his friends home after the party.

The building contractor sank the beams in concrete to make the building safe.

The rock concert will conclude at 1:30 A.M.

I disagree with the way some people dispose of, or discard, their empty cans and gum wrappers.

We watched with disbelief as he made the rabbit disappear.

The little boy will discover a Santa Claus disguise when he looks into the old trunk.

Mom dislikes disorder, and she is always making me clean my room.

I could not think of a good excuse for my low score on the math exam.

She tried to explain to the clerk why she wanted to exchange the gift.

You must exhale into the balloon to make it expand.

They walked through the exit of the spaceship to explore the world beyond.

Story 11:
Prefixes *con-, dis-, ex-*

The Family of Ants

Experts consider the life of the ant to discover more about it. Few people disagree, and most would concur, or agree, that ants live like humans in many ways. Some live in towns or villages. The queen or mother ant lays the eggs and is treated with extreme care by the workers. She controls the colony or village. Some ants are builders and construct nests. They may construct a nest or shelter from their own bodies. Farmer ants grow food, and tend other insects the way people tend cattle.

Some ants excrete something they contain in their bodies to mark their nests and to make trails for other ants to follow.

Don't expect to meet an army of ants in your backyard, but army and driver ants may move by the thousands to conquer anything in their path. In constant motion, they disappear quickly and build a new nest each night. The sting of the Australian bulldog ant can cause great discomfort also.

If you were to discuss the ant with your friends, it could be hard to convince them that people live anything like the tiny ants who disturb picnics. But it is true. With a little study, you would discover that the ant has been around for millions of years. Except for their looks, the ant may be like humans in many ways.

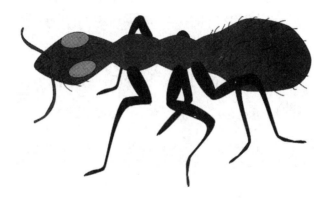

Word List 12:
Prefixes *de-*, *in-*

de-

debar	deform	deprive
debark	degrade	derail
debate	degree	derive
debrief	deice	descend
decal	delay	descent
decay	delete	describe
decide	delight	deserve
declare	deliver	design
decline	deluxe	desire
decode	demand	despise
decoy	demean	despite
decrease	demise	destroy
decry	demon	destruct
deduct	demote	detach
deface	denote	detail
default	deny	detain
defeat	depart	detect
defect	depend	detest
defend	depict	detract
defense	deplete	develop
define	deplore	device
deflate	deport	devise
deflect	deprave	devote

in-

inboard	index	infield
inborn	indirect	infirm
inbred	indoor	inflame
inbreed	induce	inflate
incense	induct	inflect
incise	indulge	inflict
incite	inept	influx
incline	inert	inform
inclose	inexact	ingest
include	infancy	inhale
income	infant	inject
increase	infect	injure
indeed	infer	injury
indent	infest	inlaid

Word List 12 (continued)

inland	inspire	intent
inlay	instance	intern
inlet	instant	intrude
input	instead	invade
inquire	instep	invalid
insane	instill	invent
inscribe	instinct	invert
insect	insult	invest
insert	insure	invite
inset	intact	invoice
insist	intake	involve
inspect	intend	inward

Sentence List 12:
Prefixes *de-*, *in-*

I detest people who insult me.

I got so cold the last time I went camping that I intend to invent an indoor campground.

If you deflate the tire tube, it will decrease in size.

When you inflate the tire tube, it will increase in size.

They will develop a new device to detect planes flying overhead.

Please describe your feelings as the plane began its fast descent.

The infant had a very intent look on her face as she tried to reach the rattle.

In infancy, a baby will hold his breath and not inhale when placed underwater.

I am afraid that if the store does not deliver my new bike soon, Mom and Dad may decide I really don't need it.

Story 12:
Prefixes *de-*, *in-*

Birds That Don't Fly

Have you ever heard anyone describe a bird that flies under water or runs faster than you can pedal your bike? Does this sound insane? Well, it isn't. The penguin uses its wings to push itself through an inlet of water so that it can rest inland on the rocks. The ostrich can run as fast as 35 miles an hour. Neither of these birds can fly. Here are a few details about other birds that do not fly.

The emu does not try to defend itself when in danger. Its instinct tells it to depart or run away as quickly as it can.

The kiwi will inhale the smell of a worm through the nostrils at the end of its beak, and then insert its long beak into the ground to get dinner.

The demise of the dodo bird came soon after it was discovered on an island in the Indian Ocean. This bird did not develop a fear of humans and soon began to decrease in number. Finally, humans did destroy all of these birds. The dodo is now extinct.

The rhea of South America is very tall. This helps the mother to spot enemies and ensure the safety of her chicks.

One funny-looking bird can defend itself with a crash helmet on its head and spikes on its feet. This strange bird is the cassowary (CASS-uh-ware-ee).

The design of these birds is not for flying. Many of these birds do not have the right kind of breastbone for flying. Instead, they find food and protect themselves in other ways.

Prefixes: Review Story

The Unusual Bats

People may compare bats to "flying foxes." They sleep by day and compete for food at night. Some bats can see at night, but most use sound waves or echoes to hunt. These bats read sounds so well that even human sonar does not compare. Bats use their own sounds to guide them through the forest and to reveal insects or other prey to feed on. If humans could detect with their own ears the complex display of sounds that bats produce, they would most likely react with surprise. But the human ear cannot detect these sounds. These unusual animals produce more sounds more often than any other group of mammals.

Some types of bats include fruit bats, tomb bats, hammerhead bats, whitelined bats, and spearnosed bats. The whitelined bat weighs no more than three dimes. Its home on the side of a tree may often expose it to plain view. One colony may consist of 40 bats. The whole colony leaves to feed at night and then returns at dawn. Two males may bark at each other and shake or snap a gland under their wing in a fight for space. In this strange display, the males may shake their wings many times. Scientists presume that this shaking causes the gland to disperse some scent or odor. When the females return to the roost, the males stop fighting and begin to sing. Scientists have been able to record these songs and reveal just how complex they really are.

Bats hunt and eat many things. A fishing bat may impale a small fish in an instant. Other bats have a tongue that protrudes and extends to lap nectar from plants. Bats can consume at night most kinds of food that birds hunt and eat during the day.

Only in the past 30 years have humans begun to extend their knowledge of the bat and its ways. Scientists still have much to learn about the unusual bats.

Word List 13:
Suffixes -*ion*, -*ive*

-*ion*

abrasion	discrimination	junction
action	discussion	legislation
addition	distinction	lesion
adhesion	diversion	limitation
admission	division	location
affliction	edition	lotion
ambition	education	mansion
attention	election	mention
attraction	elevation	mission
auction	emotion	mutation
aversion	equation	nation
caption	erosion	notation
caution	evacuation	notion
circulation	eviction	nutrition
citation	evolution	objection
combination	exception	obligation
communication	excursion	occlusion
concession	exemption	occupation
condition	expansion	operation
confession	expensive	option
confusion	explosion	ovation
connection	expression	partition
construction	extension	passion
convention	fiction	pension
conversation	fission	perception
correction	flotation	percussion
creation	formation	permission
deception	fraction	persuasion
decision	function	population
declaration	ignition	position
deduction	imagination	potion
definition	imitation	probation
delusion	impression	production
depression	induction	profession
description	information	protection
destruction	intention	punctuation
detection	invasion	question
determination	invention	radiation
dictation	inversion	ration
direction	invitation	

Word List 13 (continued)

-ion (continued)

reaction	salvation	television
reception	sanction	tension
reduction	satisfaction	tradition
reflection	section	vacation
regulation	selection	variation
relation	session	version
reproduction	station	vision
revolution	suction	

-ive

abusive	excessive	positive
active	executive	productive
attractive	expansive	reactive
captive	expensive	relative
cooperative	impressive	representative
defensive	inventive	repulsive
destructive	locomotive	
elective	objective	

Sentence List 13:
Suffixes -*ion*, -*ive*

The new building was attractive to some and repulsive to others.

I need to make a correction to this division problem or the fraction will not be correct.

Defensive driving will help keep the traffic on our highways in much better condition.

A good education may help you to become a more productive person.

I have a relative who was very active in the election of our president.

The expression of your emotions can help get rid of tension and anger.

The construction of the bridge was very expensive.

The television version of this book of fiction was not very impressive.

Story 13:
Suffixes *-ion, -ive*

Diving in "Inner Space"

A new focus of attention has been given to the expansive reaches of "inner space" in recent years. Skin and scuba diving have become an attractive sport to active people of all ages seeking information about the seas. Men and women like Jacques Cousteau have become concerned about the protection of the ocean and its resources as humans begin their exploration of this new world.

Divers must be fit and in very good condition. They must have excessive knowledge of the ocean and of the reaction of the human body in these strange conditions. Divers must also have training in first aid.

A diver must have the right tools for diving. Scuba gear can be purchased or rented, but either way it is expensive.

For a diving session in the cool waters off the California coast, it is necessary to wear a wet suit, a dry suit, or both to prevent excessive loss of body heat. A weight belt must be worn to offset the positive effect of the body and the wet suit that causes one to float. A diver also needs a face mask with a good seal, a snorkel, a set of boots and regulation fins, and a flotation vest. Gloves are an option. A scuba tank and a regulator are used to breathe underwater. A diver should also carry a knife and compass for direction. A float and a flag are used to caution boats and other divers. There are other tools in addition to these for taking pictures, fishing, or studying.

A good diver never dives alone, obeys all safety rules, and leaves the ocean as he or she found it so that it will remain productive and attractive for many years to come.

Word List 14:
Suffixes -*able*, -*ment*

-*able*

accountable	distractable	recoverable
admirable	durable	redeemable
adorable	employable	reliable
agreeable	enjoyable	remarkable
available	honorable	renewable
capable	knowledgeable	respectable
changeable	liveable	retrainable
cleanable	lovable	suitable
comfortable	movable	touchable
conceivable	notable	treatable
curable	payable	washable
dependable	questionable	
desirable	readable	

-*ment*

agreement	disappointment	judgment
amazement	disarmament	movement
amendment	discontentment	pavement
amusement	discouragement	payment
appointment	disenchantment	placement
argument	displacement	punishment
arrangement	employment	replacement
assignment	enjoyment	resentment
basement	equipment	settlement
concealment	excitement	statement
department	government	treatment
development	instrument	
disagreement	investment	

Sentence List 14:
Suffixes *-able, -ment*

After payment was made for tickets at the amusement park, we began our day of excitement and enjoyment.

The adorable little girl picked up the lovable puppy and kissed its nose.

The dog was quite capable of finding a comfortable spot on the pavement to sleep.

I bought a durable pair of jeans at the department store.

The doctor is very knowledgeable about the treatment of sick children.

The basement was too dark and dirty to be suitable for living.

My teacher said that the assignment was not readable.

I would be agreeable to a settlement of this argument.

To our amazement, the injured cat made an admirable attempt at movement toward its master.

Story 14:
Suffixes *-able, -ment*

Archery

Archery has played a notable role in human development. Early humans used their archery skills for protection, as a means of getting suitable food, and for their own amusement and enjoyment. They had to have sure judgment and quick smooth movements. The bow was also used throughout the world as an instrument of music.

Today archery is an enjoyable sport that is available to the whole family. It is also conceivable that poor posture, if caught at a young age, may be curable through regular practice of the sport on the archery range.

Archery tackle refers to the equipment used by the archer while shooting. The statement, "Athletes will be as good or poor as their equipment," applies to archery. Matched arrows and bows must be suitable to the individual using them. Equipment may be purchased from a respectable, reliable archery shop. Equipment from a department store is a poor investment. Fiberglass arrows may be best for beginners and are quite durable. There is disagreement about what is the best bow. A good recurve bow is probably the most dependable bow on the market. It is usually desirable for a beginner to use a lighter bow than a skilled archer. Other available tackle includes a bow sight, a finger tab, and an arm guard.

Archery has its place in history, literature, art, and religion. There is also agreement that it will have a place in the future.

Word List 15:
Suffixes -*ful*, -*less*, -*ness*

-*ful*

armful	doubtful	peaceful
awful	dreadful	playful
bashful	fearful	powerful
beautiful	forceful	restful
cheerful	graceful	truthful
colorful	hateful	useful
cupful	helpful	watchful
deceitful	hopeful	wishful
delightful	joyful	

-*less*

careless	flawless	priceless
cheerless	friendless	sightless
colorless	helpless	sleepless
doubtless	homeless	speechless
effortless	hopeless	thoughtless
fearless	noiseless	

-*ness*

brightness	humanness	quickness
directness	illness	sadness
emptiness	kindness	sickness
fullness	lateness	softness
gladness	loneliness	sweetness
goodness	madness	thickness
happiness	neatness	weakness

Sentence List 15:
Suffixes *-ful*, *-less*, *-ness*

The fearful child stood motionless in the noiseless room.

The graceful dancer did a joyful dance of happiness.

The delightful sweetness of the cake kept me speechless.

I am doubtful that this dreadful emptiness in my stomach will be gone after just one apple.

I love to watch the beautiful ocean because it makes me feel so restful and peaceful.

The playful puppy was homeless.

I am hopeful that you will be truthful.

He spoke in a powerful voice and flashed a watchful look toward the sky.

Story 15:
Suffixes -*ful*, -*less*, -*ness*

The Match

Bob: Hi! Ready for a restful tennis match?

Tim: Sure! Beating you is always effortless.

Bob: Effortless? You're the one with the hopeless backhand.

Tim: Ha! And you have the quickness of a turtle on the court.

Bob: Enough of this talk. Let's play tennis. Hey, that was really a forceful serve! I'd better keep a watchful eye on you.

Tim: What an awful shot. I'm just careless. I act like I have an armful of bricks. Thoughtless!

Bob: To be truthful, I'd be grateful for a little weakness on your part. I just can't seem to get my flawless game together today.

Tim: That's wishful thinking!

Bob: I am rather graceful today, aren't I?

Tim: Dreadful is more like it. Well, that's the match. Better luck next time!

Bob: Thanks, that was fun. It was a good match. That last shot of yours was priceless. Let's get a soda.

Tim: Fine! You showed no weakness today. That was a good workout. Let's play again tomorrow.

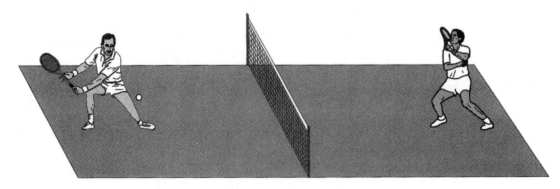

Word List 16:
Suffixes -*al*, -*ous*

-*al*

additional	formal	political
alphabetical	functional	postal
bifocal	historical	regional
brutal	hysterical	rehearsal
central	legal	terminal
chronological	musical	tribal
coastal	numeral	typical
electrical	personal	
focal	physical	

-*ous*

ambitious	glorious	poisonous
courageous	gracious	previous
dangerous	humorous	prosperous
delicious	joyous	religious
enormous	mysterious	studious
envious	nervous	various
famous	numerous	

Sentence List 16:
Suffixes *-al, -ous*

That enormous slice of cake was delicious.

The mysterious story was not easy to understand.

The lovely, gracious queen became famous for her numerous religious speeches.

The central coastal region has examples of the typical sea life in this state.

Some tribal customs seem brutal and involve physical pain.

I have always been nervous before my previous speeches, but today I will remain calm.

There will be a rehearsal of the historical play in the central lobby at 8:00 A.M.

This enormous list must be put in alphabetical order.

Story 16:
Suffixes *-al, -ous*

Sailing on Ice

Iceboating or hard-water sailing is a regional sport because you need cold weather to do it. Central and eastern New York get cold enough for a typical day of iceboating. The cold wind can be brutal, so the captain must be courageous.

Sailing on the ice can be dangerous and requires about the same physical strength as sailing on water. A typical iceboat glides on three metal runners. There are various boat styles, as numerous ambitious boaters build their own iceboats.

Racers wear functional safety equipment such as helmets and goggles. The boats may look a little humorous sailing along the ice, but their captains say they get a glorious, joyous feeling of personal freedom while iceboating.

Suffixes: Review Story

Another Way to Ride

Horse vaulting provides excitement and enjoyment for sports lovers all over the world. This team sport demands the gracefulness of a gymnast, the quickness in movement of a hockey player, and the courageous ambition of a high diver. The German version of this impressive sport was brought to the United States over 24 years ago. News of this remarkable sport spread with unbelievable rapidness.

There are now about forty additional U.S. teams in the competition. Reaction to the sport has been excellent. After many rehearsals, the precision riding of these teams is flawless and leaves audiences speechless.

Beginning riders may be nervous before a national competition. After a while, the riders lose their tension and provide enjoyable entertainment with their remarkable routines. Each team member must do a set of special exercises and is then able to do an original program. To be successful, the team must work together.

Word List 17: Syllabication

abominable	compassionate	elevation	indignation
additional	completion	emotion	inducement
adjoining	composition	emphatic	industrial
allergic	compressed	evacuation	information
alphabetical	concentration	evaporate	inhabitant
alternately	confidential	evolution	initiate
amplifier	congregation	executive	intelligent
anthropologist	continent	expedition	intention
anticipation	continual	experience	intervals
apparatus	contribution	explosion	intimidate
apparition	contributor	extension	intricate
application	conventional	extraordinary	invasion
apprehensive	convulsively	fantastic	investigate
archaeologist	correspondent	fertilizer	investigating
armadillo	craftsmanship	flotation	irritated
arrogantly	decapitated	formation	isolation
artifact	decaying	frustrating	jettisoned
artificial	declaration	generosity	lacerate
association	decompression	geologist	legislation
astronaut	defiance	gravitational	librarian
astronomical	definition	gravity	limitation
atmosphere	delicatessen	hallucination	limitlessly
barnacle	delicious	historian	listlessly
barometer	demonstration	horizontal	locomotive
barometric	descended	hurricane	luminous
barracuda	description	ignition	malignant
bedraggled	detection	ignorant	malingering
beneficial	deteriorate	illuminated	manuscript
bibliography	detestable	imagination	meditation
bicentennial	devouring	imaginative	melancholy
binoculars	diameter	imitation	melodious
calamity	diminutive	immaculate	miraculously
casserole	dinosaur	immediate	monotonously
centimeter	diplomatic	immobilize	mysterious
charity	disintegrate	immortality	neighborhood
circulation	distributor	implication	obligation
circumstance	duplicate	impossible	occupation
collapsible	egotistical	inconvenience	ominous
combination	electrical	incredible	paleontologist
commercial	electricity	incredulous	parasites

Word List 17 (continued)

particles
pedestrian
perception
permission
perspiration
persuasion
pestilential
petition
phenomenon
photographic
population
position
potato
precision
preparation
prescription
presentation

presently
proficient
publisher
radial
rapidly
ravenous
refrigerate
regression
regulate
relative
reluctant
representative
reproduction
reproductive
repulsively
residential

respiration
revolution
satisfaction
sensibilities
sensitivity
sincerity
sombrero
specifications
spectacle
speculation
stalagmite
statistics
submicroscopic
substantial
superficial
television

testified
testimony
theoretically
tolerance
tradition
tremendously
trillions
ultimately
uncontaminated
unimaginable
universe
unreasonable
unrelenting
variation
vicinity
visibility

Sentence List 17: Syllabication

The amplifier made the music louder.

The archaeologist studied the bones of the dinosaur and the other artifacts found near the caves.

Sara is a kind, compassionate person.

The twelve contributors contributed five hundred dollars to the charity.

That delicatessen has delicious potato salad.

After the explosion there was an evacuation of the building.

The horizontal lines on the television screen make it impossible to see the picture.

The intricate puzzle is very frustrating.

The hurricane did substantial damage to our neighborhood.

The barometric pressure is falling rapidly.

Story 17: Syllabication

A Black Hole in Space

Do black holes really exist? The answer may lie beyond our present imagination.

In our galaxy there are trillions of stars. Most of them are unnamed. At any given time, some of these stars are dying. Some consume themselves, some explode, and others contract or draw in upon themselves. When a decaying star contracts, the matter of which it is made is tremendously compressed. The star shrinks limitlessly. It theoretically shrinks past pinpoint size, to submicroscopic size, to zero volume. Its surface gravity rises. This unrelenting gravity or gravitational whirlpool sweeps luminous gases and star particles into its core. Scientists don't know what happens ultimately. Maybe a new presently unimaginable universe is formed.

If the earth were to collapse from a diameter of nearly eight thousand miles down to two thousand miles, its increased gravity would cause a 175-pound man to weigh almost one and one-half tons. At a diameter half the size of a golf ball, the earth would become a black hole.

When a star becomes a devouring darkness, a ravenous force, nothing can ever again escape, not even light. Because nothing can escape, there is no way an observer investigating the immediate vicinity of a black hole could report back to us. Ultimately black holes could eat up all the matter in our galaxy.

Do black holes really exist? Many scientists believe that black holes are the completion of the evolution of stars that were once many times the size of the sun.

Prepositional Phrases

This appendix contains a list of prepositional phrases that may be used in teaching some of the most common words in the English language as well as the most common prepositions and nouns words. Some teachers object, perhaps rightly so, to the teaching of basic sight words or any high-utility word in isolation. For students who are having difficulty with any of the most commonly used prepositions, you may wish to use these phrases as you would the sight word phrases in Appendix A-5. You may also make an audio tape of the phrases to be sent home with students who are having difficulties with these words. The tape may be made as follows:

1. Copy the first page so that you will have it for further reference.
2. Number the first 10 to 15 phrases of the copy you have made. (Once you have worked with a student for a short while, you will know how many he is capable of learning. If you find that you send 15 phrases on an audio tape home and the student has easily mastered all of them, send home 20 the next time. Increase these to the maximum that the student can successfully master in the time between meetings.) Place a 1 by the first phrase, a 2 by the second phrase, and so on. Then make an audio tape with a script much the same as the one that follows:

"You will hear some phrases on this tape recording. First you will hear a number and then you will hear the phrase. Look at each word as it is pronounced on this tape recording. There will then be a short pause for you to say the phrase. Be sure to point to each of the words as you say them. Number one, *about his dog* (pause), be sure to point to each word as you say it. Number two, *about my cat* (pause); Number three, *about dinner....*"

It is important that the student point to each word as it is pronounced. This way the student makes the connection between the spoken word and the written word. The following are commonly used phrases. Most of the words are also in the Fry (1972) list of the 600 most frequently used words in reading and writing the English language.

REFERENCES

Fry, E. (1972). *Reading instruction for classroom and clinic.* New York: McGraw-Hill.

about

about his dog
about my cat
about dinner
about my sister
about the room

after

after we've gone
after three years
after work
after his mother
after the bell

along

along the ground
along the water
along the wall
along the road
along the way

around

around the garden
around the school
around here
around eight o'clock
around the trees

as

as a house
as a girl
as a boy
as a man
as a woman

at

at the house
at the door
at the party
at the water
at the half

before

before winter
before bed
before the fire
before eight
before we go

but

but the outside
but the poor
but the yard
but his head
but her eyes

by

by the hair
by the horse
by the week
by the government
by her eyes

down

down the hill
down the side
down the front
down the street
down the stairs

for

for the law
for the doctor
for the money
for a guess
for tomorrow

from

from the cows
from her need
from my cousin
from the cold
from the story

in

in the hour
in the music
in the spring
in the picture
in his voice

into

into the box
into the floor
into the train
into the bank
into the office

like

like the wind
like snow
like you
like her hat
like a bird

near

near the fish
near the war
near the bridge
near the farm
near the airplane

next

next turn
next president
next to me
next to him
next in line

of

of the sun
of my life
of the farm
of the paper
of the church

off

off the wall
off the water
off the horse
off the table
off of it

on

on one afternoon
on Friday morning
on her smile
on the house
on her face

out

out of paper
out to study
out of school
out of line
out in public

outside

outside the country
outside the woods
outside the town
outside the third grade
outside the grocery store

over

over his clothes
over the ice
over the city
over the thing
over his name

to

to the summer
to the fair
to the state
to the world
to the house

through

through them

through his heart

through twenty

through the day

through the water

until

until the night

until they come

until tomorrow

until this minute

until he knew

up

up the window

up the river

up the table

up in the air

up to speak

with

with his suit

with my uncle

with her aunt

with a present

with the baby

Prefixes and Suffixes

Prefixes

Prefix	Meaning	Examples
a	on, in, at	alive, asleep, abed
a (an)	not, without	anhydrous, anhydride, anarchy
*ab, abs	*from*	abduct, abrogate, abstain
*ad (ac, af, ag, al, an, ap, ar, as, at)	*to*, at, toward	adapt, accuse, aggrade, acclaim, affirm
ambi (amb)	both	ambicoloration, ambivalent, ambidextrous
amphi (amph)	both, around	amphibian, amphitheatre, amphibolite
ana	back, again, up, similar to	analysis, analogy, anabaptist
ante	before, earlier date	antechamber, antedate, antetype
anti (ant, anth)	against, counteracts, prevents	antilabor, antiaircraft, antitoxin
apo (ap)	off, away from, used before	apology, aphelion, apocrine
archi (arch)	chief, extreme	architect, archenemy, archfiend

*Prefixes that appeared most frequently and accounted for 82% of the 61 different basic forms of prefixes studied by Stauffer. The italicized word represents the meaning of the prefix in the study referred to here. From Stauffer, R. G. (1969). *Teaching reading as a thinking process* (p. 348). New York: Harper & Row.

Prefix	Meaning	Examples
auto	self-propelling, self	automobile, autotruck, autobiography
*be	to make, about, *by*	belittle, beguile, befriend
bene	well	benefit, benefactor, benevolent
bi	having two, double	bicycle, bilingual, biweekly
by	near, extra	bystander, by-pass, byproduct
cata (cat, cath)	down, against	catastrophic, catacomb, catheter
centi	one hundred	centigrade, centimeter, centipede
circum	around, about	circumnavigate, circumpolar, circumspect
*com (co, col, con, cor)	*with*, together, intensification	combine, copilot, collect, confided, corrupt
contra	against	contradict, contraband, contrarious
counter	opposite, in retaliation, opposed to but like	counterclockwise, counterattack, counterpart
*de	*from*, away	deport, detract, devitalize
deca (dec, deka, dek)	ten	decimal, decade, decagon
di (dis)	twice, double	dissect, dichroism, dichloride
dia	through, across	diagonal, diagram, diagnose
*dis	opposite, refuse to, *apart*	disagree, disintegrate, disable, disengage
ec (ex)	out of, from	eccentric, exodus, exaggerate
*en	*in*, into, make	encircle, enact, encourage
enter	to go into, among	enterprise, entered, entertain

Prefix	Meaning	Examples
epi (ep)	upon, after, over	epitaph, epilogue, epicene
equi	equal	equilibrium, equilateral, equiangular
*ex	*out*	exile, exhale, exhaust
eu	well	euphony, euphonism, eugenic
extra	beyond	extraordinary, extrajudicial, extracurricular
for	very, neglect, away	forlorn, forbid, forget
fore	before, in front	forepaws, forehand, foreleg
geo	earth, ground, soil	geography, geographic, geology
hemi	half	hemisphere, hemicycle, hemistich
hexa (hex)	six	hexagon, hexapod, hexachord
hyper	over, above	hypersensitive, hyperactive, hyperacid
hypo	under, beneath	hypocrite, hypocycloid, hypodermic
*in (il, im, ir)	in, within, *into*	inbreed, instigate, infect
*in (il, im, ir)	no, *not*, without	illiterate, immaterial, insignificant, irresponsible
inter	between, with	interurban, interlock, interact
intra	within, inside of	intrastate, intravenous, intramural
intro	into, within	introvert, introspective, introduce
kilo	one thousand	kilowatt, kilogram, kilocycle
mal (male)	bad, wrong, ill	maladjust, malediction, maladroit
meta (met)	after, change in place or form	metacarpal, metabolism, metaprotein
milli	one thousand	milligram, millimeter, milliard

Prefix	Meaning	Examples
mis (miso)	wrong	misplace, misadventure, misanthrope
mono (mon)	one	monosyllable, monologue, monolayer
multi	many	multitude, multiply, multiphase
non	not	nonunion, nondemocratic, nonzero,
ob (oc, of, op)	to, upon, totally	object, occur, offer, oppose
oct (octa, octo)	eight	octopus, octagon, octopod
off	from	offspring, offset, offstage
out	beyond, excels	outtalk, outweigh, outmaneuver
over	too much	overactive, overheated, overage
par (para)	by, past, accessory	parallel, paragraph, parasympathetic
penta (pent)	five	pentagon, Pentateuch, pentane
per	through, completely	perceive, persuade, perchloride
peri	around, about	perimeter, periphery, periscope
phono (phon, phone)	voice, sound	phonograph, phonate, phoneme
poly	many	polygon, polygamy, polysulfide
post	later, behind	postgraduate, postaxial, postlude
*pre	*before*, in front (of), superior	prewar, preaxial, pre-eminent
*pro	moving forward, acting for, defending, favoring, *in front of*	progress, pronoun, prosecutor, prolabor, prologue

Prefix	Meaning	Examples
quadr	four	quadrant, quadrangle, quadrennial
quint	five	quintuplets, quintet, quintillion
*re (red)	*back*, again	review, regain, recall
retro	backwards	retroactive, retrospect, retroflex
semi	half, partly, twice in (period)	semicircle, semicivilized, semiannually
sex (sexi)	six	sextant, sexpartite, sexivalent
*sub (suc, suf, sug, sup, sur, sus)	*under*	submarine, succeed, suffix
super	above, exceeding	superior, superstructure, superscribe
sur	over, above, beyond	surcoat, surface, surbase
syn (sym)	with, together	sympathy, synthesis, symptom
tele (tel)	afar, of, in, or by	television, telescope, telephoto
trans	across	transcontinental, transport, transatlantic
tri	three	triangle, tricycle, triweekly
ultra	beyond, excessively	ultraviolet, ultramodern, ultramarine
*un	*not*, opposite	unannounced, unburden, uncrowned
uni	consisting of only one	unicellular, uniform, unicorn
under	below	underpaid, underworked, underpass
vice	in place of	viceroy, vice-president, vice-consul
with	against, away	withstand, withdraw, withhold

Suffixes

Suffix	Meaning	Examples	Used to Form
able (ible, ble)	able to, worthy of	obtainable divisible breakable	adjectives
ac (ic, al, an)	characteristic of, having to do with, caused by	cardiac alcoholic comical American	adjectives
aceous (acious)	characterized by, like	carbonaceous crustaceous tenacious	adjectives
ade	action, product	blockade limeade lemonade	nouns
age	act of, cost of	tillage passage postage	nouns
al	relating to, of, pertaining to	directional fictional dismissal	adjectives
al	action process	rehearsal arrival acquittal	nouns
an (ian, ean)	pertaining to, of, born in	diocesan Christian European	adjectives
an	one who, belonging to	artisan African American	nouns
ance (ence)	act of, state of being	continuance reference performance	nouns
ancy (ency)	state of being, act	efficiency piquancy emergency	nouns

Suffix	Meaning	Examples	Used to Form
ant (ent)	one who	accountant suppliant superintendent	nouns
ant	performing, promoting	litigant expectorant expectant	adjectives
ar	relating to, like, of the nature of	regular polar singular	adjectives
ard (art)	one who (excessively)	braggart dullard pollard	nouns
arium	place relating to	planetarium sanitarium aquarium	nouns
ary (ar)	relating to	military dictionary scholar	nouns
ate	office, function	directorate vicarate magistrate	nouns
ate	acted on	temperate determinate animate	adjectives
ate	to become, combine, arrange for	evaporate chlorinate orchestrate	verbs
ation (ition)	state of	translation realization nutrition	nouns
cle	little, small	article particle corpuscle	nouns
dom	state of being	wisdom martyrdom freedom	nouns

Suffix	Meaning	Examples	Used to Form
ed	tending to, having	cultured versed bigoted	adjectives
en	cause to have, made of	strengthen woolen wooden	nouns
en	to make, made of	deepen strengthen fasten	verbs
ent (ence)	quality, act, degree	solvent emergence despondence	nouns
er (ar, ior, yer)	a thing or action, connected with, or associated	batter beggar interior lawyer	nouns
ery (erie)	place to or for collection of	nunnery jewelry tanneries	nouns
esce	to begin	effervesce fluoresce coalesce	verbs
escent	starting to be	obsolescent fluorescent alkalescent	adjectives
esque	like, having quality or style of	picturesque Romanesque statuesque	adjectives
ess	female	patroness giantess princess	nouns
et (ette)	little, female	dinette suffragette pullet	nouns
ful	full of	hopeful playful joyful	adjectives

Suffix	Meaning	Examples	Used to Form
fy	to make, become	liquefy purify glorify	verbs
hood	state of, condition	womanhood childhood priesthood	nouns
eer	one who, calling or profession	auctioneer buccaneer profiteer	nouns
ic (ics)	relating to, affected with	alcoholic allergic volcanic	adjectives
ic (ical)	one that produces	magic cosmetic radical	nouns
ice	condition or quality of	malice justice practice	nouns
ie	small, little	doggie lassie	nouns
ile (il)	appropriate to, suited for, capable of	docile missile civil	adjectives
ing	related to, made of	farthing banking cooking	nouns
ion (sion)	result of act, state	regulation hydration correction	nouns
ise (ize)	to make, treat with	sterilize summarize finalize	verbs
ish	having	boyish purplish fortyish	adjectives

Suffix	Meaning	Examples	Used to Form
ism	act of, state of	baptism invalidism animalism	nouns
ist	practicer or believer in one who, the doer	evangelist pianist violinist	nouns
ive	related to, tending to	creative massive amusive	adjectives
ize	to become, become like	Americanize crystallize socialize	verbs
kin	little	catkin manikin napkin	nouns
le (el)	small, a thing used for for doing	icicle handle mantle	nouns
less	without, lacking	careless hopeless painless	adjectives
ling	young, small	duckling hireling suckling	nouns
ly	in a way, manner	softly quietly hoarsely	adverbs
ment	concrete result, state, process	embankment development amazement	nouns
ness	state of being	happiness cheerfulness hopefulness	nouns
ock	small one	hillock bullock paddock	nouns

Suffix	Meaning	Examples	Used to Form
or	state of, does certain thing	pallor grantor elevator	nouns
orium	place for, giving	sanatorium auditorium haustorium	nouns
ory	tending to, producing	auditory gustatory justificatory	adjectives
ose	full of, containing, like	verbose cymose morose	adjectives
ous	having, full of	religious generous poisonous	adjectives
ship	state of, office, art	friendship clerkship horsemanship	nouns
ster	one that does or is	spinster teamster youngster	nouns
th	act of, state of	growth length spilth	nouns
tude	condition	certitude gratitude finitude	nouns
ty (ity)	state of, degree, quality	masculinity priority timidity	nouns
ulent	tending to, abounds in	fraudulent flocculent opulent	adjectives
ure	act, office	exposure legislature procedure	nouns

Suffix	Meaning	Examples	Used to Form
ward	in specified direction	southward seaward backward	adverbs
wise	manner, way	likewise clockwise lengthwise	adverbs
y	like a, full of	rosy fishy glassy	adjectives
y (acy)	state of, action, condition, position	jealousy inquiry celibacy	nouns

Using the Cloze Procedure

DEVELOPING, ADMINISTERING, AND SCORING CLOZE PASSAGES

In constructing **cloze passages** you could omit every third, fifth, or tenth word. However, most of the research is based on the deletion of every fifth word. Blank lines of equal length replace each of the deleted words. It should also be stressed that the commonly used percentages for determining students' independent, instructional, and frustration levels are based on the deletion of every fifth word. If every eighth or tenth word were deleted, these commonly used percentages would not apply.

Passages may vary in length depending on the grade level of the students; however, for students of ages equivalent to third- or fourth-grade level or above, passages of about 250 words are often used. The entire first and last sentences are usually left intact. If passages of 250 words plus intact first and last sentences are used, and if every fifth word is omitted, there will be 50 blanks, and every blank or answer will be worth two percentage points.

Cloze passages may be administered in a group situation much as with standardized reading tests. However, in administering cloze passages, there are usually no specific time limits for completion of the work.

For passages in which every fifth word has been deleted, the percentages for the various reading levels are as follows:

Independent Level = 57% to 100%

Instructional Level = 44% to 56%

Frustration Level = 43% or below

In scoring the passages, only the exact word omitted is usually counted as correct; that is, appropriate synonyms are not counted as correct. Research has shown that the overall percentages change very little regardless of whether synonyms are counted as correct or incorrect. Furthermore, if words other than the exact word omitted were counted, scoring would be much more difficult; that is, what one teacher might consider an adequate answer, another teacher may not, and we would tend to lose interscorer reliability. In scoring cloze passages, however, students are not usually penalized for incorrect spelling as long as there is little or no doubt about which word they meant to use.

A plastic overlay such as an overhead projector transparency can be made of each cloze passage with the correct answers appearing on the plastic overlay. When this is superimposed on the student's copy, you can readily check the number of right and wrong answers. These can, in turn, be converted to percentages. From these percentages you can then determine whether the material is at the student's independent, instructional, or frustration level.

USING THE CLOZE PROCEDURE TO PLACE STUDENTS IN GRADED MATERIALS

1. Select 6 to 12 passages from a book or material that students will possibly be using. (If the results of the test show that the book is too easy or difficult for the students, another must be selected.) Pick them randomly but equally distributed from the front to the back of the book.
2. Give the tests to 25 to 30 students in a class in which the text is commonly used.
3. Calculate the mean score on each test and then the mean of the means (see pp. 503–504).
4. Select the test that is closest to the mean of the means and throw the rest of the scores away.
5. When a test has been selected for each of the texts a teacher is likely to use, the tests can be duplicated and compiled into booklets that can be administered as group tests. When a student's score is 57% or higher, the student is reading at his independent reading level. A score from 44% to 56% is equivalent to the student's instructional reading level. A score of 43% or less is considered to be at the student's frustration level. (In a textbook, of course, one is concerned with placing the student in the textbook that is represented by the passage in which the student scored at his instructional reading level.)

USING THE CLOZE PROCEDURE TO MEET THE NEEDS OF THE STUDENTS

1. Divide the book into sections and select two or more passages from each section. The same length passages as described earlier can be used.
2. Make a random selection of the students for whom the book will be used.
3. If you are using a great number of students, you may wish to put them into a number of groups and then let each group take some of the tests. (Make sure, however, that the selection of the subgroups is done randomly).
4. If students are able to score at their instructional level on the passages from the book, then it would be considered suitable for them. On the other hand, if most students scored at their frustration level on the passages from the book, it would be considered too difficult for them.

THE RELIABILITY OF THE CLOZE PROCEDURE

The reliability of the cloze procedure will essentially depend on the following factors:

1. If longer tests are used, the students' scores will probably be more accurate, but it will take longer to correct them.
2. If a larger number of tests is used when selecting the one to represent the material, the test selected will more accurately represent the difficulty of the material.
3. Some materials are uneven in difficulty. These materials should be avoided if possible.
4. The procedure outlined here must be followed exactly or the results will not be accurate.

PROCEDURE FOR DETERMINING THE MEAN OF THE MEANS

The example in Figure B-9.1 illustrates how to find the mean of the means. In this example, there were 10 passages and five students. (In determining the mean of the means one would, of course, be likely to have more than five students.) Note that there are 10 means: 52.4, 34.6, and so on. These means were added and their total was 480.6. When this figure (480.6) was divided by the number of means (10), the mean of the means was 48.06. This figure was closest to the mean of passage number 8 (47.4). Therefore, that passage was most representative of the difficulty of the

FIGURE B-9.1

	1	2	3	4	5	6	7	8	9	10
Mary	56	42	84	12	48	34	51	47	75	49
Sam	42	41	83	10	40	30	49	50	74	42
Sally	32	36	74	18	42	41	55	51	75	45
Joe	76	26	66	26	47	31	60	38	69	39
Fred	56	28	54	41	49	33	59	51	72	54
Totals	262	173	361	107	226	169	274	237	365	229
Means	52.4	34.6	72.2	21.4	45.2	33.8	54.8	47.4	73.0	45.8

Total of the Means = 480.6

Mean of the Means = $\dfrac{480.6}{10}$ = 48.06

material. As a whole, passage 8 would be kept, and the rest of the passages would be discarded.

Passage 8 is then given to new students with whom you may wish to use the text from which number 8 was derived. If they can read passage 8 with an accuracy of between 44% and 56%, this text would be appropriate for them at their instructional reading level. If they scored at 43% or lower, the text would be at their frustration reading level. If they scored at 57% or better, the text would be at their independent reading level.

Repeated Readings Chart

The method of repeated readings is described in the introductory chapter. On page 507 is an example of a repeated readings chart in which the student began reading at 35 words per minute and, after eight trials, was reading 120 words per minute. The student also began this passage with 26 errors and, after eight trials, made no errors. To compute words per minute, count the number of words the student is to read and then determine the time it takes the student to read that passage in seconds.

The words per minute equals the number of words read divided by the number of seconds it took to read the passage, multiplied by 60. A student who reads 220 words in 110 seconds would then be reading at $220/110 = 2.0 \times 60 = 120$ words per minute. In doing repeated readings, it is recommended that you use 100 words per grade level times .75. Thus, a student in the fourth grade should read $400 \times .75$ or 300 words; a student in the fifth grade should read $500 \times .75$ or a 375-word passage; and so on.

On page 509 is a blank repeated readings chart that you may wish to detach and duplicate for students' use.

Repeated Readings Chart

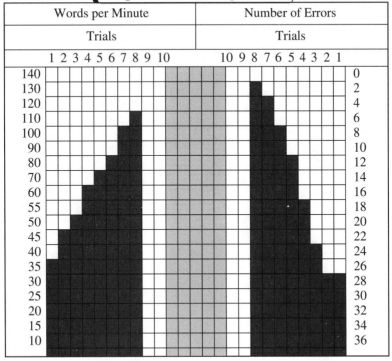

Words per Minute		Number of Errors	
Trials		Trials	
1 2 3 4 5 6 7 8 9 10		10 9 8 7 6 5 4 3 2 1	
140			0
130			2
120			4
110			6
100			8
90			10
80			12
70			14
60			16
55			18
50			20
45			22
40			24
35			26
30			28
25			30
20			32
15			34
10			36

Repeated Readings Chart

Words per Minute		Number of Errors	
Trials		Trials	
1 2 3 4 5 6 7 8 9 10		10 9 8 7 6 5 4 3 2 1	

140	0
130	2
120	4
110	6
100	8
90	10
80	12
70	14
60	16
55	18
50	20
45	22
40	24
35	26
30	28
25	30
20	32
15	34
10	36

Name of Student: _____

Number of Words in Passage: _____

Precision Reading Form and Charts

The precision reading technique is described in the introductory chapter. On page 513 is a blank form that may be used to record the student's performance during two separate precision reading trials.

At the top of the form are blank spaces to record the following information: student's name, teacher's name, date(s) of trials, the page on which the passage begins (if it was taken from a book), and the page on which the passage ends.

The form is easy to use. The numbers below the lines correspond to the sentences that the student reads. The teacher merely writes a plus (+) or a minus (−) above each line, as the student finishes the sentence, to indicate whether the student read the sentence correctly (+) or with one or more errors (0). At the completion of the reading (up to 50 sentences per trial on this form), the teacher and student count the number of pluses, then tabulate the efficiency rate.

The efficiency rate is a percentage, obtained by dividing the number of sentences read without error by the total number of sentences, and multiplying this figure by 100.

Efficiency rate = the total number of correct sentences ÷ the total number of sentences × 100.

Example: 42 correct sentences ÷ 50 total sentences × 100 = efficiency rate of 84% (or, if total of 50 sentences is always used, multiply the number of correct sentences by 2)

After the student's reading performance is tabulated, the teacher or student then completes an accuracy chart, such as the example on page 512. If the technique is used daily, the student will see improvement in her reading of the same passage over time by looking at the chart. When the student achieves 100% on two successive readings, a new, more difficult passage may be selected.

GRAPHING ACCURACY

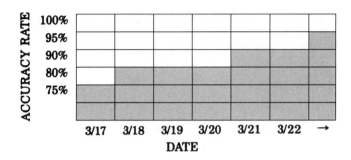

The graph begins at 75% accuracy because the student should not be reading any material at a lower rate.

GRAPHING THE NUMBER OF CORRECT SENTENCES

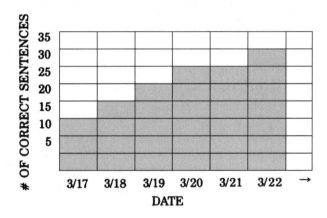

Teacher judgment should be used in deciding what constitutes an error. In some cases, for example, the teacher may choose not to count self-corrections as errors, especially if the teacher has been encouraging the student to read carefully and go back and self-correct oral reading when necessary.

This method is designed to stress accuracy over speed. Only after the student is able to read material at grade level with consistent accuracy should the technique be modified to encourage reading speed. To do this, the same recording chart is used; however, the student is asked to read for a specified time (which may be indicated in the *Time* space on the recording form shown on p. 513). At the end of the specified time, the teacher or student then graphs the number of sentences read correctly on the second chart that appears above. Before using this technique, it is suggested that you read the more complete description in the introductory chapter.

PRECISION READING FORM
AND CHARTS

Student _____   Teacher _____

Date(s) _____   Begin on _____   End on _____

_____

TRIAL # _____
Scoring by Sentences

__	__	__	__	__	__	__	__	__	__	__	__	__	__	__	__	__
1	2	3	4	5	6	7	8	9	10	11	12	13	14	15	16	17

__	__	__	__	__	__	__	__	__	__	__	__	__	__	__	__	__
18	19	20	21	22	23	24	25	26	27	28	29	30	31	32	33	34

__	__	__	__	__	__	__	__	__	__	__	__	__	__	__	__	__
35	36	37	38	39	40	41	42	43	44	45	46	47	48	49	50	

Tabulating Efficiency   [TIME: _____]

_____ ÷ _____ × 100 = _____

correct sentences   total sentences   efficiency rate

_____

TRIAL # ____
Scoring by Sentences

__	__	__	__	__	__	__	__	__	__	__	__	__	__	__	__	__
1	2	3	4	5	6	7	8	9	10	11	12	13	14	15	16	17

__	__	__	__	__	__	__	__	__	__	__	__	__	__	__	__	__
18	19	20	21	22	23	24	25	26	27	28	29	30	31	32	33	34

__	__	__	__	__	__	__	__	__	__	__	__	__	__	__	__	__
35	36	37	38	39	40	41	42	43	44	45	46	47	48	49	50	

Tabulating Efficiency   [TIME: _____]

_____ ÷ _____ × 100 = _____

correct sentences   total sentences   efficiency rate

Graph Forms

ACCURACY

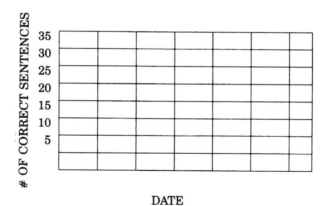

ACCURACY RATE

100%
95%
90%
80%
75%

DATE

NUMBER OF CORRECT SENTENCES

OF CORRECT SENTENCES

35
30
25
20
15
10
5

DATE

APPENDIX B-12

Charts for Graphing Words per Minute and Comprehension

This appendix is for students to use in graphing their reading rate in words per minute, as well as graphing their percentage of comprehension. As noted in the description of the precision reading technique in the introductory chapter and Appendix B-11, emphasis should be placed on *speed* of reading only after the student demonstrates an ability to read materials at grade level with consistent *accuracy*.

A number of available study-skills and reading-rate books present passages to be read by the student. These are usually followed by comprehension questions, most often 10, for the student to answer. You may wish to use the system of graphing each factor separately, which appears on page 520 or the single-chart system on page 519, which takes both percentage of comprehension and reading rate in words per minute into account. It will, of course, do the student little good to improve reading rate if comprehension suffers considerably in the process. In using the combination chart on page 520, multiply the number of words per minute by the percentage of comprehension and then graph the combination of these two factors. On page 518 you will find a sample of Fred's reading scores graphed for six trials. Note that there are blank lines on the left side of the graph to be filled in by the student. The lines have been left blank because every student will tend to read at a different rate. As the student gains in competence, he will probably improve in overall comprehension. Although percentage of comprehension may decrease as the student increases reading speed, it will usually increase after practice. Start the numbers representing the combination of the words per minute and percentage of comprehension on the third line from the bottom (as shown in Fred's example), since it is quite possible that the student may decrease in overall score slightly before beginning to increase that score. The method of computing Fred's scores is shown below the graph of Fred's reading performance. This is the system that you should, of course, use if you wish to graph the students' scores yourself.

On Fred's first trial, he read at 150 words per minute and had a comprehension score of 60%. His score was $150 \times 60 = 9,000$. This score was then put as the first trial using the third line from the bottom, in case his score might decrease in any future trials instead of increase.

Name **Fred**

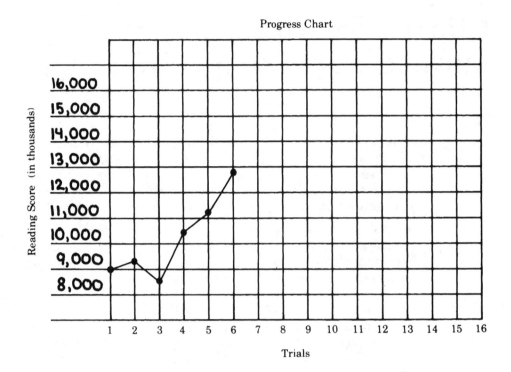

Progress Chart

On the following five trials, Fred's scores are shown below and graphed above.

Trial 2: 155 words per minute with a comprehension score of 60% = 9,300
Trial 3: 170 words per minute with a comprehension score of 50% = 8,500
Trial 4: 175 words per minute with a comprehension score of 60% = 10,500
Trial 5: 185 words per minute with a comprehension score of 60% = 11,100
Trial 6: 185 words per minute with a comprehension score of 70% = 12,950

Name _____

Progress Chart

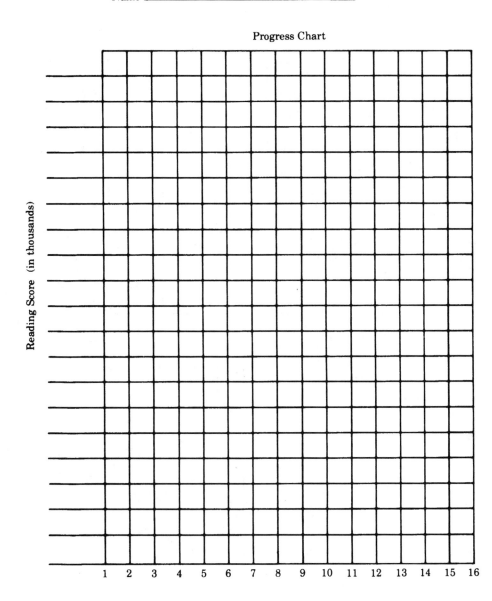

Reading Score (in thousands)

1   2   3   4   5   6   7   8   9   10   11   12   13   14   15   16

ILLUSTRATING WORDS PER MINUTE AND
PERCENT OF COMPREHENSION

Name _____

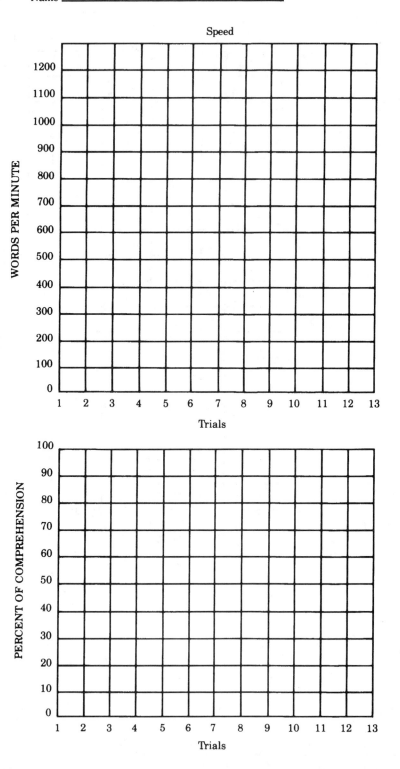

Speed

WORDS PER MINUTE

Trials

PERCENT OF COMPREHENSION

Trials

520

Suggestions for Interviewing Parents of Disabled Readers

Interviewing the parent or parents of a student with reading difficulties is important for several reasons. In the interview, you often will be able to discover certain things that parents may hesitate to put in writing. For example, in an interview parents often will give information concerning *their* perception of their child's capabilities. If the parents have other children, they will be able to give important information on their feelings concerning the child's ability to learn compared with their other children. This will provide you with important information, not only about the child but also about the parents' feelings toward the child's capabilities. It is important that parents believe that their child has the ability to learn and that they are willing to do their part in carrying out a program of remediation.

Parents can also provide accurate information on when they first noticed the reading problem. For example, if the child has had problems from the very beginning of school, it would indicate that the reading difficulties may be severe and may take longer to remediate. However, if the child suddenly started having reading problems at a later grade level, then it might indicate that the child has developed some emotional problem because of a divorce, a death in the family, or some other traumatic event. The development of a reading problem might also indicate the onset of a physical problem such as a need for eyeglasses, a hearing difficulty, or a side effect to a prescribed medication.

The initial interview should also reveal, to some extent, whether counseling is needed. The parents may need guidance to help them make the child feel confident in her ability to learn. The parents, perhaps unintentionally, may have given their child the impression that he does not have the ability to learn. The parent interview can also provide important information on whether the parents have been consistent in dealing with the child. For example, do the parents tell the child to do something and then not carry through with requiring it to be done, or is the child allowed to find excuses for not performing certain tasks?

In the initial parent interview, it is also important that you get a verbal commitment from the parents that they are willing to do such things as the following:

1. Be prompt and responsible in providing transportation to tutoring sessions, if required.

2. Follow up in scheduling appointments for physical examinations, including vision and hearing examinations, if necessary.

3. Set aside a specific time each day when the student is required to do homework assignments or recreational reading.

4. Provide a reading environment in which the student sees her parents reading.

5. Provide a quiet place where the student can concentrate on homework or recreational reading without being interrupted by brothers or sisters or without interference from a television or telephone.

6. Check to see that homework is done.

7. Take the student to the library and learn techniques for selecting books to be read for pleasure.

Glossary

Affixes   The verb *affix* means "to fasten"; the noun form is usually applied to suffixes and prefixes collectively.

Alphabet Knowledge   The ability to discriminate, recognize, and name the letters of the alphabet.

Basal Reader   A reading textbook designed for a specific grade level. These usually contain material designed to enhance specific skills, such as word-attack, vocabulary, and comprehension skills, along with teacher manuals and a wealth of other teaching/reinforcement materials.

Basic Sight Word Phrases   These are basic sight words that are grouped together in phrase units. When students learn to read these phrases quickly and smoothly, they usually transfer their ability to recognize basic sight words in isolation to reading them in context.

Basic Sight Words or **Basic Sight Vocabulary**   These are words that appear most often in reading material written for children and adults. For a student to master a basic sight word, she must recognize and pronounce the word instantly (in 1 second or less) every time she sees it. One of the most common basic sight word lists is the Dolch Basic Sight Vocabulary, which contains no nouns but is a 220-word list of "service words." In Appendix A-5, you will find a modified version of this list, along with instructions for assessing students' knowledge of these words.

Bottom-Up Model of Reading   A model that assumes the written material is the primary source of meaning, rather than the person who is reading. This model is sometimes referred to as *text-driven*.

Choral Reading   Reading done orally by two or more students from the same passage at the same time.

Cloze Passage   A reading passage of approximately 250 words in which, beginning after the first sentence, every 5th word is omitted. Students read the original passage, then fill in the exact word, if possible. Independent, instructional, and frustration levels may be calculated based on the percentage of correct words filled in.

Cloze Procedure   A process of matching students to materials at their appropriate grade level. *Cloze passages* may be used to test students' comprehension of selected passages to determine placement, to teach context clues, or to teach students to better comprehend what they read.

Comprehension   Meaning gained from what is written on a page (when read) or heard (when spoken).

Consonant Blend   Combinations of two or three consonants blended together into sounds while retaining the sounds of the individual letters; for example, *cr* in *crayon* and *pl* in *plate.*

Consonant Cluster   A term referring to both *consonant blends* and *consonant digraphs.*

Consonant Digraph   See **Digraph.**

Context Clues   Clues to the meaning and/or pronunciation of an unknown word derived from the words preceding or following that word. For example, one can use context clues to determine that the missing word in the following sentence is *dog:* The _____ was barking all night and kept me awake.

Critical Reading   Evaluating on the basis of the reader's experience the meaning and implications of what is read.

Decoding   The process of taking words in print and changing them to spoken words. This is accomplished when the reader applies one or more of the following: sight word recognition, phonics, structural analysis, and context clues.

Diagnosis   A careful investigation carried out to determine the amount and sequence of remediation needed by a student with reading difficulties.

Digraph   A combination of two letters recording (representing) a single sound. There are *consonant digraphs* and *vowel digraphs.* An example of a consonant digraph is *ph* in the word *digraph.* In this case, the *ph* stands for the /f/ sound. (When a letter is found between two slash marks, as the *f* above, it means the sound for which the letter stands.) An example of a vowel digraph is the *ea* in the word *each.* In saying the *phoneme* (sound) represented by the letters of a digraph, one does not change the position of the mouth from the beginning to the end of the sound.

Diphthong   A combination of two vowel letters that are both heard in making a gliding sound; for example, *ow* in *cow* and *oy* in *boy.* In pronouncing a diphthong sound, the position of the mouth is moved from the beginning to the end of the diphthong. (The word diphthong is pronounced: /dif/ ¢/thong/. The consonant digraph *ph* is pronounced as /f/.)

Direct Instruction   A teaching approach that is academically focused, sequential, and structured. The teacher presents information to the students and monitors the pacing and learning of the material.

Dyad Reading   An adaptation of the neurological impress method whereby proficient readers are paired with struggling readers to assist them as they read from one shared book.

Echo Reading   Also called *imitative reading;* a recommended technique for improving efficiency skills in reading. This technique can work on a one-to-one basis or with a tape recorder. Students may also use this technique when reading in pairs. The teacher reads a passage aloud; then the student attempts to duplicate the passage using the same phrasing and intonation.

Engaged Time or **On-Task Time**   The amount of time a student is involved or engaged in the learning task.

Flexible Reading   Adjusting reading speed to fit the requirement of understanding the text. The purpose for reading and the type of material to be read dictate appropriate speed.

Fluency   Beyond the ability to merely decode words, the ability to use punctuation and other cues to read smoothly and easily, with proper speed, accuracy, and phrasing.

General Sight Vocabulary or **General Sight Words**   Any word that a reader has seen many times in the past and is able to recognize instantly without using word-attack skills. This term should not be confused with the term *basic sight words*, which refers only to words that appear on a list of the most frequently occurring words.

Grapheme   A grapheme is the written representation of a phoneme. For example, the word *dog* has three distinct sounds that are represented by the graphemes *d*, *o*, and *g*. The word *straight* also has three phonemes that are represented by the graphemes *str*, *aigh*, and *t*. See **Phoneme.**

Group-Assisted Reading   A modification of the dyad reading method to be used with groups of struggling readers. The reading material is large enough for all to see, and the teacher and students read it out loud together, with the teacher pointing to each word as it is read.

Holistic Approach   A teaching-learning approach that emphasizes the wholeness of subject matter. A completely holistic approach to teaching reading would include instruction in few or no subskills of reading, and an emphasis on the teacher as a facilitator of learning rather than one who provides direct instruction. Also called *whole-language approach.*

Imitative Reading   See **Echo Reading.**

Interactive Model of Reading   A model that describes reading as being both concept- and text-driven, in which the reader and the text work together to construct meaning. The reader comprehends through the use of both decoding skills and prior knowledge.

Kinesthetic Method or **Tactile-Kinesthetic Method**   The use of touch, hearing, sight, and muscle movement to teach letters or words. The approach usually involves tracing over words with the index and middle fingers while sounding the part being traced.

K–W–L Technique   For reading in the content areas, a direct-instruction comprehension strategy in which the teacher elicits what students *know* about the subject to be read (*K*), what they *want* to learn (*W*), and finally, what they *learned* from reading the passage (*L*).

Language-Experience Approach (LEA)   The student's or group's own words are written down and used as material for instruction in reading, writing, spelling, listening, and speaking. The approach relies on children's oral language background to develop their reading skills and is considered more personalized and motivating, though less systematic or sequential, than other approaches.

Letter Knowledge   See **Alphabet Knowledge.**

Letter-Sound Correspondence   The relationship between a letter and the sound it stands for.

Levels of Reading

Independent or free reading level   The student can function adequately without the teacher's help at this level. Comprehension should average 90% or better, and word recognition should average 99% or better.

Instructional reading level   The student can function adequately with teacher guidance and yet be challenged to stimulate his reading growth. Comprehension should average 75% or better, and word recognition should average 95% or better.

Frustration reading level   The student cannot function adequately. In reading at this level, the student often shows signs of tension and discomfort. Vocalization is often present. Comprehension averages 50% or less, and word recognition averages 90% or less.

Literature-Based Reading Program   A program that uses children's stories, nonfiction pieces, and poetry to teach. This may range from an in-depth study of core literary works to extension of core work together with recreational and motivational reading that is based on the student's natural curiosity.

Meaning Vocabulary   Sometimes called simply *vocabulary;* refers to the student's knowledge of the *meanings* of words in her listening, speaking, and reading vocabularies. A large and growing meaning vocabulary is critical to reading comprehension as students progress through the grades.

Metacognition   Knowledge of one's own thought processes while reading. This implies that the student can select reading strategies that will help her to comprehend the material.

Miscue   A misreading, error, or deviation from the written text that occurs while the student is reading orally. When analyzed properly, miscues can provide clues to the nature or causes of reading difficulties.

Modeling Strategies for Paragraph Meaning   The teacher models, then directs students in the use of, a code for marking reactions to selected paragraphs. This is one of the most effective methods to teach students to improve their comprehension by monitoring their thought processes when reading.

Morphology   See **Structural Analysis.**

Neurological-Impress Method (NIM)   The teacher sits beside the student and points to each word, reading it aloud. The student follows along with her eyes and reads aloud with the teacher.

Onset   The consonant(s) at the beginning of a syllable, such as *b* in *bat* or *str* in *street*. See **Rime.**

Paired Reading   Two students read out loud, usually from the same text. The students may read simultaneously (two-person choral reading) or alternately (one student reads out loud while the other follows along silently).

Paired Repeated Readings   Students are paired. They read the selection silently, then each reads it out loud three times while the other listens and provides assistance. The reader evaluates his performance and the listener provides a critique.

Phoneme   The smallest unit of speech sound in a language. For example, in the word *dog*, there are three phonemes: /d/, /o/, and /g/.

Phonemic Awareness   Also called *phoneme awareness* or *oral phonemic segmentation;* the understanding of and the ability to manipulate phonemes. The term *phonological awareness* is also used incorrectly as a synonym for *phonemic awareness.*

Phonic Elements   Initial consonants, consonant digraphs, consonant blends, vowels, vowel combinations, or special letter combinations to be learned in the study of phonics.

Phonics   The application of *phoneme-grapheme* (sound-symbol) relationships to the teaching of reading; usually used in beginning reading because phonics is a helpful tool for decoding one-syllable words.

Phonogram   A series of letters that begin with a vowel and are often found together; for example, *all, ell, old, ime,* and so on. A phonogram is sometimes referred to as a *rime, graphemic base, word element, word family, vowel family,* or *graphoneme.*

Phonological Awareness   Awareness of the sounds that make up words, including *phonemes* (the smallest units), *onsets* and *rimes,* and *syllables.* Although phonological awareness is sometimes used as a synonym for *phonemic awareness,* it has a broader meaning.

Precision Reading   A method used to help students overcome difficulties with reading fluency. A segment of a book is selected and the student is told to practice reading these sentences as accurately as possible. Later, the oral reading of the sentences is scored and the results are graphed.

Reader's Theater   After practicing, students read their parts from a script in front of a group. The material read is highly motivating and not too difficult.

Reading Programs

   Developmental   The classroom instructional program followed by the teacher to meet the needs of students who are progressing at a typical rate in terms of their capacity.

   Corrective   A program of instruction usually conducted by a classroom teacher within the class setting to correct mild reading difficulties.

   Remedial   A program of instruction that may be carried on either inside or outside the regular classroom to teach specific reading skills to students with severe reading difficulties.

Reading Recovery   A program developed by Marie Clay for the early intervention of reading difficulties. This one-to-one instructional program is designed to help

6-year-olds overcome a slow start in reading. It is a registered trademark in the United States. Reading Recovery teachers receive extensive training prior to certification.

Repeated Readings   The student is given a selection of 50 to 200 words, practices reading it, and is timed. Reading rate and number of errors are noted. The student then rereads the selection along with a recording and is retested.

Rime   The vowel and all the consonants that follow in a syllable. See **Onset.**

Semantic Feature Analysis   A technique for teaching vocabulary that uses themes, a discussion, and a matrix to expand knowledge of word meanings.

Semantic Mapping   Organizing concepts into a cognitive structure or hierarchy for better comprehension.

Semantics   The study of *meaning* in a language.

Shared Book Experience   Also called *shared reading*, this strategy was developed by Don Holdaway to provide young children in the classroom with experiences similar to those they might experience in a warm and literate environment at home. Big books are used by the teacher to help youngsters learn to read by following along as the teacher reads with enthusiasm and runs his or her hand under the words as they are read. Repetitive, familiar texts are often used. The shared book experience is a step between reading to children and independent decoding by the children.

Story Frame   A device used to build comprehension. It provides structure to a variety of content material. In a story frame, the teacher begins a sentence about the story's content and the student must complete the sentence. Story frames may become more elaborate and deal with character, plot, and setting as students become more skilled in completing them.

Structural Analysis   Often referred to as *morphology;* the study of meaning-bearing units such as root words, prefixes, suffixes, possessives, plurals, accent rules, and syllables. As a decoding skill, the reader uses structural analysis to decode words of more than one syllable by identifying, separating, and pronouncing reliable units or parts of words.

Think Aloud   A metacognitive strategy in which the teacher models the comprehension process by explaining how she comprehends a passage while reading it aloud.

Top-Down Model of Reading   A model that assumes the person who is reading is the primary source of meaning, rather than the written material. This model is sometimes referred to as *concept-driven.*

Vocabulary   Most often, and most appropriately, this term is synonymous with *meaning vocabulary.* Sometimes it is used to refer to the number of words a reader recognizes, or the reader's *sight vocabulary.*

Whole-Language Philosophy   Reading and writing instruction that uses complete texts in communicative situations, as contrasted with focused skills practice or the use of phonics or isolated drilling of language. This philosophy or approach to reading/language instruction may also incorporate speaking, listening, and spelling, and may use materials such as newspapers, children's books, notes, and memos. It usually de-emphasizes grouping by ability and teacher-directed instruction.

Word-Analysis Skills   Sometimes called *word-attack skills*, these are the skills a reader must use to determine how to pronounce a word when it is not recognized instantly. (The three important word-analysis skills are phonics, structural analysis, and context clues.)

Word-Recognition Skills   The ability of a reader to recognize words; usually refers only to recognition by sight or recognition without the aid of word analysis.

Index